40 -

SIR RALPH HOPTON

Oxford University Press, Ely House, London W. 1

GLASGOW NEW YORK TORONTO MELBOURNE WELLINGTON
CAPE TOWN SALISBURY IBADAN NAIROBI LUSAKA ADDIS ABABA
BOMBAY CALCUTTA MADRAS KARACHI LAHORE DACCA
KUALA LUMPUR HONG KONG TOKYO

SIR RALPH HOPTON

(National Portrait Gallery, London)

SIR RALPH HOPTON

THE KING'S MAN IN THE WEST

(1642-1652)

*A Study in Character
and Command*

by

F · T · R · EDGAR

CLARENDON PRESS, OXFORD
1968

Printed in Great Britain by
Alden & Mowbray Ltd
at the Alden Press, Oxford

TO JUDITH

ACKNOWLEDGEMENTS

This Life of Sir Ralph Hopton owes much to others. I wish to thank Professor Thomas G. Barnes of the University of California, Berkeley, for his patience in directing a novice through the first stages of research, for his contributions of Materials and editorial advice and for his encouragement, first and last. To Brigadier Peter Young, D.S.O., M.C., M.A., F.S.A., of the Royal Military College, Sandhurst, equal gratitude is due for his generosity in sharing sources, as well as his expert knowledge of tactics and command. I wish to acknowledge the kindness of Dr. Ian Roy of King's College, the University of London, for several hours of profitable discussions and for giving me an opportunity to examine the typescript of his thesis on Charles I's Oxford Army. For many of the cardinal facts of Hopton's career, I am deeply indebted to Mr. Ivor Collis, Archivist, Mr. D. Shorrocks, Assistant Archivist, and Miss Christine Stone of the Somerset Record Office, Taunton.

Appreciation and thanks are also due to the following people who have been most helpful with suggestions, services, contributions, and criticism:

Professor George H. Guttridge, University of California, Berkeley
Professor Sheldon Rothblatt, University of California, Berkeley
Professor John S. Coolidge, University of California, Berkeley
Professor Robert Ashton, University of East Anglia
Dr. Robert Latham, Royal Holloway College, University of London
Mr. Taylor Milne, the Institute of Historical Research
The staff of the Public Record Office
Mr. Roderick Barman, solicitor
Dr. R. W. Hunt, Keeper of the Western MSS., and Dr. D. M. Barrett, the Bodleian Library, Oxford
The staffs of the Reading Room and the Manuscripts Room, the British Museum
The staff of the War Office Library
The National Portrait Gallery, London, for permission to reproduce Sir Ralph Hopton's portrait
The staff of the Victoria and Albert Museum

viii ACKNOWLEDGEMENTS

Percy Hamilton Seymour, eighteenth Duke of Somerset
Mr. Harold Dodd, Town Clerk, Wells
Mr. A. S. Hanson, Librarian, King's School, Bruton, Somerset
Mr. F. B. Stitt, County Archivist, and Mr. R. A. McKinney,
    Assistant Archivist, Staffordshire Record Office, Stafford
Mr. P. L. Hull, County Archivist, and staff of the Cornish Record
    Office, Truro
The Reverend P. G. Harrison, vicar of Great Torrington, Devon
Mr. Richard Sawyer, architect and surveyor, Winchester, authority
    on the battle of Cheriton
The staffs of the Devonshire Record Office and Exeter City Library
The staffs of the Bristol Record Office (the Council House) and City
    Library
The staff of the Devizes Museum, Devizes
The staff of the Hampshire Record Office, Winchester
The staff of the Sutro Library, San Francisco
Eyre and Spottiswoode, Ltd., publishers of *The Great Civil War*, by
    Lieutenant Colonel Alfred H. Burne and Lieutenant-Colonel
    Peter Young, for permission to use carbon tracings of three
    maps: the battle-grounds of Lansdown, Roundway, and Bristol.

Special thanks are due Miss Jean Gates, for much useful advice
and assistance; and Professor Harold E. Aikins of Northern Illinois
University, with whom I toured the West Country in the summer
of 1956, the starting point for many researches and inquiries in that
region.

Finally, I wish to convey thanks to my mother, my wife Judith,
and my friend Leonard Tearle Zimmerman for devoted editorial
assistance; and to Miss Agnes Conley for typing the manuscript.

F. T. R. EDGAR

Berkeley, California
All Souls' Day, 1966

CONTENTS

LIST OF MAPS

ABBREVIATIONS

Add. MSS.: Additional Manuscripts, British Museum
A.P.C.: Acts of the Privy Council of England
Black, *Docquets* . . . W. H. Black, *Docquets of Letters Patent*
B.M.: British Museum
Cal. C.A.M.: Calendar of the Committee for the Advance of Money
Cal. C.C.: Calendar of the Committee for Compounding
Cal. Clar. S.P.: Calendar of Clarendon State Papers
C.J.: Journals of the House of Commons
C.S.P.D.: Calendar of State Papers, Domestic
C.S.P.F.: Calendar of State Papers, Foreign
C.S.P.V.: Calendar of State Papers, Venetian
C.R.O.: Cornish Record Office
Devon, Repts. & Trans.: Reports and Transactions of the Devonshire
    Association
D.N.B.: Dictionary of National Biography
E.H.R.: English Historical Review
Harl. MSS.: Harleian Manuscripts, British Museum
Harl. Soc.: Harleian Society Publication
H.M.C.: Historical Manuscripts Commission
J.S. Army H.R.: Journal of the Society for Army Historical Research
L.J.: Journals of the House of Lords
N. & Q.: Notes and Queries
N. & Q., Som. & Dor.: Notes and Queries, Somerset and Dorset
P.R.O.: Public Record Office
Som. Arch. & Nat. Hist.: Somerset Archaeological and Natural
    History Society Proceedings
S.P.: State Papers (Domestic, unless otherwise indicated)
S.P. Clar.: Clarendon State Papers
S.R.O.: Somerset Record Office
S.T.C.: Short Title Catalogue (Donald Wing, ed.)
T.T.: Thomason Tracts
Wilts. Arch. & Nat. Hist.: Wiltshire Archaeological and Natural
    History Magazine

CHRONOLOGY

1596 Ralph Hopton born at Witham Friary, Somerset. Baptized 13 March, Evercreech

1614
    14 Feb. Admitted to Middle Temple

?1616? Admitted to Oxford, probably Lincoln College

1620 To wars in Palatinate; episode with Queen of Bohemia

1621 M.P. for Shaftesbury

1623
    18 Mar. Marries Elizabeth Capel Lewin (1591–1646)

1624 With Mansfeld expedition as Lieutenant-Colonel in regiment of Sir Charles Rich

1625
    Jun.–Aug. M.P. for Bath (still on continent during first half of session)
    Jul. Brought back to go on Cadiz expedition
    Nov. Declines to go on Cadiz expedition

1626
    2 Feb. Made Knight of the Bath at Charles I's Coronation

1628 M.P. for Wells

1629–39 J.P. and Deputy Lieutenant in Somerset

1639 Captain of royal bodyguard troop in North

1640
    Apr.–May M.P. for Somerset

1640–2 M.P. for Wells

1642
    10 May Votes for Strafford's Attainder
    1 Dec. Presents Grand Remonstrance
    4 Mar. Committed to Tower for two weeks, one day before Militia Ordinance
    12 Jul. Leaves Beverley with Hertford for Somerset to execute commission of array
    1 Aug. Incident at Shepton Mallet

B

4 Aug. Stawell at Marshall's Elm; 'first blood' in the west

5 Aug. Declared delinquent by the House of Commons

6–7 Aug. From Wells to Sherborne, Dorset

30 Aug. Declared traitor by House (following publication of 'certain words' spoken by him at Sherborne)

24 Sep. Parting of Hopton and Hertford at Minehead

1643

19 Jan. Defeats Ruthin at Braddock Down

22 Jan. Saltash, fortified by Ruthin, taken by Hopton

10 Feb. The Commons orders search of house at Witham

20 Feb. Property 'sequestered' by House and seised to William Strode (of Devon)

23 Apr. Action at Launceston

25 Apr. Hopton intercepted by Chudleigh at Sourton Down

16 May Defeats Chudleigh at Stratton

4 Jun. Joins Hertford and Maurice at Chard

5 Jul. Meets Waller at Lansdown. Severely wounded. Siege of Devizes

13 Jul. Wilmot's victory against Waller at Roundway Down. Hopton, wounded and immobile, sends Cornish troops from Devizes

24–27 Jul. Siege and storming (26 Jul.) of Bristol; capitulation of the city

4 Sep. Created Baron Hopton of Stratton

29 Sep. Council of War at Oriel College, Oxford. Cadre of a new western army; nucleus of army in south-eastern counties

1644 Defeated by Sir William Waller at Cheriton Wood (near Alresford)

Summer. With King. Retreat into Cornwall, pursued by Essex

1645

26 May Warrant from King making him General of the Ordnance

1646

15 Jan. Takes command of army under Prince of Wales, whom he serves as Councillor and Lieutenant-General

16 Feb. Defeated by Fairfax at Torrington

2 Mar. The Prince, Hyde, and Culpeper leave Land's End

14 Mar. Capitulation to Fairfax at Truro

1650 Eliminated from Council at Breda because he opposes accommodation with the Scots

1652
   8 Oct. (N.S.) Dies at Bruges of ague 'in honorable poverty'
1661 His body returned to Somerset and buried in the churchyard at
   Witham Friary. But the record of the location of his grave is
   missing

NOTE

The Office of the Lord (or Captaine) General of an Army

A man of an undaunted Courage & authoritie, severe and austere in his command, who ought to be greatly honored, feared, and respected, a man full of resolution, and magnanimity in the daie of Battell, and constant and resolute in desperate cases, happie in his dessignes and enterprises, and above all religious, invocating God to be propitious unto him, and to give a blessing upon his dessignes, to give him knowledge, policie and understanding, how to order and Governe his Armie well, that he may keep it under good discipline, and to make it not onely capable of vanquishing, but also Victorious, which depends onely upon the Almighty power of the Lord of Hoasts, and that neither good, nor bad successe should make him change, or alter his countenance, but upon the hottest services, to give out his orders and directions with temperance and moderation. . . . A brave Generall also considers, that the force of an Armie consists not in the multitude of men, but in Valliant and well experienced souldiers, and officers, which are well instructed, and trained up in the use of armes, and knowes thar Victorie consists not in many Troupes but . . . in observing of good order, and discipline choosing of advantages of wind, sunne, and ground. . . .

—Henry Hexham, *The Three parts of the Principles of the Art Military* (12–13).

'I will strive to serve my Sovereign Lord the King.'
—Ralph, Lord Hopton

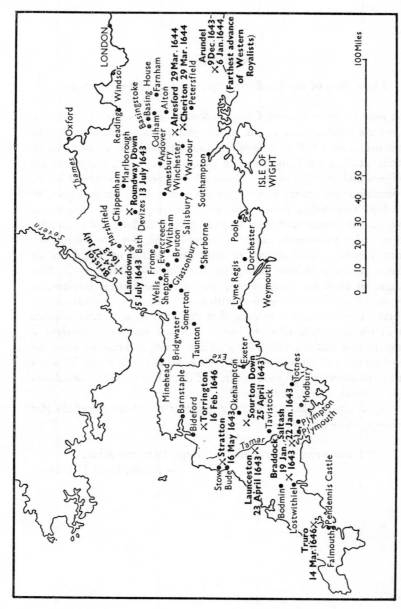

Map 1. Sir Ralph Hopton in the West
July 1642–March 1646

I

THE EARLY YEARS:
Apprenticeship in War

(1596–1625)

THE figure of Ralph Hopton depicted by an unknown artist, as it appears framed in the National Portrait Gallery, has much in common with many of Van Dyck's Caroline gentlemen. The tufted lip and chin, the straight hair worn to the nape of the neck, the dark suit with starched collar and cuffs, the grave pensive eyes present a visage and pose as much removed from arresting individuality as from the stereotypes of 'dour Puritan' and 'laughing Cavalier'. It is hard to think of this man going noticed in a crowd. And yet he displays a quality of self-abnegation that belongs to nearly all first-rate military commanders.

Caroline portraiture, for all its similitude, may in some ways be more revealing than Caroline biography. Despite a long list of 'worthies', English 'Lives' in this period are mainly dependent on incidental mention in official sources or the thumb-nail sketches of contemporary biographers. The multifarious diaries and private correspondence of the next century are lacking. So, too—except in the theatre and a few raconteurs—is the instinct for social history, the delight in life and manners for their own sake, the reflective mood that sustains the detailed analysis of individual character and temperament, the penetrating inwardness and self-absorption that a little earlier on the Continent had already begun to find voice in Montaigne. We know the seventeenth-century man mainly as a man of action in his role as privy councillor or M.P., soldier or divine. We know little of his schooldays, of his domestic life, hardly anything about his 'state of mind' or 'exact words' at a given time and place. The relish for personal idiosyncrasy appears sometimes in an antiquary like John Aubrey; but, Pepys's *Diary* aside, there is little at this time to compare with the *Life of Samuel Johnson* or *The Education of Henry Adams*.

For the background of the Hoptons, a few facts must suffice. The ancestor of the Somerset branch was Sir Arthur Hopton I of

Westwood, Suffolk, and master of Cockfield Hall, near Saxmundham.[1] He was present at the christening of Edward VI, an indication, perhaps, of his standing at court.[2] His eldest son, Sir Owen, was Lieutenant of the Tower under Elizabeth. His second son, Sir Ralph I, was founder of the family fortunes. This Ralph was probably the 'Mr. Hopton' mentioned as being in Thomas Cromwell's service in the 1530's. In 1538 he received a lease of part of the property of Witham Friary in the hundred of Frome in Somerset. In May 1540 he received a lease 'of the demesne lands of Aysbury or Aishebury, Berks.', parts of the lands that had lately belonged to Glastonbury Abbey.[3] Four years later he received a full grant of Witham and also acquired Ditcheat and other Glastonbury lands in Somerset and Berkshire.

The original grant was confirmed on 18 May 1552:

> A lettre to the Chauncellour of thaugmentacions to make out a booke of the Kinges Majesties gyft unto Sir Rauf Hopton and his heyres, of a pasture and certain woodes called the Halt in the Countie of Somerset, parcell of the late desolved House or Priorie called the Charterhouse of Wittham.[4]

Thus 'Monastic lands . . . made the Hoptons'[5] and the holdings continued to increase. The second Sir Ralph was to hold lands in six counties.[6] Meanwhile, the family star continued to rise in the royal service. Ralph I was Marshal of the Household to Henry VIII, Edward, and Mary, becoming Knight Marshal in 1547: sufficient proof of durability, or flexibility, in an age of rapid transitions. It can

---

[1] Sophia W. Bates-Harbin, *Members of Parliament from the County of Somerset* (Taunton, 1939), 120; F. G. Emmison, *Tudor Secretary: Sir William Petre at Court and Home* (Harvard University Press, Cambridge, 1961), 248.

[2] J. Gough Nichols, *Literary Remains of Edward VI* (London, 1857), i. cclxii.

[3] *Letters and Papers, Foreign and Domestic, Henry VIII*, xv, Entry 733, Sect. 46 (May 1540).

[4] *Acts of the Privy Council of England*, 1552–54 (London, 1891 ff.), 51; *Calendar of the Patent Rolls, Edward VI* (London, 1926), iv. 299 (25 May 1552). Edward, Duke of Somerset, had enjoyed brief tenure of Witham Friary before his attainder.

[5] Thomas Garden Barnes, *Somerset, 1625–1640: A Country's Government During the Personal Rule* (Harvard University Press, 1961), 19.

[6] Mary Frear Keeler, *The Long Parliament, 1640–41: A Biographical Study of Its Members* (Philadelphia, 1954), 222. Six English counties before the war: Somerset, Wilts., Kent, Essex, Hereford, Monmouth. To these were added the lands in Norfolk and Suffolk which Hopton inherited from his uncle, Sir Arthur Hopton, in 1650. Ralph also held lands in Glamorganshire, and the Glastonbury lands in Berks. also must be included. The number of ten counties is less significant than the dispersal of the manors throughout the Marches, the west country, and the south-east, suggesting a broad and diverse pattern of regional interest and influence.

be conjectured, though not conclusively proved, that he had reservations about Queen Mary's Spanish consort, Philip II. Though his patent was reconfirmed in August after Edward VI's demise in July 1553, a deposition was later made 'relative towards words spoken by Sir Ralph Hopton concerning the coming in of the Prince of Spain and the Spaniards',[1] and he appears on the Pardon Roll in October.[2] He survived in office till 3 June 1556 when he laid down his patent, having failed to appear before the Council to answer charges of absenteeism.[3] He was restored, however, by Queen Elizabeth upon her accession and continued in that office till his death in 1572, serving also as M.P. for Heytesbury in 1559. It is possible that he may have helped to win preferment for his elder brother Sir Owen as Lieutenant of the Tower; and his whole career may provide an enlightening commentary on the initiative of younger sons. Certainly the roles of these Hopton brothers serve as interesting precursors to the career of Sir Owen's great-grandson, the second Sir Ralph.

The two succeeding generations represent a brief decline in national prominence, if not in public service. The first Sir Ralph left no sons as heirs. His only child was a daughter, Dorothy. In the collateral line his brother Sir Owen had a son, Sir Arthur Hopton II, K.B., who inherited his uncle Ralph's lands, which leads to the assumption that they were entailed. This Sir Arthur fixed the family seat at Witham. He had five sons: Owen, Robert, Henry, Thomas, and Arthur. The eldest, Owen, married his cousin Dorothy, the daughter of Sir Ralph I. The second son, Robert, inherited the property; the third, Henry, is mentioned only in the will of Lady Dorothy Hopton (d. 1597), widow of Sir Ralph I;[4] the fourth, Sir Thomas, became a gentleman pensioner of the court and acquired lands in his own right;[5] the fifth son, Sir Arthur Hopton III, K.B., was sheriff of Somerset and ambassador to Spain throughout the Civil War.[6] His embassy and his nephew Ralph's command in the west represent the high point of Hopton prestige and influence; as they were both childless men, their deaths, within two years of each

---

[1] *C.S.P.D.* 1547–1580, 58 (33).

[2] *Calendar of the Patent Rolls, Philip and Mary* (London, 1937), i. 439 (12 October 1553).

[3] *A.P.C.* 1554–56, 203, 236, 279.

[4] *Prerogative Court of Canterbury*, 'Cobham', 74: 'Owen and Henry sons of my nephew, Arthur Hopton.'

[5] Keeler, loc. cit.

[6] *Complete Peerage* (of George E. Cokayne), 12 vols., Vicary Gibbs *et al.*, eds. (London, 1910–59), vi. 577.

other, mark the extinction of the line. In a little more than a hundred years, stretching from the Reformation almost to the Restoration, four generations in a family of 'new gentry' made themselves quietly useful to four Tudor and two Stuart sovereigns, sank roots in new soil, acquired substantial holdings in land, and finally attained positions in the privy council and high offices of state. One fact should be noted: none of the Hoptons seem to have won prominence at the bar, in the church, or in business. They rose through civil and military service. And as their lands never diminished,[1] so their good name, even with Sir Ralph I's temporary suspension, seems never to have been impaired or impugned.

Robert Hopton of Witham married Jane, widow of Sir Henry Jones and daughter of Rowland Kemeys, of Vandry, Monmouthshire. They had six children: two sons, Ralph and William; and four daughters, Katherine, Rachel, Mary, and Margaret. William, born in 1598, apparently died some time between 1619, when he is mentioned as a student at the Middle Temple,[2] and 1623; his name is absent from the genealogies.

The oldest child, Ralph, was born at Witham in March 1596. The exact date is uncertain, but he was baptized on the thirteenth of that month at Evercreech Church.[3] In some ways it was an auspicious time to be born. The spirit of the Armada days ran strong. The bravado of Raleigh and Essex was a national tonic. 1596 was the year of a successful assault on Cadiz. Only a few sober minds might reflect that the Queen was old; that factions united about her might not rally round the throne forever. No one could predict that the next Cadiz expedition, that of 1626, would be a disaster,

[1] There can be little doubt that the lands increased. On 14 June 1553 Sir Arthur Hopton I was granted a yearly rent of £18. 9s. from the 'house and site of the late priory of Blyborough, Suff., manor of Blyborough . . .', etc.—*Calendar of the Patent Rolls, Edward VI*, v. 79. For an inventory of Ralph, Lord Hopton's lands taken in 1650 by the Committee for Compounding, see Appendix IV.

[2] William Hopton, Esq., is a shadowy figure. According to the often-inaccurate *Alumni Oxonienses*, Joseph Foster, ed., 4 vols. (Oxford and London, 1891, 1892), 745, he matriculated at Queen's College, Oxford, 5 Dec. 1617, aged fifteen. Apparently he took no degree, but left after two years' residence. He is described as the second son of Robert Hopton, Esq., of Witham, Som. Elsewhere, he is mentioned only in an MS. of the Dean and Chapter of Wells, dated 13 Sept. 1616: 'The office of surveyor of the manors of the bishop granted to Robert Hopton, esq. and his assigns, for the lives of himself and of Ralph and William his sons.'—H.M.C., *Calendar of the MSS. of the Dean and Chapter of Wells*, ii. 371 (f. 118d.).

[3] *Complete Peerage*, vi. 576. See 'Hopton Pedigree' in Genealogical Notes of H. Hobhouse; and MS. of the Rev. Frederick Brown, ix. 138, at S.R.O., Taunton. These MSS. are of immense value.

partially responsible for breaking up that unity for yet a generation more.

Hopton's formative years are barely mentioned, but the stereotype of a simple man of action is modified by hints of amazing precocity. Lloyd's *Memoirs* report:

> His education was such, that he learned to pray as soon as he could speak; and to read, as soon as he could pray, before three years old he read any character or letter whatsoever in our Printed Books, and within a while, any tolerable Writing Hand; getting by heart, at four years and a half, five or six hundred Latine and Greek words, together with their Genders and Declensions.[1]

Educated at a country grammar school, he 'very early showed a great aptitude for study, especially languages'.[2] The grammar school in question was probably King's School, Bruton, five miles from Witham.[3]

For his higher education the only reliable record notes that on 14 February 1614 'Ralf Hopton, son and heir of Robert H. of Witham, Somerset, Esq.' was admitted to the Middle Temple,[4] standard procedure for a gentleman's son in that day. As for his residence at Oxford, recent commentators,[5] following Lloyd, affirm he attended Lincoln College, but do not indicate that he took a degree. He is supposed to have studied under Robert Sanderson, later Bishop of Lincoln, whom he remembered gratefully for instilling habits 'of considering matters proposed to him leisurely and soberly, of recollecting the proper circumstances of a business pertinently, '. . . of searching into the bottom of things quickly . . . .'[6] In the Brown MSS. at Taunton he is referred to as a graduate of Lincoln.[7] Anthony Wood refers to him as a gentleman-commoner of the same college.[8] Yet his name appears neither in Foster's *Alumni* nor in the matriculation register. If, however, he did not intend to graduate, it was unnecessary for him to matriculate. He could simply have

---

[1] David Lloyd, *Memories of Excellent Personages.* . . . (London, 1668), 341.
[2] Ibid.
[3] According to Mr. A. S. Hanson, Librarian of the King's School, Bruton, Som., the only other grammar schools in the area were those at Sherborne and Shaftesbury, about nineteen and fifteen miles respectively from Witham. Mr. Hanson reports no extant registers containing names of boys. The first boy mentioned by name is a scholar in 1638.
[4] H.A.C. Sturgess, *Middle Temple Register* (London, 1949), i. 101.
[5] Firth, Cokayne, Sealy.   [6] Lloyd, loc. cit.
[7] Brown MS., loc. cit.
[8] Anthony Wood, *Fasti Oxonienses* (London, 1815), ii. col. 152.

remained in residence for two or three years. A probable date for his entrance is 1616. It was the year in which Pembroke, Hopton's future patron, became Chancellor of Oxford and in which King James, moving against Calvinism, advised young divines to study the Fathers.[1] It is more admissible if we acknowledge that Hopton came to the Queen of Bohemia in 1620 'fresh from Oxford'.[2] But when the average age of matriculation was between fifteen and seventeen, it was unusual to enter the University at the age of twenty after a year or two at the Inns of Court.

Whatever the exact dates it is most likely that he did attend Lincoln: it had been the college of his great-uncle Sir Ralph I and also of his uncle Arthur. Since Sanderson in the late 1610's was a Fellow of Lincoln and University Proctor, it is also likely that Hopton knew him. If the commentary on their contacts is accurate, the wisdom he gained from him was less the scholar's than that of the man of affairs. His collegiate experience was perhaps not dissimilar to that of a modern youth who needs it mainly for seasoning, social polish, and contacts. Indeed, it would seem that the University was a kind of afterthought, lately arrived at and casually assumed, as though he were merely waiting for the campaign to open.

To a student of twenty-four, somewhat older than his fellows, the Palatinate struggle may have come as a relief. For this he had to thank the tortuous policy of pacific King James, who would not openly side with the Elector Frederick against the Emperor, but who was quite content to let him use English volunteers. Many of the 2,000 who, on 22 July 1620, set sail with Sir Horace Vere for Holland, and many of those who followed for several years, represented the first families of the realm. 'The young nobility so throng for officers' places that the experienced officers are thrown out.'[3] From the upper ranks of the peerage came the

dissolute and reckless Earl of Oxford, fresh from his dissipations at Venice, and the sturdy, half-Puritan Earl of Essex. In this enterprise there was room alike for the spirit which twenty years afterwards animated the Parliamentary bands, and for the spirit which inspired the troopers who followed Rupert to the charge.[4]

Cutting their fighting teeth in the campaigns of the Low Countries

[1] Isaac Walton, *Lives* (London, 1825), 366–7.
[2] Robert S. Rait, *Five Stuart Princesses* (New York, 1902), 118.
[3] *C.S.P.D.* 1619–23 (London, 1858), 159 (1 July 1620).
[4] Samuel R. Gardiner, *History of England to 1642* (London, 1887, 1891), iii. 365.

and the Rhineland, these youthful warriors acquired a first-hand acquaintance with war that their countrymen had not known since the days of Elizabeth; lamentably, for the moment, their martial sinew was thrown away in the service of a weak and vacillating government and an utterly lost cause. But unlike the 'lost generation' of Essex, these veterans, blooded abroad, were to form the generation of leadership—as M.P.'s, J.P.'s, and deputy lieutenants—in the years ahead. Above all they were to form the cadres of armies that, in their significance to England itself, would make the Palatinate wars seem like a remote frontier skirmish.

These wars round out Ralph Hopton's apprentice years. The high point, though it may be regarded as a kind of sugar gloss on the crust of a hard campaign, came early. Within three months he was in Bohemia. The 'winter kingship' of Frederick was coming to an end. His defeat at Weissenberg on 8 November left him and his Queen-Electress, the Lady Elizabeth, virtually defenceless. Her escape from Prague was full of hazard; harassed by Cossacks and by faithless servants who plundered the baggage, she was in bad plight. In the week-long journey to Breslau, when the roads became nearly impassable, she rode postilion behind an obscure ensign, exactly her own age, in experience little more than a cadet, who remained her champion till death, whose lifelong and perhaps only boast was the service he had rendered her.[1]

With periodic leaves, which included a short term in Parliament in 1621, he spent the next five years on the continent, officially under Count Mansfeld, but undoubtedly considering it his lady's service, and rising from ensign to the rank of Lieutenant-Colonel in Sir Charles Rich's fourth regiment of foot by 1624. That year saw a dwindling of levies from England among the gentlemen volunteers and soldiers of fortune. James, since the breakdown of negotiations for a Spanish marriage, was now involved in continental affairs to the point of using conscripts. Late in the year they embarked to join Mansfeld, presenting a scene far different from that of the young nobility fighting for place in 1620:

It is lamentable . . . to see the heavy countenance of our pressed men, and to hear the sad farewells they take of their friends, showing nothing but

---

[1] Mary Anne Everett Green, *Elizabeth, Electress Palatine and Queen of Bohemia* (London, 1855, 1909), 167. The only contemporary record is a marginal note in Lloyd, 342. Presumably Lloyd, who personally knew Hopton, got it from him first-hand. There is no mention of the incident in the Queen's letters in the State Papers.

deadly unwillingness to the service; and they move pity almost . . . in regard of the incommodity of the season, the uncertainty of the employment, and the ill-terms upon which they are like to serve.[1]

The new system of recruiting gave Hopton a profound distaste for the bungling methods of bureaucracy, no more evident than when applied to the complicated task of fitting out, victualling, and paying an army in the field. Though this is a matter for conjecture, he must have developed a peculiar sympathy for men thus brought, willingly or not, under the arbitrary rule of others, a mixture of paternal tenderness and fraternal camaraderie that made their interest his. At the Wells quarter sessions in January 1627 one John Byshopp, a former pressed soldier, was presented: in serving under Hopton he had lost the use of one of his hands. Hopton, not himself sitting on the bench, appeared in person to confirm this; and Byshopp was awarded compensation of five marks yearly.[2]

On 30 November 1624 the privy council ordered Hopton to receive 250 foot from the Lord Lieutenant of Somerset, Pembroke, and to convey them to Dover by 24 December, there to embark them for use in Mansfeld's service. In the same warrant his colonel, Rich, was authorized to bring 250 out of Essex; and 200 more from Sussex were brought in under the very young Captain George Goring.[3] Also serving under Rich was Sir William Waller,[4] married a year before to a Devon heiress. Goring and Waller were to loom large in Hopton's Civil War career: the first as his bitter enemy, though fighting on the same side; the second as his greatest friend and most formidable Parliamentary opponent, prevented by conscience and the exigencies of war from displaying more than tokens of the personal esteem he never lost for Sir Ralph.

But when a man is proposed by a Secretary of State for special assignment his apprentice days are over. In 1625, England, following the death of the cautious James and the accession of his less politic son, planned, in keeping with a long and honourable tradition, another attack on Cadiz. On 25 May Secretary Conway wrote to Sir Dudley Carleton, English ambassador to the Netherlands, 'to move Mr. Hopton to change his employment under Mansfeldt and

---

[1] Gardiner, v. 282–3.

[2] The Rev. E. H. Bates-Harbin, ed., *Quarter Sessions Records for the County of Somerset* (London, 1908), ii. 30 (20).

[3] *A.P.C.* 1623–25, 386; S.P. 84: 121, f. 301.

[4] John Rushworth, *Historical Collections. . . .* (London, 1680–1722), i. 153.

to go with the fleet', with similar letters to Sir Edward Cecil, destined to command the expedition, and to Hopton himself.[1] This letter is worth quoting. It shows very well how Hopton, not yet thirty, was regarded by his contemporaries, and reflects incidentally the low esteem in which the Palatinate armies were held:

Sec. Conway to Mr. Ralph Hopton: When I first had the good fortune to meet you at Prague I took special notice of your great worth and virtue, and would desire your advancement in that noble way of a soldier you have applied yourself to. According to the freedom I desire to hold with you I must declare to you my opinion, that for a gentleman of your estate to live in an army so unsettled and uncertain is little better than to be a courtier or game-ster, who depends too much upon fortune, and [such employments] are safer for those that want than for such as have much to spare. There is now in my judgment a fair opportunity to change that uncertainty for a far more hopeful employment in the forces to be now sent forth from hence, where your services and merit may have a more immediate and ready passage to His Majesty by those noble friends of yours, who will be eyewitnesses of your carriage and favourable reporters to His Majesty.[2]

Conway wrote to Hopton again on 29 June and sent a letter to Mansfeld for his leave.[3] A week later he wrote to Mansfeld about the leave again.[4] This 'wire-pulling', while it might indicate the push of an interested patron or faction, must mean that Hopton, at twenty-nine, had obtained a reputation as a 'good man' for great ventures. He arrived on 20 July at Deal. Finding it 'necessary to avoyd Canterbury, for the great infection', he arrived at Court and delivered his letters to Lord Conway, who 'brought me to My Lord Duke who both together brought me presently to the King. . . .'[5] What followed in the next two or three months must be conjectured. Conway's ingratiating letter would indicate that pressure was brought for Hopton to take a place in the Cadiz fleet. But it sailed without him. In October he was back in the west country. On the twelfth of that month he wrote to Carleton from Salisbury asking for advice about his service with Mansfeld. He explained that he

had some cause to feare that the fleet is none of the best vitualled fo a long voyage and I confesse the miseries we suffered in the last journey (though I

---

[1] *C.S.P.D.* 1625–26, 27, No. 88.
[2] Ibid. 1625–49 (Supplement, London, 1897), 15.
[3] Ibid. 1625–26, 49, No. 98.
[4] Ibid. 54, No. 9.   [5] S.P. 16/4/111

could hazaad myself willingly enough) makes me afrayd to have charge of men where I have any doubt of the means to support them . . . .[1]

In the same letter he complains that his 'expectation of a press for 600 men to reinforce his company under Count Mansfeldt is not realized'. He wants to know if he is bound to return. If not, he begs for his discharge.

The discharge came. Hopton returned to Somerset and the life of a country squire, living at Evercreech Park not far from his father Robert at Witham. Within a few months, at the Coronation of Charles I on 2 February 1626, he was made a Knight of the Bath. Though his farewell to arms was only withdrawal from war service, it might seem that his life henceforth would be one of honourable retirement and comfortable domesticity. Somehow, in between battles, he had acquired a wife. On 18 March 1623 at Little Hadham, Hertfordshire, he married Elizabeth, widow of Sir Justinian Lewin and daughter of Sir Arthur Capel. Born in 1591, she was five years older than her husband; she died in 1646, six years before him.[2] Though they had no children, she was reputedly a woman of wit and beauty, well fitted to be a soldier's wife and often accompanying her husband on his campaigns.

[1] S.P. 16/7/71.   [2] *Complete Peerage*, vi. 576–7.

II

THE YEARS OF LEADERSHIP IN PEACE

(1625–1642)

THE second period of Hopton's life is significant because his role, if not his main activity, was chiefly political. Even his most effective position, that of deputy lieutenant, was one bestowed largely on civilians, functionally entwined with the post of J.P. This political career can be divided into three phases: early parliamentary experience (1621, 1625, 1628); local service as deputy lieutenant and J.P.; and service in the Parliaments of 1640–2.

The parliamentary apprenticeship began when he was on leave from the wars. In assessing it we cannot ignore the figure of William Herbert, third Earl of Pembroke, a powerful peer, always 'ready to promote the pretences of worthy men',[1] an experienced privy councillor, Lord Chamberlain of the royal household, later Lord Steward, and in 1621 a joint commissioner of the Great Seal. That year he also became lord lieutenant of Somerset and Wiltshire.[2] As such, and as a substantial landowner, the borough of Shaftesbury was in his pocket. From Shaftesbury to the Parliament of 1621, in which his father Robert sat for Somerset, went young Hopton, possibly picked on the expulsion of Thomas Sheppard, an incumbent.[3] In Pembroke he had a powerful patron, but like most fledgling M.P.'s he spent most of his time silently serving on committees. For his first specified assignment he sat on one to investigate defective carding machines, which had proved of 'much prejudice to the poor, and to the clothiers'.[4] Trade relations with the Dutch seem to have entered the picture. Other items involved the transfer of a trust;[5] relief of a fine enforced by a decree made contrary to an Act of

---

[1] Edward Hyde, Earl of Clarendon, *History of the Rebellion and the Civil Wars in England* (Macray edition, Oxford, 1888), i. 120–1.
[2] *Complete Peerage*, x. 413–14; Violet A. Rowe, 'The Influence of the Earls of Pembroke on Parliamentary Elections', *E.H.R.* l. (Apr. 1935), 242–56.
[3] *N. & Q., Som. & Dor.* ii. 90–91; *Cobbett's Parliamentary History* (London, 1806), i. col. 1171. The early volumes of Cobbett must be received with caution.
[4] *C.J.* i. 548.   [5] Ibid. 556 (16 Mar. 1621).

Parliament;[1] enforcement of the laws of Henry VIII relating to Wales;[2] a statute designed to control mistakes in pleading;[3] and 'An Act to avoid Extortions of . . . Comptrollers',[4] in which he sat with the Burgesses of all the Port Towns. This work, routine as it was, gave him a nodding acquaintance with the workings of the Exchequer and the Court of Wards.

Later he was added to the committee meeting to deal with recusants,[5] a subject in which he seems to have taken considerable interest. At least it was in this connexion that he first voiced a recorded opinion. The case was that of the Roman Catholic Edward Floyd, who had spoken in most disparaging terms of the Elector and Electress Palatine. In a hurly-burly of suggested penalties, Hopton, in a spirit of moderation, advised the House to suspend judgement till Floyd's papers were examined, which, after all, might aggravate his offence.[6] For a junior member this response shows some maturity in judging the temper of the House and trying to control its immediate impulse. To be sure, Floyd was sentenced the same day. Considering that his revered Queen of Bohemia had been clinging to his waist less than six months before it is to Hopton's credit that he was not crying for vengeance with everyone else.

In service again with Mansfeld, Hopton missed the 1624 Parliament. His second term came in the Parliament of 1625 when he was a member for Bath, but for the first half of the session he was still absent on the continent, and the *Journals* do not mention him at all. It is presumed, however, that he continued to enjoy the patronage of Pembroke, who remained lord lieutenant until his death in 1630, and afterward that of his brother, the fourth earl, Philip. In 1628 Sir Ralph was returned again, this time for Wells, his own backyard, so to speak. If precedence in committee listings meant anything he had moved up in prestige: instead of being near the bottom in a list of eighty he was named on one occasion almost immediately after all the privy council and Sir Edward Coke, sitting, with others, to frame a bill into 'An Act to avoid suspicion of Injustice in any member of the Commons House of Parliament'.[7] The issues seem to have grown more complex and, to us, perhaps more familiar. Now he was concerned with 'An Act for Confirmation of Letters Patents,

---

[1] *C.J.* i. 600 (1 May 1621). [2] Ibid. 551 (13 Mar. 1621).
[3] Ibid. 602 (2 May 1621). [4] Ibid. 611 (7 May 1621).
[5] Ibid. 617 (11 May 1621). [6] Ibid. 600 (1 May 1621).
[7] Ibid. 874 (24 Mar. 1628).

made by the late King's Majesty'[1] and again with the presentments of recusants.[2] There is a fragmentary reference to the fact that he sat on a committee meeting with the Lords to discuss tonnage and poundage.[3] In the midst of other grave constitutional and religious questions and a sense of privilege that tends at times to be clubby and exclusive, his association with the Act for 'free Liberty to marry at any time'[4] strikes a relatively gay note. The Act itself, following the precedent of a Commons Bill presented in 1584 which was never read in the Lords, is important in showing the puritan reaction to the remnant of Catholic practice involved in the issuing of banns.[5]

On the basis of this uneven experience it is hard to make a summary statement about Hopton's early parliamentary career. It was educative. He was directly involved in the discussion of national issues and measures of reform; once at least, in Floyd's case, he had won notice by arguing for a cooling-off period. But it is presumed that he had no great enthusiasm for politics. Though later known as the 'Ancient Parliament Man', in the sense that his experience went back twenty years, he never seems to have absorbed much parliamentary tradition. Probably he was influenced only moderately by fiery reformers like his fellow Somersetman Sir Robert Phelips. When in 1633 Sir Robert, for his own political advantage, tacked about and professed the 'King's interest' in supporting church-ales and the revival of Sunday sports, Sir Ralph took the side of the Sabbatarians and the puritan preachers.[6] In 1631 he had signed an order for the suppression of alehouses.[7] In both cases, it is possible that a personal sense of decorum as much as political considerations may have influenced his decision.

Though for the decade 1629–39 he sat officially at no more than twelve general sessions of the peace,[8] his magisterial position gave him a variety of roles to play in county administration. He was chosen as treasurer of the hospitals of the eastern division.[9] He was suggested as a 'fytt master' for one John Collens, a weaver's apprentice who

---

[1] Ibid. 903 (23 May 1628).   [2] Ibid. 896 (12 May 1628).
[3] Ibid. 874 (21 Mar. 1628).   [4] Ibid. 887 (22 Apr. 1628).
[5] J. E. Neale, *Elizabeth I and Her Parliaments* (London, 1957), ii. 77, 356.
[6] Barnes, 90 and n. 101.
[7] *Quarter Sessions Records for the County of Somerset*, ii. *Charles I, 1625–1639*, the Rev. E. H. Bates-Harbin, ed. (London, 1908), 144 (28). In 1635, however, he and his father Robert allowed their woodward to sell beer to their woodcutters without a licence. See Barnes, 193, n. 49.
[8] Ibid., *passim*.   [9] Ibid. 99 (1).

had been starved and ill used.[1] His duties extended to resolving problems of personal libel:

Sir Ralph Hopton ordered Christopher Howie after Evening Prayer at Evercreech Church, June 24, 1629, in the presence of the minister and twenty more of the sufficient inhabitants, to openly acknowledge and confess that he had much wronged John Robbins by using many scandalous speeches and evil reports of him, the said Robbins, in accusing him of witchcrafte and of theft in stealing a sack; and to ask his forgiveness, and to promise that he would never offend again, but would henceforth behave and carry himself toward him as a good Christian ought to do.[2]

This view of Hopton as an arbitrator and administrator is offset by a side-glance at him in another capacity: in a sketch of John Ogilby, John Aubrey mentions that 'he [Ogilby] taught two of the Lord Hopton's [then Sir Ralph's] sisters to dance; and Sir Ralph taught him to handle the pike and musket'.[3] Whether strictly true or not, apart from the charm of the incident and the reflection that Ralph was probably not much of a dancer, we know that his martial enthusiasm and prowess were not wasted in the 'peaceful' years. From 1629 he was, concomitant with his duties as a justice of the peace, also a deputy lieutenant of the militia,[4] a post which he likely received by virtue of his social position and grace of the lord lieutenant Pembroke as well as his martial experience. At any rate, through sheer energy and ability, he soon established it as his very own. It is possible, indeed—and it is a major hypothesis of this study—that the lieutenancy, along with his role in the Long Parliament, may be Hopton's chief claim to political consideration. The course of the Civil War depended upon the readiness of the militia and upon which factions were able to control it: Ralph Hopton, as the most experienced leader the Somerset trained bands had, was the man, if any there was, who could sway them to rally round either flag.

His pre-war reputation was greater because of obstacles, tragic and sometimes ludicrous, that proved the bane of lesser men. It began with personnel: the inadequacies of civilian command; the rivalry between men of predominantly civilian and men with some military background; dislocations caused by wars that never quite came off. In the summer of 1626 the privy council, facing conflict with both France and Spain, began sending into every county veteran officers and

---

[1] *Quarter Sessions Records for the County of Somerset*, ii. 178 (3).
[2] Ibid. xxx.   [3] Aubrey, 220.   [4] Barnes, 317.

sergeants from the Low Countries, who volunteered to spend three months each year training the local bands. In Somerset the eminent Sir Robert Phelips, colonel of the Bath regiment, whose ego had been wounded by what he considered a breach of official punctilio, took umbrage and refused to allow the sergeants to train his regiment.

A more rational deputy, Ralph Hopton's father Robert, tried to soothe him; but to no avail. In July Phelips was out as justice of the peace. About the same time he was dropped as a deputy lieutenant, and as a corollary to this he was also relieved of his regimental command.[1] With a considerable following in Parliament, he could have exploited the situation as an abuse of prerogative threatening military despotism, or at least the encroachment of sinister 'outside' influence, technically needful but pernicious to the rights of Englishmen. Most of the regimental commanders, however, liked the four sergeants who had been sent to their county, and the local companies wanted them to remain after the first year. If they did not have a lasting effect it was due in great measure to the issue of funding 'outsiders', seized by the local opposition to court policy. Hugh Pyne, deputy *custos rotulorum* (and so chairman of quarter sessions) declared in his charge to the Easter quarter sessions grand jury in 1626 that the contribution to the Low Country sergeants was an 'extortion'.[2]

In some of his conclusions Phelips was not far wrong, but the real threat in the late 1620's came not from despotism but from anarchy. The fiascos at Cadiz and at Rhé threw another kind of 'veteran' on the counties: the pressed men who, since the end of 1624, had made up the levies for the Continent. Though many came of good yeoman or artisan stock, they had lost their roots and became the immediate responsibility of the deputy lieutenants. These gentlemen were forced to billet their charges on the local populace. The dislocations of private lives made both the deputies and the veterans odious in the eyes of the people, who could easily be led to regard them as hirelings of a tyrannical Crown.[3]

Such an attitude was unfortunate, because it was transferred to the militia itself. A truly local organization of 'friends and neighbors'

---

[1] Ibid, 249.

[2] Ibid. 70. Hugh Payne was later called up and examined by the Justices, including Robert Hopton, for 'divers malicious and undutiful speeches against his Majestie's royall person and dignitie'. See 'A letter directed to Sir John Stawell ... Robt. Hopton, Esq., & others', dated 16 February 1627/8, *A.P.C.*, 1627 *Sept.–1628 June* (London, 1940), 297–8.

[3] Ibid. 258.

failed to receive local support, as evinced, among other lapses, by the chronic failure to pay the muster master.[1] In the late 1620's and throughout the 1630's Hopton was the only remaining deputy lieutenant with real military experience.[2] His perseverance was more than devotion to duty: the eye that had detected the Cadiz debacle was now focused on a development threatening actual catastrophe. Indeed the military system displayed terrifying inadequacies, particularly in the middle echelons of command where easy-going lords lieutenant failed to maintain effective liaison between the Council and the deputies. The lord lieutenant, in theory, was the King's personal representative in the shire, charged with mustering the county's forces and executing martial law in times of invasion and rebellion; his office was intended to bind crown to country in military matters as that of the judge of assize did in the judicial sphere. Unlike the judges, however, he seldom followed a circuit; he was often a non-resident in the county or too far removed to attend musters in person.[3] Thus, there was no 'national' militia; it was not controlled from the top. Each county unit, or fragment thereof, was potentially at the mercy of local factions; or, more advantageously, in a position to bid for favour. It is to Hopton's undying honour that, until the issue clearly became one of rebellion, he refused his allegiance to any of them.[4]

Indeed, he was one of many men who could see national issues like ship money not in terms of factional advantage but as a matter of conscience, who, while never denying the King's right,

felt the weight of ship money on their hearts as well as on their backs. To these souls even the barest connection with ship money must have been abhorrent at times. As in the forced loan, they had to make the choice between the claims of their neighbors and their King, the choice that was no choice at all. It is easy to undervalue the power of these sentiments, easy to underestimate the importance of such consciences. But the nation was on the threshold of an era when men responded to the dictates of conscience.[5]

As the lotus years of the thirties slipped away Englishmen approached the greatest challenge to conscience in their history. In 1637 the Scots rose against the Laudian liturgy. The following year they subscribed a covenant against popery, extended to include episcopacy. In 1639 the King, to crush this rebellion, advanced with an armed force

[1] Barnes, 263–5.   [2] Ibid. 261.   [3] Ibid. 99, 102, 279.
[4] Ibid. 35–36.   [5] Ibid. 242.

towards the Tweed, guarded by the Earl of Pembroke and Montgomery's regiment of horse, in which Hopton commanded a troop.[1]
As the Scots poured into England the militia was called out for what
to most of its members amounted to foreign service. After fifteen
years of omissions and miscalculations, of seeing war as a 'May
Game', its morale had all but disappeared. Pay, as usual, was in
arrears. There was a natural disinclination to fight co-religionists.[2]
Hopton himself was not wholly committed. Though he supported
the Established Church and was wary of too much indulgence for
Roman Catholics, he was quite tolerant of Protestant Dissenters
and at least saw no reason why Episcopalians and Presbyterians could
not lie down together, a point of view he was able to retain even
after the 'Scots Treason' of 1647 and for which Edward Hyde was
later to rebuke him.[3] But properly incensed or not, nothing, in a
military view, could excuse the mutiny and outrage that in a properly
trained and seasoned militia would never have occurred. Under the
prevailing system a host of Hoptons might have proved ineffectual.

   In the spring of 1640 Charles, as one on a sinking ship, convoked
the Short Parliament that it might bail him out. Still trying to help
him launch the lifeboats, Hopton, sitting for Somerset, entered upon
new paths of leadership. On 16 April he was appointed to a committee
of the House

to examine and consider of all questions to grow and arise [in] this Parliament
about Elections, Returns, or other Privileges of the House; and to report their
opinions and Proceedings therein, to the House, and have Power to send for
Records and Witnesses, and to hear Counsel. . . .[4]

On 1 May he was appointed to the committee for reformation of
'divers Abuses in Ecclesiastical Courts'.[5] He was caught up in events
to an extent which his earlier parliamentary career had not even
hinted at. When the Long Parliament met in the autumn and he
returned to sit again, this time for Wells, his role became for the first
time more political than military. A politician in the strict sense he
could never be. Impervious to subtleties of thought and diction,
innocent of theory—neither lawyer like Hyde, nor philosopher like
Falkland—he generally followed the lead of these men[6] in the
practical matters of parliamentary management, with occasional

---

[1] Clarendon ii. 14–28; *C.S.P.D.* 1625–49 (Suppl), 607. Hopton is listed among
the 'King's Servants' for 1639 and 1640.
[2] Barnes, 278.   [3] *Cal. Clar. S.P.* i. 420–1, No. 2770.
[4] *C.J.* ii. 17.   [5] Ibid.   [6] Sealy, 87.

advice from Sir Simonds D'Ewes. Nor can it be said, despite the statement that Somerset was the only rich and populous county with a majority of members supporting the Crown,[1] that the man who preserved his trained bands from becoming the tools of faction aligned himself at this early stage with any political clique. Broadly speaking, he was a reformer who became a Royalist about the time of the Grand Remonstrance in November and December 1641. With respect to established authority, 'renovation, not innovation' might have been his creed.

This preference for 'known ways', however, did not necessarily include any great sense of parliamentary usage and tradition, as D'Ewes took pains to point out. And yet in the Commons debates he was referred to as 'that Ancient Parliament Man'. Such titles, used to indicate a previous speaker, were not as a rule carelessly or gratuitously bestowed: as the exclusive property of a single individual they were drawn from some personal quality or from the position which the member occupied in the House. Here it may be taken as a sign of seniority: out of 500-odd M.P.'s in the Long Parliament Hopton was one of 156 who had been sitting in 1621.[2] 148 members of the Long Parliament had sat in two to five previous Parliaments.[3] Hopton had sat in four of them. It may therefore be of some significance that Hopton's colleagues, even though their title may represent merely a token of honour and affection, thus acknowledged him as a man of experience in the parliamentary field. In lieu of political theory, party, and 'sense of the House' Hopton could display at least personal respect, conscientious regard for the commonweal, a moderate approach, and a hard sense of reality. In the light of his record it can even be argued that his position was important enough to qualify as 'leadership'. At the very least, until propelled by extraordinary events, he reflects, in regard to most of the 'big' issues, the broad middle segment of House opinion. His own stand can be taken almost as a common denominator.

As might be expected, his attitude was conservative where prerogative and particularly the Church were concerned, reformatory with respect to suppressing abuses perpetrated by the King's servants. Ship money might have weighed upon his conscience, but it is indicated that he looked upon it as an inherent right of the Crown

---

[1] R. N. Kershaw, 'The Elections for the Long Parliament of 1640', *E.H.R.* xxxviii (October 1923), 507–8.

[2] Keeler, 16.   [3] Ibid. 15.

that an Act of Parliament could not take away.[1] The Scots War was the King's War and deserved a loyal subject's support: on 21 November 1640 he subscribed £1,000 security for the City on money sent to the north.[2] As for the Church, his main line was to push reform but defend episcopacy. While not opposed to indulgence or even toleration for the more orthodox Protestant Dissenters, he moved on 1 December that 'some course might bee taken to suppress the growth of poperie . . .'.[3] So far he was on tolerably safe ground. But on the question of the episcopate itself—its political rights, or its very existence—he could take a clearly controversial stand. On 8 February, reacting to petitions for the abolition of episcopacy, he joined Digby, Falkland, Hyde, and Culpeper, Selden, and Waller in supporting reformation without abolition.[4] On 10 March he defended the right of the bishops to sit in the Lords; for 'If you take away their voice in parliament, then they shall be concluded in Ecclesiasticall matters without their consent, which noe subject ought to be by the law of the lande'.[5] In May when the *Protestation* was first drafted it contained a promise to maintain the 'true reformed Protestant religion'. Hopton moved to insert the clause, 'as it is now established in the Church of England'. The Root and Branchers objected, and the result was a compromise to mention the doctrine of the Establishment but not the discipline.[6]

Hopton, then, supported the basic constitutional structure as embodied in the Prerogative and the Established Church. But with respect to specific reforms he may be counted a member of the popular party. On 23 November he struck at the Lord Keeper by moving that 'the Finches might bee sent for as delinquents'.[7] Lord Finch had already been impeached, among other counts, for having, as Chief Justice of the Common Pleas in 1637, exerted pressure from the bench upon the judges of assize to render an opinion maintaining the legality of ship money. His younger brother Edward, vicar of Christ Church, Newgate, was impeached also.[8] By 15 April 1641 Hopton was prepared to move against the mighty Strafford himself, declaring that 'To fram, authorize, and practice things not

[1] *Journal of Sir Simonds D'Ewes, From the beginning of the Long Parliament to Strafford's Trial*, Wallace Notestein, ed. (Yale University Press *et al.*, 1923), 123 and n. 22. Hereafter *D'Ewes*, Notestein.

[2] Ibid. 52. [3] Ibid. 91. [4] Gardiner, ix. 281.

[5] *D'Ewes*, Notestein, 56. [6] Gardiner, ix. 353.

[7] *D'Ewes*, Notestein, 56.

[8] Clarendon iii. 15, n. 2; Barnes, 226 & n. 43.

law is to subvert law. If the actuall e[vidence], bee a sufficient proof of his endeavour to subvert the law, hee hath donn it.'[1] By December he was ready for what may be regarded as the climax of his parliamentary career and perhaps as the parting of the ways. On the first of that month he headed the delegation that presented the Grand Remonstrance to the King.[2] Sir Edward Nicholas, the new Secretary of State, insinuated that he did so unwillingly, 'having before declared his judgment against it', but that his colleagues compelled him to obey. Nicholas, however, who was more conservative than Hyde or Hopton, may be taken as the voice of Royalist officialdom. Though his own views of the Remonstrance can be surmised only from his concern about popish practices in the Church, Hopton was a proper spokesman: the King, despite his abhorrence of the document, 'gave especial Respects to Sir Ralph'.[3] Hopton's report was delivered to the House in due course (2 December):

last Night in the Evening the Committee appointed to attend his Majesty in this Particular, came to Hamptoncourt ... And within a Quarter of an Hour, the King sent a Gentleman to call us in; with Directions that none should come in but the Committee alone: who did all of them present themselves upon their knees: And myself, in obedience to the order of the House in the Absence of another designed for that Service, did begin to read the Petition.... The first Observation his Majesty made was at the Part of the Petition that chargeth a malignant Party with a Design to change Religion: To which his Majesty said, with a great deal of Fervency, 'The Devil take him, whosoever he be, that hath a Design to change Religion.' I then proceeded; and when I came to that Part of the Petition for reserving the Disposal of the Lands of the Rebels in *Ireland*, &c. his Majesty was pleased to say, 'We must not dispose of the Bear's Skin till he be dead.' After the Petition was read, his Majesty desired to ask us some questions: We answered, 'We have no Commission to speak any thing concerning this Business.'[4] Then, said he, you may speak as particular men. Doth the House intend to publish this Declaration?' We answered, We could give no Answer unto it. 'Well then (said he) I suppose you do not now expect an answer to so long a Petition. ... I shall give you an Answer to this Business with as much speed as the Weightiness of the Business will permit.'[5]

[1] Sir Ralph Verney, *Notes of Proceedings in the Long Parliament*, John Bruce, ed. (London, 1845), 48.   [2] *C.J.* ii. 328.

[3] *Journal of Sir Simonds D'Ewes, From the First Recess of the Long Parliament to the King's Withdrawal from London*, Willson Havelock Coates, ed. (Yale University Press *et al.*, 1942), 223, n. 1. Hereafter *D'Ewes*, Coates.

[4] A familiar Stuart tactic. Cf. James I breaking down the corporate nature of a judicial body by interrogating the judges individually in Peacham's Case (1615).

[5] *C.J.* ii. 330.

Granted the importance of this trust, it is indicated that Hopton acted more as the servant than as a leader of the House. He was more concerned with reform than with parliamentary privilege as such. But he saw the roots of that privilege. At the end of the month, in a discussion concerning security for the delivery of certain towns to the Scots, he said that 'wee should have no securitie unles wee had the publike faith . . .'.[1]

In the first days of January 1642 the situation was still fluid. Though the Remonstrance had created a rift which the Militia Bill later was to make apparent, it is safe to say that those members who were neither 'Root and Brancher' nor within the purlieu of Pym's influence were still in an accommodating mood, amenable to compromise and reconciliation with the King. In his study of Edward Hyde's politics, B. H. G. Wormald has designated these men as 'nonviolent' parliamentarians. But at the same time, he says, they could not be called 'conservatives' or even 'moderates', for they were in no way defecting from the ideals of the Long Parliament.[2] The difference between Hyde and Pym was one not of aim but of method. If we accept this view as plausible, we may assume that Hopton, as a follower of Hyde, could have been counted on to support any reasonable change that might be justified in terms of the public interest. And if his intellect was sometimes incapable of sifting the subtleties of debate, if his disagreements with members of opposite persuasions were often too deep to be bridged, his personal esteem for an adversary on that account was never diminished. He stood up for Sir Edward Dering, M.P. for Kent, one of the Root and Branchers, to whose view that the bishops should be shorn of their political privileges Sir Ralph was staunchly opposed. Dering had made indiscreet remarks about members of the House, which moved to expel him. Hopton spoke out and declared that he should be retained 'because of his great parts'. Sir Simonds D'Ewes rose and denounced this proposition; the expulsion was carried out.[3]

5 January 1642 was another day of choice for moderate men. The King's invasion of the House in search of the Five Members brought many of them into line as a continuing opposition. Sir Ralph Hopton fell into line on the other side. When Sir Harbottle Grimston,

---

[1] D'Ewes, Coates, 371.
[2] B. H. G. Wormald, *Clarendon: Politics, History and Religion* (Cambridge University Press, 1951), 45–46
[3] John Forster, *Arrest of the Five Members by Charles I* (London, 1860), 228–9.

in the peroration to a vehement speech, suggested that members of the House should not be impeached except through legal prosecution by the whole House,[1]

Sir Ralfe Hopton excused the Kings coming hither with soe great a number and soe unusually armed, because wee our selves had divers of our servants attending in the Lobbie without the doore of this howse armed in an unusuall manner also with Carabins and Pistolls, that the speech his Majestie made was full of grace and goodnes, that hee did not thinke wee would appoint a grand committee to goe into London nor would hee have had us to have adjourned at all.[2]

Hopton's response is used by the Whig historian Forster to refute Clarendon, who had argued that after the King's intrusion the Commons was exclusively in the hands of the popular party, the King's men remaining silent. On the contrary Sir Ralph 'contradicted everything that was said without scruple'.[3] At this time it can be said that Rushworth's title of the 'King's Servant' replaces that of the 'Ancient Parliament Man'. On 20 January, as in retaliation, the House took up the bill for putting the militia under parliamentary control. The man who had kept his trained bands out of politics for fifteen years now saw the ironic prospect of having them arrayed against him.

Hopton's response to the crisis appears to have been largely unpremeditated, even, at times, reflexive. He could be called a 'parliamentarian' at a stage when 'Parliament' was virtually synonymous with 'Country': the interest of the whole.[4] Sympathetic to reform, his temperament defied parliamentary managers, for he had no 'sense of the meeting': especially, it might be added, when managers and meetings seemed to be pointing toward 'alteration in the old ways' and 'long continued vast change'.[5] Hence, in the three months between the Remonstrance and the Militia Bill, with pressures and provocations mounting on both sides, his own choice of allegiance was hardly surprising. His royalism, always latent, was bound to emerge when the crunch came. It had three roots: first, his non-Laudian high Anglicanism, akin to Falkland's, manifest in Hopton's

[1] Forster, *Arrest of the Five Members* . . . , 275.
[2] *D'Ewes*, Coates, 386.
[3] Forster, *Arrest of the Five Members* . . . , 293.
[4] Perez Zagorin, 'The Court and the Country: A Note on Political Terminology in the earlier Seventeenth Century', *E.H.R.* lxxvii, No. 303 (Apr. 1962), 310.
[5] Wormald, 185–6, citing *S.P. Clar.* ii. 369.

aligment with the 'Episcopal Party' and his defence of the bishops; second (in common with his colleague Culpeper),[1] a concern for the militia and a recognition of the need on the King's side for a show of strength; and third, it would be hard to deny, a sense of personal loyalty to the throne itself.

The last phase of Hopton's connexion with the Commons, extending over the next year, was one of increasing alienation. There had been some foreshadowing of this at the time of the Remonstrance. A procedural problem had arisen in the case of Geoffrey Palmer, a member who, with Hyde and others, had protested against this measure. Picked as a scapegoat, Palmer was accused of faction and sedition; it was suggested that he either be sent to the Tower or put out of the House. There was a discussion as to which question should be put first. Hopton said that the Tower should take precedence. He argued that expulsion was the greater question; if it were put first, the lesser question of the Tower could not be put. Sir Simonds D'Ewes rose and rebuked him severely: 'He wondered to hear such from an ancient parliament man, for it was not the putting and voting of one, two, three, or four questions there that made the judgment of the House.' D'Ewes' somewhat cryptic pronouncement obscures the main issue, which was whether a member could 'protest against the sense of the House': that is, officially dissent from a majority view after the vote had been taken. Hyde himself, admitting that he knew of no precedents for such a situation, asked permission before voicing his objections.[2]

Sir Simonds, of course, was not infallible; but it may be that Sir Ralph, even after five Parliaments, was still not up on his parliamentary procedure. At any rate he had better reason than most to be aware of it. For he continued to 'contradict everything without scruple', and as a result in March he followed in Palmer's steps for two weeks' imprisonment in the Tower, one of the very few members of the Long Parliament to receive such accommodation. This action took place during the debate on a new Declaration (on 4 March) in which Hopton

gave great offence, laying an Imputation upon the Committees of both Houses 'That the Tenth Clause of the Declaration, prepared and brought in from the Committees of both Houses, did accuse the King, for being an Apostate from his Religion, not only in his own Person, but endeavouring to bring his

---

[1] Ibid. 62.
[2] John Forster, *The Grand Remonstrance* (London, 1860), 350–1.

People to the same Apostasy and Idolatry,' or Words to that Purpose, and did desire, that such things might not pass without very good Proof, whereas no such thing could be collected out of that Clause.

Resolved, That Sir Ralph shall be brought to the Bar, and there receive this sentence of being sent to the Tower. Sir *Ralph Hopton* was accordingly called down; and kneeling at the Bar, Mr. Speaker pronounced sentence against him accordingly, That he was adjudged to be sent to the *Tower*, there to remain a Prisoner, during the pleasure of the House.

Ordered, That no Motion shall be made for the Enlargement of Sir Ralph Hopton, but between the Hours of Two and Four.[1]

From the record it is fairly clear that Hopton was imprisoned by the House, not under 'protective custody' through a royal *mittimus*; and that the House took every procedural precaution against a too early or easy release. On this occasion, though, Sir Simonds D'Ewes stood up for Sir Ralph. When Sir Walter Erle, M.P. for Weymouth, moved that Hopton should not be 'enlarged' except in a full house, D'Ewes pointed out the injustice and changed it to simple petition.[2] This gesture, however, was insufficient to curtail two weeks' imprisonment. On 5 March, the day after his commitment, the Houses passed an ordnance appointing new parliamentary lords lieutenant for the militia.[3]

Hopton's active career in the House was almost at an end. From the time of his release in the middle of March we hear little of him. On 11 June at York Charles I, countering the Militia Ordinance, decided to issue commissions of array directing the trained bands to place themselves under officers of his own choosing.[4] By July Hopton, under this authority, was back in Somerset.

On 5 August Parliament took steps to clarify his status:

Resolved, upon the Question,

That Sir *Ralph Hopton* shall be disabled to sit as a member of this House, during this Parliament . . .

Resolved . . . That new Writs shall be sent for new Elections of Burgesses to serve in this House . . . in the Place and Stead of Sir *Ralph Hopton*. . . .[5]

Resolved, That Sir Ralph Hopton [*et alios*] be forthwith sent for, as Delinquents.[5]

Thus ended Hopton's connexion with the House of Commons. Four days before these resolutions, he had raised his King's standard at

---

[1] *C.J.* ii. 467. [2] Forster, *Arrest of the Five Members* . . . , 226–7.
[3] Gardiner, x. 171. [4] Ibid. 202. [5] *C.J.* ii. 708.

Shepton Mallet in Somerset. Before the month was out the Commons had initiated full-scale vengeance against its 'Ancient Parliament Man'. On 29 August 'An Information of some Words spoken by . . . Sir Ra. Hopton . . . at Sherborne in Dorsetshire, was this Day read; and ordered to be printed'.[1] Next day it was Resolved . . . that . . . Sir Ralph Hopton shall be accused, by this House, of High-Treason, in the Name of Themselves, and of all the Commons of England'.[2]

The records hint that Hopton may have had his defenders. On 18 October a pamphlet entitled 'The Examination of Sir Ralph Hopton, &c.' was referred to the Committee for Printing, which was ordered to summon printer and author as delinquents.[3] The examination was alleged to have taken place on 14 October, and was supposed to have included Sir John Winter, Sir John Stawell, and two other knights, all, along with Hopton, upon their knees at the bar of the House to answer articles of high treason. It is probably spurious, since Hopton was recruiting in Cornwall all through October; and may be taken as a Royalist tract, as it has him answering the charges of unlawfully raising troops and money by replying that this was done by warrant and commission of the King.[4]

On 10 February 1643 it was

Ordered, That the Deputy-Lieutenants, and the Committees in *Sommer-settshire*, do presently disarm the Houses of Sir *Ralph Hopton* at Wytham . . .

---

[1] Ibid. 747. Probably reported by John Ashe of the Parliamentary committee in Somerset. See A. R. Bayley, *The Civil War in Dorset, 1642–1660* (Taunton, Barnicott and Pearce: The Wessex Press, 1910), citing, p. 46, H.M.C., Portland MSS., i. 47; *C.J.* ii. 701, etc.

One George Leddoze, merchant of Dorchester, being examined by two J.P.'s, declared he had been taken for a spy and examined at Sherborne Lodge by Poulett, Hopton, Stawell, and Sir Henry Berkeley. When asked whether he were for King or Parliament, he replied 'for both'. Poulett said all Parliamentarians who were for the militia (being under their own control) were proclaimed traitors and 'crop-eared rogues', and that Sir Walter Erle (M.P. for Weymouth) was the wickedest rogue of them all and 'one of the Devil's limbs'. Hopton and the others agreed, and Sir Ralph said further that God was plainly with the Cavaliers in protecting so small a number; that those who took up arms for Parliament were 'blood-sucking robes [rogues?]'. When told there were six great guns in Dorchester, he declared they belonged to him.

[2] Ibid. 749.   [3] Ibid. 816; *S.T.C.* (Wing) 3724.

[4] *The Examination of Sir* Ralph Hopton, *Sir* John Winter, *Sir* John Stawell, *with two other Knights, upon their knees at the Barre, in the House of Commons, the 14 day of this instant October* (1642) *With the Articles of high Treason exhibited against them by the House of Commons* (London, 1642), *passim*. On 19 October the Houses appointed the Earl of Pembroke as Lord General of the western counties 'to raise Forces and march with them' against Hopton. See Bayley, above, 61.

and of all other malignant and disaffected Persons in that County; and send up such malignant and disaffected Persons as they shall find in any of the said Houses standing upon their Guard, in opposition to the Ordinances and Proceedings of Parliament.[1]

Ten days later he suffered forfeiture, under the name of 'sequestration', and his lands were taken up by Act of the House:

Whereas Sir *Ralph Hopton*, in a hostile and rebellious Manner, with a Multitude . . . hath lately invaded . . . the County of Devon; and committed . . . many . . . Outrages, . . . almost to the Utter Impoverishment and Destruction of that County, and the Inhabitants thereof . . . And, amongst others suffering in that kind, *Wm. Strode*, Esquire, a member of the House of Commons, hath been plundered and robbed, and his Goods violently . . . taken out of his House, . . . The Commons in Parliament assembled, taking the same into serious consideration, . . . and holding it agreeable to the Rules of Law and Justice, that the Estates of such as have, in any sort, been Wrong, should be liable and subject to make satisfaction and Reparation; and the Complaint and Loss sustained by the said Mr. *Strode*, do *Order* and *Declare*, That both the real and personal Estate of the said Sir Ralph Hopton shall be forthwith seized and sequestred; . . . and full Power and Authority is hereby given unto the above named *Wm. Strode*, . . . to make such reasonable allowances for the . . . gathering the Rents and Revenues of the same. . .[2]

Thus, in a little more than a hundred years, these lands had passed from the Church to the King, then to the King's man, and now to Parliament and the Parliament's man: ironically, Strode was the member who, in November 1641, had urged the House to command its own forces, an argument leading directly to the Militia Bill of March.[3] In 1646, just before her death, the Lady Hopton petitioned for an allowance out of her husband's estate, a request which was considered 'reasonable'.[4] Later Hopton tried to compound, without success; not until 1672, twenty years after his death, were his sisters, by order of the Lords, properly possessed of their inheritance.[5] A cycle had ended. For the ten years that were left to him he was to know little rest. Landless, a reputed traitor by declaration of Parliament, eventually a man without a country, he had only his good name and profession of arms, sufficient in his case to see him through the years of crisis and exile.

---

[1] *C.J.* ii. 965.   [2] Ibid. 977–8.   [3] Gardiner, 86.
[4] *C.J.* iv. 664.   [5] *L.J.* xi. 53, 96.

III

THE KING'S MAN IN SOMERSET:
The August Days at Wells and Shepton Mallet

(1642)

WHEN Charles I finally raised his standard at Nottingham on 22 August 1642 civil conflict had been simmering, and sometimes exploding, for several months. On 23 April the King had been turned back by Sir John Hotham from the gates of Hull. On 11 June the commissions of array had gone out, and on Sunday 10 July the Parliamentarians fired on the Royalist entrenchments near Beverley, Yorkshire. The ordnance played about briskly all morning; in the afternoon a troop of Royalist horse commanded by Sir Thomas Metham of Lord Lindsey's regiment sallied out of the works towards Hull and burned three windmills,[1] not returning till the following morning. On Tuesday 12 July William Seymour, Marquis of Hertford, left Beverley with a party of gentlemen for the west. On 15 July first blood was shed at Manchester.[2] On 26 July Parliament refused to surrender the arms at Hull. When the King received this refusal two days later,[3] the fact was patent that henceforth he could retain his prerogative only through force of arms. But we may still suspend using the phrase 'civil war' until the strife becomes continuous on something like a national basis.

The war of words, of pamphlets, came first. The great question was whether subjects might take arms and resist their King on the pretext that he was subverting religion and the laws, and whether Parliament might officially sanction such rebellion and take such measures as might be necessary to support it. The key issue was that of the Houses placing control of the militia by ordinance in their own hands. A Royalist pamphleteer accused them of imitating the methods of the Papists and asked if they did not have a 'silent thought

---

[1] B.M., *T.T.*, E. 107 (32): *Exceeding Good News from Beverley, Yorke, Hull, and Newcastle,* Parliamentary correspondence from Beverley dated 16 July 1642, printed London 20 July. This is the starting point for Hopton's own narrative, *Bellum Civile*, q.v., p. 1.

[2] Gardiner, x. 214.

[3] Clarendon, v. 420–3.

of infallibility in that great Councell . . .'.[1] On 28 July a Parliamentary apologist thought the point 'strange ground for such an uncouth dismall war', and wondered that the King should have 'sole interest' in the garrison towns, without 'generall' advice and consent. He could not see why the entrusting of the militia into 'faithfull' hands should be counted oppressive, when at the same time the King was granting commissions 'as illegall and vexatious and dangerous . . . as the Ship-Scot was'. Virtually equating Parliament with the State, he accepted the maxim that 'He which serves the State faithfully, must needs serve the King faithfully, (it is to be wished, the contrary were true) . . .'.[2] Thus, a change in the subordinate officers of the militia did not flout the ultimate authority of the King. If this was granted, and the militia removed as the main bone of contention, there was no excuse for blood.

But such sophisms, much as they may have turned in many men's minds, were of little weight to resist the final resort to arms. By August Parliament was gathering force in the east; the King, moving down from York, was making progress in the north. The question now was: which way the west?

On 14 June 1642 a petition addressed to the Lords and Commons arrived from the 'Knights, Gentry, Clergy, and Freeholders of the County of Somerset'. Thanking the Houses for their 'care and pains', they begged that order might be maintained; that the Established Church should be retained and obeyed until the King and the Parliament, with a synod of divines, made alterations; that an account should be given as to the expenditure of previous monies, since Parliament was demanding more and the country was becoming impoverished; that, since there was no agreement on how to settle the militia, it should be used 'as in the time of Elizabeth' until a law could be made. Above all, they pleaded that a civil war was worse than disputes about a 'malignant party'.[3]

This appeal is typical of early seventeenth-century Englishmen at their best. It shows their high-mindedness, patience, gravity; their moderation and reverence for tradition; their sense of commonweal. Perhaps it shows also their comparative lack of complexity and

[1] H. Fern. D. D., *The Resolving of Conscience*, etc. (Cambridge and London, 1642), 3.

[2] Henry Parker, *The Danger to England Observed, upon its deserting the High Court of Parliament* (London, 28 July 1642), 3.

[3] *Cobbett's Parliamentary History*, ii. cols, 1366–7.

sophistication,[1] though no more than that of most people still on the fringes of great events. But in another way it may be misleading, for it implies a unanimity which in fact did not exist.

Immediately preceding the petition was a letter from Alexander Popham, Member for Bath, to his father Sir Francis, Member for Minehead, which explained something of its background:

Honoured Father,
The next day after you went out of this country, this Petition inclosed was sent to divers Places, for to procure Hands to it; it hath been read in several Churches, by the Ministers of these Towns. Sir *Francis Dorrington* [Doddington] sent it to *Bath*, and writ a Letter to *George Wilb*[erforce] and *Dick Chapman*, for the advancement of it; all *Sir Charles Barklye's* Friends, and *Sir Ralph Hopton's* labour for the Advancement of it. Some of *Bath* gave me Notice of it, whither I did repair; the Mayor and aldermen called a Council, and sent for me: The Petition was then read. They asked my Opinion: I told them, there were great Aspersions laid upon the Parliament in it, and desired to know who sent it to them. They told me *Sir Francis Dorington*. I thought it my duty to give you Notice of this, that some Way may be thought on to nip this in the Bud; for otherwise it will set us together by the Ears. There are many earnestly for it, but as many violently against it. It will wait on you, God willing, on *Monday* next at Littlecott [Wilts.] I humbly beg your Blessing.

Hunster [Dunster]   Your ever dutiful and obedient son,
   11 June   Alexander Popham
   1642
                  The Petition is thrown aside at Bath,
                  and yet Hands to it.[2]

This letter implies that public opinion in Somerset was extremely mixed, but that it tended perhaps towards becoming a moderating curb on Parliament. Indeed Popham's admonition to 'nip this in the Bud' would indicate much more. It shows also that Parliament was accepting his report at face value by merely repeating his own word 'aspersions' as their only recorded excuse for not permitting the petition to be heard. In short, that body depended very much on its local observers and commentators; the success of its strategy depended to no little extent not only on accurate reporting but on the leverage which such correspondents could give to county opinion. Popham's

---

[1] Wallace Notestein, *The English People on the Eve of Colonization* (New York, 1954), 30–35.
[2] *L.J.* v. 133.

advice to the mayor and council of Bath may well have had something to do with the defection of that city from the Royalists five or six weeks later.

Before describing the failure of the Royalist rally in Somerset, it is necessary, then, to consider briefly the nature of public sentiment. One source of conflict lay in a cleavage within the ranks of the county notables. The gentry were an amorphous body, but could be divided roughly into two groups. One consisted of the older families dating at least from the Reformation and owing their prosperity in the first instance to the King's service and bounty. The other included men of more recent affluence, rising largely through successful farming and the cloth trade,[1] which might provide an economic base for social advancement and political preferment. The first group, with some exceptions, was generally well affected to the King. The few dissidents were men like the Horners of Mells and the Pophams of Littlecote, Parliamentary and puritan. They became the leaders of the local opposition to the King. This group was rich, vocal, cohesive, and on the whole much better led than the Royalists.[2] Clarendon himself admits this, though he excuses the Royalists by saying that the King's counsels were all 'with great formality deliberated before concluded: and then, with equal formality and precise caution of the law, executed . . .'.[3]

The Parliamentary position was deceptive. Numerically two-thirds of Somerset's members in the lower house could be called Royalists. But the most influential of these were on the verge of being expelled. For the important boroughs the Royalists had Wells, but the Parliamentarians had Bath and divided the honours of Taunton and Bridgwater.[4] To offset Sir Ralph Hopton sitting for Wells and Sir John Stawell for the county there was Sir Francis Popham, sitting for Minehead, soon to be succeeded by his fifth son Edward; and, more important, the old knight's second son Alexander (he who was to be one of Cromwell's Lords and Councillors of State) sat for Bath. Ralph Hopton had been a deputy lieutenant in Somerset; under the new order, Alexander Popham was a deputy lieutenant for Parliament.[5]

---

[1] Barnes, 6; Mildred Campbell, *The English Yeoman* (New York, 1942), 217, 345.

[2] Ralph Hopton, *Bellum Civile: Hopton's Narrative of His Campaign in the West, and other papers*, C. E. H. Chadwyck-Healey, ed. (For Somerset Record Society, Frome—pub. London, 1902), xxii.

[3] Clarendon, vi. 5.   [4] Gardiner, frontispiece; Keeler, *passim*.

[5] *D.N.B.* (Oxford, 1908), xvi. 141–3.

As colleagues in the Commons they had both pushed for reform. Hopton, tolerant of Presbyterians, had had no qualms about pressing Sabbatarian legislation for the puritans. Now the two men were to be recruiters for different causes altogether.

We may proceed, then, to the constitutional issue, which did indeed turn on that 'precise caution of the law' of which Clarendon was so fond. The issue was one involving the King's prerogative right to control the militia. This right Parliament had assumed by ordinance. The King, in retaliation, had issued commissions of array, acting on the basis of an old statute dating from the reign of Henry IV. Both measures were denounced by the leading lawyer of the day. John Selden argued that the commissions were illegal, since the original statute had been repealed. The ordinance had even less justification: according to Selden, it was 'without any shadow of law'.[1] Clarendon himself called the commission a 'thing not heard of', even though founded on statute. He thought the King would have done better to use the 'old known way' of lord and deputy lieutenant.[2] In fact the commission became a prime ingredient of Parliamentary propaganda. It was argued that a great part of the estate of every farmer or substantial yeoman would be taken from them; that the poorer sort would have to pay a tax for one week's labour to the King; and that all would be slaves to the lords. In other words, England would become like France. These allegations were not without effect. Also, some Parliamentary advantage was gained from the document's being printed in Latin:[3] only the educated could construe it for themselves. At any rate, it is safe to say that allegiance was not won strictly on points of law, as to some extent it was a few months later in Cornwall.

This, then, was the state of affairs in Somerset at the time when the Marquis of Hertford was sent out from York to raise the western counties for the King. He held an extraordinary commission under the Great Seal, which he was to keep secret until he found 'by the growth [or] extraordinary practice of the Parliament in raising forces that the commission of array was not enough . . .'.[4] Perhaps an extraordinary commission was necessary, for the marquis, in a military sphere, was something less than ordinary, being 'not fit for much activity and fatigue, and . . . wedded so . . . to his ease that he loved his book above all exercises'.[5] He and his brother, Francis,

---

[1] Clarendon, v. 365. [2] Ibid. 364. [3] Ibid. vi. 4.
[4] Ibid. v. 385, 443. [5] Ibid. iv. 296.

Lord Seymour of Trowbridge, were mere ribands on the plain buff coat of soldiering. But among the Cavaliers that rode with them were some whose names would grow and resound with the war. There was Sir John Stawell of Cothelstone, whose estate was second to none in the county of Somerset. There was Sir Hugh Pollard, back from an uncompleted voyage to the Netherlands: on his way thither to raise levies for the royal cause he had fallen in with a King's ship from Holland bearing arms and returned with it safely, though pursued by Parliamentary vessels.[1] And there was Sir Ralph Hopton, out to save what he could from the militia he had trained for over fifteen years.

But before this train even reached Somerset there came a premonition that the Commons' strength might prove a hard nut to crack. In the last days of July they came to the marquis's seat of Marlborough in Wiltshire, wherein lay Hertford's main estate and his brother's house. Upon the arrival of the illustrious lord, the populace broke down the church doors and seized the magazine, which they refused to yield. The Royalists, being but a small force, could do nothing.[2] Resistance, if not completely open, was more than passive.

At this point it is almost ludicrous to shift the scene to Bath, where the Somerset autumn assizes were sitting. On 25 July, approximately the same time Sir Ralph Hopton was in Marlborough, he was called upon, as one in the commission of the peace, to settle a civil dispute.[3] Was it referred to him when at last he did arrive? A more weighty question is whether Hopton might have made a harangue at Bath similar to the one he made some months later at the quarter sessions in Cornwall, where he saved the county for the King by pointing out the legal shortcomings of the Parliamentary deputy lieutenants. Had the Somersetmen been as susceptible to legal logic as to partisan persuasion, he might have swayed them. But Bath's preference for Parliament was never in doubt. Martin Sanford, the high sheriff, who had given assurances of fidelity to the King, quickly disclosed his 'treacherous intencions' in allowing himself to be 'guided by an undiscreete sonne'.[4] Bath, therefore, was unsuitable as a Royalist rallying-point.

Two other possibilities were Bristol and Wells. Strategically, the Royalist occupation of Bristol this early in the war would have

---

[1] *D.N.B.* xvi. 564.　　　　　　　　[2] Hopton, 1–2.
[3] P.R.O., Assizes 24/21, f. 50.　　　[4] Hopton, 2.

provided a base for a war of greater manoeuvre through more effective co-ordination with the King's forces. It might have prevented the costly siege of July 1643. Bristol, however, was a 'municipal' county outside Somerset's jurisdiction. Its Parliament deputies were Royalists, but rumour went that its sentiments were otherwise. On the other hand, Wells, it was thought, was unquestionably Royalist; and it had the advantage of a central location. This, in fact, was its undoing, for it was easier to surround from east and west. The more hopeful considerations, however, prevailed, and Wells was 'unhappily chosen'.[1] Here the 'error of uneffective and unfinished considerations began betymes, and hath to[o] constantly attended the business throughout'.[2]

Hertford's initial strength when he went to Wells points up the Royalist tendency to be heavy in horse while remaining relatively deficient in foot. The units had been raised by individual gentlemen. John Digby, son of the Earl of Bristol, had raised one troop; Sir Francis Hawley of Buckland, another. Sir John Stawell, who in 1643 was to become one of the strongest proponents of a Royalist 'Western Association' to balance Parliament's Eastern Association,[3] raised three regiments of horse and two of dragoons at his own charge. Hopton, also, at his own expense, had raised a troop. To complete this array, John, Lord Poulett of Hinton St. George, Lieutenant-Colonel Henry Lunsford, and other gentlemen had brought in only a hundred foot.[4] This cadre, it was hoped, would soon be augmented by the trained bands. Yet, by the time the marquis was driven out of Wells, he had raised and retained only 900.[5] The breakdown is hard to determine, since most accounts are incomplete or else inclined to exaggerate. One alleges the Royalists had approximately 500 horse,[6] but the figure is inadmissible. When they reached Minehead in September desertion had trimmed their ranks to 160,[7] and the defection of two-thirds of such a force is unlikely. As for the opposing numbers, before Bedford's arrival they reached a peak of over 15,000, though only about 7,000 were finally joined to the earl's army.[8] At any rate, whether or not the royal cause was popular that summer in Somerset it failed of support. In trying to describe its failure

---

[1] Ibid. 2–3.   [2] Ibid. 3.
[3] Clarendon, viii. 257.
[4] Hopton, xxii; Clarendon, vi. 6; *D.N.B.* xviii. 1007.
[5] Gardiner, x. 216–17.   [6] *D.N.B.* xvii. 1272.
[7] Hopton, 18.   [8] Gardiner, loc. cit.

we need to look closely at events in Wells and its environs during the first week of August, and particularly at the role played by Hertford's right-hand man—one might as well say the King's lieutenant in the west—Sir Ralph Hopton. Essentially it is his story.

When Hopton went out to Somerset to execute the commission of array perhaps it was not quite the beginning of a new career but rather the termination of an old one. More than ever his role was political as well as military: unless the militia could be won over, or until separate cadres could be formed, he was essentially a recruiter, trying to persuade 'friends and neighbours' to rally round his flag. It may be worth noting again that Hopton and Hertford were both in Somerset before the end of July, although Hertford's 'extra-ordinary commission' received at York had been post-dated so as not to become effective till 2 August. By that date Sir Ralph had already raised a troop of horse at his own cost, the first jostlings between the forces had occurred, and the first blood in the west was about to be shed. Hopton, however, was on his own ground: his official relations with Hertford were hardly different from those he had held with Pembroke, his lord lieutenant of Somerset a dozen years before.

With the Royalist commissioners receiving the musters of the trained bands at Wells, the Parliamentary committee met six miles to the east at Shepton to plot a countermove. According to their own account 'wicked . . . Incendiaries of that place' petitioned Hertford, asserting the meeting was to 'fire their houses and make the streets run with blood'. Hertford sent his deputy to investigate. Hopton was delayed by the slack appearance of volunteers to go with him and by an order from the Council of Wells to take with him no troops but only private gentlemen. Finally he set out with three troops of horse, one of dragoons, 100 foot, and 28 country gentlemen, perhaps 360 men at the very most. He arrived at Shepton between ten and eleven in the morning to discover, if not 'wicked incendiaries', at least 160 or 200 'honest men well arm'd'. Seizing all the arms and ammunition he could find, he then tried to read the petition.

At this point he was ordered to desist. The dissenter was one William Strode, not the fire-eater of 'Five Members' fame, though he had sat in the Long Parliament.[1] A sound Presbyterian from

---

[1] 'Five Members' Strode was from Devon, where he sat for Beer Alston, and died in 1645. The other Strode was a Somersetman, lived in Barrington, sat at

Barrington, equally opposed to bishops and commissions of array, he was now a temporary resident of Shepton Mallet; and it was he who, as one of the Parliamentary deputy lieutenants, was responsible for the presence of the armed men there.

As a damper for this spirit, Hopton seized both his person and his horse, forcing him to alight and arresting him on suspicion of treason. Though he would have done better to keep his prisoner in his own custody, he turned him over to the constable and then read the petition. Strode called on the people to obey the King as guided by Parliament, not by evil counsellors. This done, Hopton rode out of town and 'raised many men'; but many others, 'without request', private gentlemen and plain freeholders, poured in as a *posse comitatus* for Parliament. The constable at Shepton to whom Hopton had committed Strode ran away with him. The weakness of the Royalist position was manifest. Finally the Parliamentary committee sent two gentlemen into the fields to interrogate Hopton. He took them to Wells, where the marquis informed them that the protest meeting was illegal. The committee, apprised of this, retorted that so, too, was the commission.[1] So far it was mainly a war of words.

But they were loaded words, and it could be argued that the failure of the King's men at Wells in August was due in no small

---

[1] Hopton, 4–6, note; Clarendon, vi. 6; *C.J.* ii. 265; *Victoria History of the Counties of England: Somerset*, W. Page, ed. (London, 1911), ii. 205. In Clarendon the marginal date for the Shepton incident is Wednesday 3 August, based on a letter of John Ashe, printed by the Lords on 12 August. But I think a close reading of *Bellum Civile* will confirm Monday 1 August as the true date. This account is based on a letter to Parliament signed by eight members of the Somerset committee. It was received by 5 August, the date on which Hopton was disabled from sitting in the Commons.

---

one time for Ilchester, and died in 1666. His revolt had begun as early as 1636. In that year he had refused to pay ship money; after one of his cows was seized for the tax, he replevied it. In November of the same year he was examined by the King and in December called before the Privy Council, though he refused to attend on account of illness. Later the job of examining him seems to have been deputed to the Bishop of Bath and Wells. Strode replied with a long argument in writing about the illegality of the proceedings. See *C.S.P.D.* 1636–37, pp. 205, 216, 222, 341, 400–1, 405, 552; and an article by Thomas Serel, 'On the Strodes of Somersetshire', in *Som. Arch. & Nat. Hist.* xiii (1865–6), Pt. 2, pp. 14–15. The last source refers, pp. 10–11, to a return from the judges of assize in Somerset in the 1630's with suggestions as to proper persons for the office of Sheriff. Strode and Sir John Horner, among others, were declared unfit.

measure to the epistolary efforts of men like John Ashe,[1] whose first
Parliamentary experience had come in the Short Parliament where
he sat for Westbury, Wiltshire. It had elected him again to the
Long Parliament. An active member, he served on the committee
concerning scandalous ministers. In 1642 he pledged £10 weekly for
the duration of the war. Though moderate as far as the orders of the
House permitted, he incurred the hatred of the Royalists by his work
in dealing with sequestrated estates. His own property included at
least two manors in Somerset and Wiltshire and much of the parish
of Freshford. Yet, not surprisingly, despite his holdings, he was
never received by the gentry, who, because of his clothier connexions,
might readily brand him an upstart. Social and religious bias cannot
be ruled out in considering his activities as a member of the Parliamentary committee in Somerset.

The 'August Days' at Wells and Shepton Mallet have been
described from the Royalist standpoint by Hopton in his *Bellum
Civile*, a straightforward, factual narrative compressing the main
events into a few pages. It does not, however, mention the Royalists'
return to Shepton on 3 August. For more perspective we must turn
to a letter written by Ashe at Freshford on 7 August, which was
received, read, and recorded at Westminster on 9 August. Since the
ends of the lines are torn, it is at times highly ambiguous. The style,
however, in places is inflammatory enough to warrant the assumption
that Westminster was impressed.

Tuesday 2 August had passed with watchful waiting. The Royalist
position was growing perilous. Popham and Horner were drawing out
12,000 men for Parliament, many from Devon, Dorset, and Bristol.[2]

---

[1] Ashe (1597–1659), a Presbyterian elder, lived within the county at Freshford,
though he sat for Westbury, Wilts. The eldest son of a wealthy clothier, James Ashe,
of Westcombe in Batecombe, he had followed his father's trade and secured numerous
landed estates. In 1637 he was described as the 'greatest clothier in England'. A
collector for the 1627 loan, he was reported as defaulting on the whole amount
assessed him, thus setting an example of resistance. About ten years later he was
summoned by the Attorney-General to answer for attacking ecclesiastical abuses
and charged with being the confederate of William Prynne, J. Bastwick, and Henry
Burton in publishing and distributing such libellous works as *News from Ipswich*
and *A Divine Tragedy Lately Enacted*. His crime was knowing the contents of the
volumes, which, late in 1636, he had distributed in Somerset and elsewhere.
In January 1637 he was called to London, but allowed to return under bond
to Somerset because of the thousands of workers dependent on him. A Star
Chamber prosecution was threatened, but the records tell only of the trial of the
principals. Later Ashe protested against the soap monopoly and ship-money assessments. See Keeler, 91–92.

[2] Clarendon, vi. 7.

Next day, the third, Hopton's men came back to Shepton to recon-
noitre. According to Ashe, they rode through the town up to the
Mendip Hills, frightening the people, who sent scouts to warn Ashe,
Alexander Popham, and the other Parliamentary gentlemen to look
after themselves, 'for that these Cavaliers were coming to destroy
us'. Coming down the hill again to Shepton, they stayed to roister in
the taverns:

> Some of their Cavaliers, marching about the Town, found out all . . . .
> Religious Mens Houses that were there; those Houses they broke into,
> plundered, ... robbed, especially of all Arms and Ammunition; and
> made the Owners, with . . . . Wives and Children, to forsake their
> Houses, and hide themselves, for Fear of . . . ., and never durst to
> return Home until Yesterday; but, after the . . . ., refreshed themselves,
> and the Cavaliers done their said Pranks, they dep . . . . to *Wells*,
> when they had ordered the Billeting of 100 of their Troope . . . . [ellipses
> in original, document fragmentary].

'Upon this their bold March and Bravadoe', Sir John Horner
called together his neighbours and tenants, supplied them with
weapons, and marched them off to rendezvous with Alexander
Popham, who had mustered 1,000 men in arms. On Friday 5 August
they all marched together to Chewton, four or five miles north-east
of Wells, with the 'great vast Mendeep' between them. To them
came the trained bands from that quarter of the shire, including
Popham's regiment, 'doubled Twice over, by Means of Volunties'.
There came also 300 horsemen out of Wiltshire; 300 'lusty stout
Men, of very good rank and Quality' from Bristol, all on horseback;
and a company of 250 or 300 foot from Gloucestershire—all
volunteers. There were two wains loaded with powder, bullets, and
match and two more with four small field pieces, including carriages
and ramrods, all sent from Bristol contrary to the orders of the mayor
and the sheriff. Despite the lack of expert soldiers and commanders,
the troops, even without food or drink, 'could not be stayed, but
would march over the Hill, which was near 4 Miles, [until] they
came in Sight of *Wells* . . .'.[1]

It might be assumed that Mr. Ashe drew the original stereotype
of the 'swaggering Cavaliers', a term which is used synonymously
with 'Incendiaries' and 'Delinquent Gentlemen'; and it is intriguing
to compare these tavern roisterers with the committee's forces lying
by night in the open and spending the time in 'Prayer and the singing

[1] *L.J.* v. 278–9.

of Psalms'. In a word, his reports, of dubious value as records of fact, show considerable ingenuity as propaganda. He emphasized the 'Love and Affection of all the Country, with 8 & 10 miles Distance' toward the Parliament, and indicated that this love plus the violent tactics of the Cavaliers would make it impossible to put the commission of array into effect. But just in case, he begged the presence of the Earl of Bedford with three or four hundred horse.[1]

Thursday 4 August the Parliamentary noose began to tighten as a force under John Pyne of Curry Mallet moved up toward Wells from Taunton. From the exposed position, perhaps, it was only a matter of time, but Sir John Stawell, that man of 'notorious courage and fidelity',[2] took three troops of horse and fourteen dragoons and went to protect the road between Wells and Glastonbury. With him were Lieutenant-Colonel Henry Lunsford, who had come with Hertford from York; Captain John Digby, Sir Francis Hawley, and Edmund Wyndham, a gentleman of the King's Privy Chamber and Pyne's brother-in-law.[3] In all, the Royalists numbered eighty men. Riding toward Somerton they came to Marshall's Elm and discovered, in a cornfield two miles away, a Parliamentary host of 600 men drawn up against them.

The number of the opposing force was gleaned from a messenger whom they apprehended as he tried to approach Pyne with information from William Strode to the effect that another Parliamentary army had already mounted the Mendip Hills north of Wells. An hour later Stawell decided to parley. By agreement, he, Hawley, and Sir John Poulett, son and heir apparent of Lord Poulett, met at the Elm with Pyne, who was accompanied by Captain John Preston and a Captain Sands. Stawell urged the 'disaffected party' to reflect that 'they would not by their advancing beginne a civill warr, but prevayled not . . .'.

Meanwhile, Lunsford, showing his tactical skill, had divided the horse into three squadrons, drawn up on the brow of the hill to hide the thinness of their ranks. Stawell commanded the centre, Digby the right wing, Hawley the left. The uneven ground was natural camouflage for all but their heads and a few swords. The fourteen dragoons were divided into two equal squads and placed in two quarry pits, one on each side of the road, about 150 paces in front of the

[1] *C.J.* ii. 228–9.   [2] Clarendon, viii. 146.
[3] Wyndham had married Christabel, Pyne's sister. See *The Visitations of Somerset in the Years* 1531 *and* 1573, F. W. Weaver, ed. (Exeter, 1885), 67.

horse. Lunsford, standing by one of the pits, took charge of this van. The Parliamentarians advanced; the Royalist dragoons fired and killed John Osmond, who led the attack, with a shot in the head. As the whole body staggered, Lunsford signalled Stawell; the Royalist horse charged, and the enemy line broke. Seven Parliamentarians were killed on the spot; eighteen died later from wounds. There is no record of Royalist casualties.[1] Stawell's exemplary moderation and mercy prevented further deaths. He was satisfied with having taken sixty horse and several high-ranking prisoners, among them Preston and Sands.[2] First blood had been shed in the west.

The way to the south, then, was still open; and back in Wells that same day preparations went forward to meet the advance from the north. Hopton and Sir Edward Rodney of nearby Rodney Stoke negotiated with the corporation for munitions. It was delivered to them out of the stores in the city's magazine for £30 deposited in the hands of the mayor.[3] The bargaining power of the Cavaliers had improved considerably since Marlborough. Indeed, Parliamentary intelligence of 1 August reported that the mayor, Robert Morgan, had delivered the keys of the magazine to 'Sir Francis Doddington, a delinquent'.[4] Doddington was to become Hopton's adjutant at a later phase in the war.

The climax came on the night of Friday 5 August as a Parliamentary army gathered on Mendip above Wells. Writing a few days later Ashe reported gleefully on volunteers from Hopton's own neighbourhood 'unto his very gates', who lay that night upon the hills above Wells, fasting and praying:

> Sir John Horner and Master Alexander Popham with his two valiant brothers [Edward and Hugh] and Sir John Horner's youngest sonne, with many others, lay all that night in their Armes upon fursbushes in the open fields, the old Knight often saying that his furs-bed was the best that ever he lay upon.[5]

Ashe's narrative reads like an account of Sir Thomas Erpingham—

---

[1] For an account of Lunsford's ambuscade, see B. M. *King's Pamphlet*, E. 112, No. 33.

[2] Hopton, 7–9.

[3] City Clerk's Office, Wells: MS. 'Acts of the Corporation of Wells', 4 Aug. 1643. The account gives:
    300 lb. of powder at 12*d*.
    300 doz. of bullets at 2*d*. a lb.
    600 yds. of match at 1*d*.

[4] Hopton, 7, note.   [5] Ibid. 10, n. 1; *L.J.* v. 278–9.

that 'good old knight' in *Henry V*—mixed with one of Gideon prowling above the tents of the Midianites.

Meanwhile the Royalists were astir. With a host mounting against them, they were suffering serious depletions in their own ranks: the deficiencies of the trained bands were showing up at last as, in the dark of night, they left their posts and ran away. Deciding not to wait on events, Hertford ordered a move, handing the order to Hopton for execution. The first of many retreats, it was carried out through 6 and 7 August, taking the troops by way of Glastonbury and Somerton to the castle at Sherborne in Dorset.[1] Here they remained a month and half, being joined by Sir John Berkeley, Colonel William Ashburnham, and other officers.[2] The only reason that can be alleged for this delay is that they were a small force with enemies everywhere and cut off from any help; either to advance or retreat might be to invite disaster.

In the meantime, however, their hand was being forced. On the same day as they arrived at Sherborne, Ashe's appeal had been answered, and Bedford's troops were on the march to 'impeach the recourse' between north and south as well as to 'strengthen the Ordinance of Parliament for the apprehension of the Marquis Hertford . . . and Sir Ralph Hopton . . . who are declared delinquents in both Houses [Hopton had been disabled from sitting in Commons on 5 August] for enforcing the execution of the Commission of Array'. At the same time Sheriff Sanford of Somerset, he who had shown his 'treacherous intencions' at the assizes in Bath, was directed to act with a *posse comitatus*.[3]

Thus it was open war between Parliament and the Royalists of the west, and the puritan trumpet had sounded in a call to arms against

that Legion of Devils . . . that heap . . . of scrum, and drosse, and garbage of the Land . . . made up of Gebal and Ammon and Amaleck, . . . of Jesuits and Papists, and Atheists, of stigmaticall and infamous persons in all kindes, with that bloody and butcherly Generation, commonly knowne by the name of Cavaliers. . . .[4]

The John Ashes of the Parliamentary committees did their vituperative best. But the King's standard, too, had been raised. Just before

---

[1] Hopton, 10.   [2] Clarendon, vi. 7.
[3] *C.S.P.D.* 1641–43, 366, No. 104.
[4] *Anti-Cavalierisme, or, Truth Pleading as well the Necessity, as the Lawfulness of the present War . . .* etc. (London, 1642), *passim*.

the battle of Edgehill, on 23 October, he addressed his troops in a ringing charge and exhortation that goes far to explain why men like Hopton served him, if indeed it does not hint at the sort of man Hopton was:

> You are called Cavaliers and Royalists in a disgraceful manner: . . . that should produce in you all a nobly mounted anger . . . You are called Cavaliers in a reproachful signification. . . . They call all the Kings Troopers cavaliers; but let them not know that the valour of the Cavaliers hath honored that name . . . and now let it be known in England as well as Horseman or Trooper, it signifying no more but a Gentleman serving his King on horseback, shew yourselves therefore now courageous cavaliers, and beat backe all . . . aspersions cast upon you by the Enemy. Let them know and discerne that for your King you dare adventure youselves, and for the eternall reward of a just acquired honour.[1]

About the same time, Bedford's reception in Wells indicates that Royalist sentiment there may have been stronger than some would have been led previously to believe. A fortnight after Hertford's retreat Strode of Shepton Mallet wrote to Mayor Morgan and the city council desiring entertainment for 'Our Lord Lieutenant of this county, the noble Earle of Bedford'. (Hertford was, or had been, lord lieutenant of Somerset for the King.) The letter was signed also by Alexander Popham and John Ashe. It stated further that though some thought 'your Towne is verie ill affected to the peace of the kingdome', the Parliamentary committee had assured Bedford that 'hee shall fynde as faythfull servyce amongst you as in any Towne in this Countye'. Somewhat reluctantly, it is inferred, the citizens provided a hogshead of claret to go with the entertainment, which the earl could not have deemed satisfactory. Moreover, Strode pointed out, the city was by no means enthusiastic about providing adequate arms for the 'safetye of his Majesties person, the Parliament, and Kingdomes'.[2] The intimation is that the Royalists are actually considered as rebels against the King's weal as well as the commonweal.

Perhaps the good people of Wells did not think so. If they had not openly and heartily endorsed Hertford, this may have been partly because they were not impressed by him and also because they were

---

[1] *Three Speeches Made by the Kings most Excellent Majesty: The first to divers Lords and Colonels in His Majesties Tent, the second to His souldiers in the field; the third to His whole Army* . . . etc. (London, 1642?). See *The King's Speech to his Souldiers*, 5.

[2] Serel, 11–13.

intimidated by the hordes levied from outside the county. Since the bulk of the Parliamentary troops seem to have been drawn from Wiltshire, Gloucestershire, and Bristol, it would appear that Royalist sentiment was defeated by a combination of propaganda and external pressure. At any rate, the town did not go out of its way to help Bedford, who took his time coming on; and if this did not depress him, it is certain that Hopton's horse gave him pause. The night attacks forced him finally to withdraw. But reverses elsewhere led to a Royalist council of war at which Hertford decided to retreat towards Wales that he might more readily communicate with other King's forces and perhaps harass Bristol.[1] The retreat had already been ordered when the marquis decided to make it by way of Minehead. Presumably it was well known that there would be coal boats from Swansea which would take them directly to Wales.

Hopton submitted to this new command, but none too gracefully. Indeed, it is possible that he had reached a point where his deputy's role was beginning to weigh on him. Hertford had no professional knowledge whatsoever of tactics or strategy. Hopton, more effectively perhaps than when he had argued in Parliament with D'Ewes and Sir Harbottle Grimston, urged him to consider the disadvantages of this particular move:

It being a much longer marche, and over a verie ill country for carryages, and worst affected to the service, Taunton being just in his way at that tyme, a strong Garrison of the Parliaments, and Dunster Castle being then held against him, and there being a possibilitie many wayes that his expectacion of Welch-boates might fayle him, which afterwards did. . . .[2]

But the marquis persisted in his resolution. The last week in September, tailed by Bedford, they picked their way to Minehead through a generally hostile country. Hertford reproached Sir Ralph with the cowardly character of his countrymen; Hopton tried to excuse them and pointed out that, after all, Bedford had even more deserters.[3] At Minehead there were only two boats; so

upon Sir Ralph Hopton's advice and request, the Lord Marquesse with all the Voluntiers, the foote, the baggage, . . . tooke passage for Wales, leaving the horse (being a hundred and ten) and the dragoones (about fyftie) under the command of Sir Ralph Hopton. . . .[4]

Remaining with him were not only officers like Colonel Ashburnham and Major Walter Slingsby but eminent civilians like Sir Henry Killigrew and Sidney Godolphin, all members of his council of war.

[1] Hopton, 17.   [2] Ibid.   [3] Ibid. 18, n. 2.   [4] Ibid. 18.

Bedford, though only four miles away when Hertford and Hopton parted, was content with having expelled the marquis, assuming no doubt that Hopton's little band would be picked up by the committees of militia in Devon or Cornwall. He must have felt that he had extinguished all hope of raising an army for the King in the west.[1] Save for Hopton, he might well have been right.

It is uncertain whether Sir Ralph had cleared his plan with the marquis or whether it was clear even to himself at the time of parting. In effect he was no longer Hertford's lieutenant-general of horse and chief of staff, but a commander on his own. For many months he was generally out of touch with other Royalist forces until his great victories in the first half of 1643—at Braddock and Launceston, Stratton and Lansdown—brought him a barony and finally command as field marshal of a new western army.[2]

But in the early autumn of 1642 as Hopton and his band of 160 horsemen worked their way down towards Cornwall, the future must indeed have appeared troubled and uncertain. Cornwall was reputedly Royalist, but sharply divided, and the Parliamentary committees had already gone to work. The Royalist cause in the west was by no means hopeless, but many a King's man must have felt like Edward Hyde writing ten years later to Secretary Nicholas on the death of Hopton, with 'heart ready to break and to despair of seeing better times, bringing other melancholic thoughts . . . which I am . . . obliged to shake off'.[3] It is fair to say that the pessimism of his mourner never tormented Sir Ralph himself. He was used to retreats: they embraced his fondest memories and first considerable exploits in arms. A retreat swung in an arc became an advance. And so the going down into Cornwall, as to an unknown land, doubtless was fraught with more hope than fear. No longer a deputy lieutenant of Somerset, no longer in fact anyone's deputy, Hopton was ready for his new role as 'King's Man in the West'.

---

[1] Clarendon, vi. 34.

[2] William Henry Black, ed., *Docquets of Letters Patent*, 1642–1646 (London, 1837), 85: 'A Commission directed to Ralph Lord Hopton Feild Marshall of the westerne Army. . . .'

According to *The Shorter Oxford Dictionary*, p. 965, the rank was first conferred in the British Army in 1736, its earliest use being in Germany in 1614. In the seventeenth century, it was more a functional title than an official military rank. An equivalent might be: 'tactical commander'.

[3] *Clarendon State Papers*, R. Scrope and T. Monkhouse, eds. (Oxford 1767–86), iii. 108 Letter of Hyde to Nicholas, No. 44, dated at the Palais Royal, 26 Oct. 1652.

IV

THE KING'S MAN IN CORNWALL:
Watch on the Tamar

(September–November 1642)

'WE live in a kind of twilight . . . a cloudy and foggie clime of sadnesse and uncertainty. . . .'[1] This bleak comment by the pamphleteer Jonathan Pym was one echo of a note that sounded many times that year. But feelings of gloom could not impede action to avert, to delay, or, at the last, to mitigate the force of the approaching storm. Shortly after the Somerset petition to the Houses of Parliament on 14 June a similar petition was presented to the King at York from 'forty-three gentlemen and seven thousand esquires, free-holders, and inhabitants'[2] of Cornwall. More succinct in substance, more apologetic, even obsequious, in tone, its burden was similar, though less explicit: 'Never to suffer Your Subjects to be Governed by an Arbitrary Government, nor admit an alteration in Religion.' And the signers offered themselves as 'most ready to maintain and defend with their lives and fortunes, Your Majesties Sacred Person, Honour, Estate, and lawfull Prerogative against all persons whatsoever . . .'.[3]

The militancy of these last lines is in striking contrast to the moderation of the Somerset message. It would be hard to deny that the 'Arbitrary Government' here mentioned means Parliamentary government. Yet it is just to suppose that the Cornish, no less than the Somersetmen, were anxious for peace; and the petition expressly mentions their prayers for the reconciliation of the Throne with the Houses.

Appreciating this general wish and hope, the Commons had moved with firm but cautious policy to win control of a county which for three hundred years had maintained itself as a land apart, a 'country'

---

[1] Jonathan Pym, *Some few and short considerations on the present Distempers* (London? 1642?), sheet 1 (no pagination).

[2] Mary Coate, *Cornwall in the Great Civil War and Interregnum, 1642–1660* (Truro 1933, 1963), p. 31, citing Rushworth, op. cit. iv. 638–9.

[3] Ibid. 355.

in more than the local sense of the word. This was true even where a substantial segment of its people stood, directly or indirectly, in a state of clientage to the Crown. Forty-five manors, the hereditary fief of the King's eldest son as Duke of Cornwall, had established a degree of monarchial influence among a considerable class of officials and tenants. Yet not all of them joined the King when the crisis came. The remoteness of the peninsula had bred an autonomy, a parochialism, further strengthened by ethnic and linguistic traits that made the River Tamar more than a physical boundary. During the Civil War the old Celtic tongue was still being spoken from Truro to Land's End.[1] Through the years native independence had accommodated itself to overlapping lines of authority: royal, ducal, municipal, and private. Living thus among multiple and often conflicting jurisdictions, it is small wonder that the litigiousness of the Cornish had passed into a proverb. For Parliament to cope with such a county in political and military terms and win its allegiance was a venture the success of which might be the measure of success anywhere in the kingdom.

On 11 July 1642, the day after the exchange of fire between the Parliamentarians and the Royalists near Beverley, the Commons issued an order 'for staying of Horses going to *Yorke* out of Cornwall . . .'.[2] On the 12th Hertford and his troop of mounted gentlemen left Beverley for the west. Without straining for coincidence, it is possible to imagine an appeal from the King's men on the fringe.

The Houses had cause for uneasiness. Among their adversaries in the peninsula counsels were pending that might upset all their plans. On 21 July Lord Mohun at Bocconoc, in a jocular vein, wrote to Francis Basset, Esq., of Tehidy:

> To lett you see what an Impudent beggar I am, I have sent this bearer to you, for the Barrell of Gunpowder, you promised mee, And Likewise to give you notice that the Commissioners of Array doe meet at Lostwithiel Wednesday next [27 July] Pray doe mee the honour to meet your friends Sir Nich: *Slanning*, Sir Bevill *Grenvile* and Mr. [John] *Arundle* of Trerise heer a Tuesday, where we shall conferre about some busines concerning settling of this County. . . .[3]

The same day on which the Lostwithiel meeting was to take place the Commons began taking steps to assert its own authority. Some of

---

[1] Ibid. 2.   [2] *C.J.* ii. 669.
[3] C.R.O.: Bassett MS., p. 49, No. 12.

the Cornish members—Sir Richard Buller, Sir Alexander Carew, Mr. Thomas Arundell, Mr. Francis Buller, Mr. Richard Erisey, and Mr. Francis Godolphin of Trevenegue—were enjoined to go down to Cornwall and execute the Ordinance for the Militia. On the next two days the Houses nominated Richard Erisey, John Trefusis, Nicholas Trefusis, and Humphrey Nicolls to be deputy lieutenants for Cornwall. The committee was warned, however, to use all means to preserve the peace.[1]

But the meeting of 'friends' at Bocconoc and Lostwithiel had set the wheels of war in motion to the extent that preparations were already being made against what now appeared to be the inevitable day. On 9 August the Lords informed the Commons of intelligence that five or six gentlemen had joined together to execute the commission of array in Cornwall, and that three of them—Sir Nicholas Slanning, Sir Bevill Grenvile, and Mr. John Arundell—were Members of Parliament. That same day came a letter from Launceston in which the Parliamentary committee reported that these three had, at the assizes, published the King's proclamations concerning Hull and the militia, contrary to the orders of the House. Along with the sheriff, Sir John Grylls, they were sent for as delinquents; and Slanning was disabled from sitting. A general ordinance enjoined lords lieutenant and deputy lieutenants to employ the full power of the counties to disarm and pursue all countenancers of the commission of array, specifically mentioning Hertford and Hopton.[2]

When on 24 September he left the marquis at Minehead, Hopton must have known that he had no other choice but to descend the peninsula. It was a risky move, but here he was hemmed in: Bristol at his back, Barnstaple in front of him, Taunton on his flank— Parliamentary strongholds all. He knew that only Cornwall could be counted on to provide a sure haven and perhaps a launching point for offensive action. Cornwall was a good seventy miles away by the coastal roads, perhaps fifty miles cross-country.[3] In either case the ride down might take the better part of two days, or a day and a night; and it was not likely they would be able to obtain fresh horses on Exmoor. Setting off without further delay, the cavaliers crossed the Exe near Dulverton and came that Saturday night to Exford

---

[1] *C.J.* ii. 698, 700.   [2] Ibid. 714, 715.

[3] The English mile in the seventeenth century was slightly longer than the present mile—2,428 yds. as opposed to 1,760 today. See *The Journeys of Celia Fiennes*, Christopher Morris, ed. (London, 1947), xxxix. In this present work distances are given in terms of modern mileage.

and then to the village of Chittlehampton, five miles from Barnstaple, From here they were guided by a servant of Sir Ralph Sydenham, member for Bossiney in the Long Parliament and chief agent for the Earl of Bath at Tavistock.[1] It would appear that they kept in touch with other Royalists while on the march.

Hopton's eye for country, his capacity for taking advantage of the ground in battle, was of little use, since a good part of the retreat took place during the night. West of the Exe he held no lands; his local and personal influence would have been negligible. The principal towns were against him. Passing near Torrington he came within two miles of a large enemy force.[2] His success in evading a disastrous encounter must be put down to a combination of sound instinct and plain luck. The local Parliamentarians seem to have been more concerned with securing their own position and by no means eager for a direct confrontation of strength.[3]

On Sunday 25 September Hopton's horse crossed into Cornwall and came to Morwenstow, the house of Sir Bevill Grenvile, perhaps the most esteemed of all the notables in the county. Since June he had been one of the most active members of the commission of array; and, presumably, his hospitality afforded the cavaliers a breathing-space that they had not enjoyed since Sherborne. But their commander could not pause long. One of the Parliamentary leaders, Sir Richard Buller, had issued a call from Saltash on the Tamar estuary for the militia to gather on 28 September at Bodmin, accusing the Royalists of entering Cornwall in a warlike manner.[4] To forestall the mustering of the trained bands was imperative. Sir Ralph and his band spurred on toward Bodmin. It is likely that they made slow time on the narrow, ill-kept road from Bude and Stratton to Camelford, proceeding at a quicker pace on the main road from Camelford to Wadebridge.[5] Their manoeuvres were successful. At St. Columb, within twenty-four hours and from two small hundreds alone, the Royalists were able to raise nearly a thousand men in arms.[6] On 27 September Hopton's party arrived at Bodmin to find that Buller had retired to

---

[1] Hopton, 19, n. 1; Roger Granville, *The History of the Granville Family* (Exeter, 1895), 230; Coate, 25.
[2] Hopton, loc. cit.
[3] It is likely that Parliamentary cavalry at this stage was hardly adequate to cope with three troops of Royalist horse.
[4] Coate, 36.
[5] See Coate, p. 1, for a description of Cornwall's roads.
[6] Hopton, 20.

Launceston. Plainly the Parliamentarians were unprepared to fight at this juncture.

It was then that Hopton and Grenvile decided on a bold move: to ride on to Truro and present their case at the Michaelmas quarter sessions for Cornwall, appealing to the county in terms of strict legality, within a very framework of law.

When he arrived at Truro, Hopton, at a rough estimate, had covered 150 miles since leaving Minehead less than a week before. He knew he had to answer the presentment that had come in against him for bringing 'divers men unknowne . . . into the County *contra pacem* etc.'.[1] Indictments also had been preferred against Buller and his committee for their 'rowte and unlawfull assembly' at Launceston. Clearly the Cornish were in no haste to be swayed by either side, and certainly not by force. The quarter session ordered John Grylls the sheriff to raise the *posse comitatus* and disperse the assembly at Launceston. Meanwhile, Hopton, on the last day of the sessions, being Saturday 1 October, appeared to answer the charge that he had acted against the peace. It is a pity that no transcript can be found of his speech, for it was a turning-point in the fortunes and designs of the western Royalists. Hopton had conceived that 'the exact prosecution of the course of lawe and submission to it, was the best foundation that at that tyme could bee taken for his Majesties affayres'. Before a petty jury 'of men of very good quality' he produced his commission and pleaded his case. Whatever his arguments, it can be surmised that his personal character did no damage to his cause. The jury considered and

after . . . a leasurable and legall debate of the busines, Sir Ralph Hopton and his company were not only acquitted of the Indictment, but also the Jury in open Sessions, declared, that it was a great favour and justice of his Majesty to send downe ayde to them who were already mark'd out to distruction, and that they thought it the duty of every good subject as well in loyaltie to the King as in gratitude to them to joyne with them, and stand close by them to the utmost hazard of their lyves and fortunes.[2]

The King's man, then, had scored on points of legal precision, a far cry from his attempts to read a simple proclamation in the market place at Shepton Mallet. He must have seen, too, that the trained bands were in such a state of disarray that improvisation must be made. New deputy lieutenants had been appointed by Parliament.

---

[1] Hopton, 20.   [2] Ibid. 21.

But a supplementary force existed in the *posse comitatus*, under the control of the sheriff, which theoretically included all the able-bodied men in the county. Though the words 'trained bands' (or 'Militia') and *'posse comitatus'* were sometimes used interchangeably, strictly speaking the first phrase pertains only to the active part of the *posse*, that part organized in regiments and subject to regular training. The *posse* proper was simply the residue of the county's available manhood. The most significant difference lay in the lines of authority. For the *posse*, it was the sheriff; for the militia, it was the lord lieutenant.[1] Both offices formerly had been appointive by the King. Now the lieutenantcies had been taken over by Parliament, and in some cases the Houses also had been able to bring the shrievalties into line. Thus, in Somerset Sheriff Sanford had been directed to aid with a *posse comitatus* the Earl of Bedford, lord lieutenant of the county.

With the lines of authority confused in the active militia, it was a blessing to the Royalist cause to have a staunch partisan in the person of John Grylls, high sheriff of Cornwall. Upon the orders of the sessions he executed warrants for summoning the *posse* on 4 October to Moilesbarrow Down near Lostwithiel. The muster brought out 3,000 peasants, badly weaponed and untrained,[2] revealing to Hopton as he reviewed them, if he had not known it before, that the whole system of county levies was in need of a drastic overhauling. But for the moment he had no time to innovate. Buller was at Launceston in confederation with Sir George Chudleigh and others in Devonshire. Threatening letters from Chudleigh to Hopton had removed the last hopes for an accommodation.[3] Organizing his forces into regiments, Sir Ralph marched to the Tamar and occupied Launceston, Buller fleeing before him (6 October). Crossing Polston bridge into Devon, the Parliament-men fled on to Plymouth. The Royalists moved down the river and took Saltash. The Tamar was now a battle-line.

Meantime, Grenvile, deputizing for Hopton while Sir Ralph descended the estuary, viewed trends with great discontent. As he wrote to his wife, he had wanted to 'fetch those traitors out of their

---

[1] These differences are explained in a note by Brigadier E. Foster Hall, *J.S. Army H.R.* xxxix. 110.

[2] Hopton, 21–22. According to the Tremayne MS. (C.R.O.) the *posse* had 10,000 men ready; 4,000 marched at once in arms (pagination sparse). Their arms were old, but not necessarily unserviceable.

[3] Hopton, 22.

neast [*sic*] at Launceston or fire them in it'. But it transpired that 'som of our faynter brethren' had persuaded Sheriff Grylls to attempt a conference on 12 October with a dim hope of composing matters, a meeting which, apparently, was indefinitely postponed. Sir Bevill complained that some of his neighbours had not joined the *posse*, abstaining from the legal course of assisting the sheriff, as directed by statute. Though vowing they were 'punishable by the Lawe in a high degree', he said he would do what he could to save 'some of the honester sort, yett others shall smart'.[1]

Sir Bevill's chagrin has some poignancy. A quicker, more decisive blow conceivably might have shortened the period of seven months that was to elapse before the Parliamentary forces were expelled from Cornwall. But the *posse* had reached an impasse. There was a supply problem: lack of munitions; and a legal problem: the *posse*, being, in effect, the sheriff's army, could not be drawn out of the county, or at least Hopton had doubts that it could without commission. The cumbersomeness of the old military system, its ineffectiveness for anything more than a kind of expanded constabulary duty, must have come home to him as forcefully as it had during the Scottish war.

His task, then, after the *posse* had been dismissed, was to raise a force of volunteers, well trained and properly equipped not only to throw the enemy out of Cornwall, but to make an offensive thrust into the enemy's own territory. A good army must be based on a proper recruiting system, clearly defined and organized units, strict mustering, and stern discipline.[2]

As for financing this army, the 'sinews of war' might come from several sources: trade, assessments, voluntary contributions, and sequestrations. For the first, the Cavaliers had an invaluable ally in Queen Henriette Marie, who organized in France and Holland the exchange of Cornish tin for munitions.[3] Secondly, the commissions of array recognized at least three possible objects of assessment: recusants,[4] Parliamentary commissioners,[5] and those who because

---

[1] Victoria and Albert Museum, South Kensington: MS. letter dated at Bodmin 12 Oct. 1642 from Sir Bevill Grenvile to his wife Grace at Stow.

[2] Michael Roberts, *Gustavus Adolphus* (London and New York, 1958), 201.

[3] Coate, 38.

[4] See the 'Extraordinary Commission of Array granted to the Marquis of Hertford', dated at York 2 August 1642, in Rushworth, iv. 672–4. Technically, recusants were disabled from bearing arms, but the law was easily evaded.

[5] See the 'General Instructions to the Commissioners of Array' in Rushworth, iv. 682.

of some bodily weakness were incapable of bearing arms.[1] Thirdly, to pay the troops (and with Hopton prompt payment was a maxim)[2] there was the necessity for personal sacrifices on the part of the Royalists themselves. Grenvile, Slanning, John Arundell of Trerice, and Charles Trevanion of Caerhayes mortgaged their estates and sold their plate.[3] Sir Richard Vyvyan, Jonathan Rashleigh, and Francis Basset gave or lent a total sum of £414.[4] Finally, these contributions were considerably augmented by £2,000 sent to them from the King's sequestrator, Sir George Strode.[5]

Meanwhile, Lord Mohun, who had not been present with the *posse*, made a special trip to Oxford, where he obtained the King's commission for himself, Hopton, Berkeley, and Ashburnham, or any two of them, in Hertford's absence to command in chief all the Royalist forces raised, or to be raised, in the six western counties of Cornwall, Devon, Somerset, Dorset, Wiltshire, and Hampshire, and in the cities of Bristol and Exeter.[6] A joint commission might have created problems, but at least the functions of three of the chief officers had been clearly defined: Hopton was lieutenant-general of the horse, Berkeley commissary-general, and Ashburnham major-general of the foot. Public spiritedness suppressed ill will;[7] there is no reason to infer any cavilling that the generals were not 'of Cornish crew'.

For all practical purposes the authority was Hopton's. No doubt Grenvile and Godolphin gave him invaluable service as liaison with the county worthies. It is not unlikely that Sir Bevill suggested the

---

[1] See the 'Commission of Array for Devon', dated at Beverley 19 July 1642 in Hopton, 105.
[2] Lloyd, 343.   [3] Granville, *The History of the Granville Family*, 246.
[4] Coate, 38.
[5] S.P. 16: 511:66 (Oxford, 8 Dec. 1645): warrant under privy seal to Exchequer. In October 1642 Sir George Strode paid to Hopton £2,000 to be disbursed for payment of the Cornish army, for which he had not received a legal discharge. The Exchequer was required to strike a tally for this sum 'as paid in full of the £7,000 payable by Sir George Strode, and to charge the same as issued to Ralph, Lord Hopton by way of imprest upon accompt for payment' of the Cornish forces. Strode was wounded at Edgehill. See *Cal. C.C.* 1060; Clarendon, vi. 94. Sequestration appears to have been the most lucrative though not the steadiest source of income. In the Basset MS., p. 2, a letter to Sir Francis Basset from Secretary Edward Nicholas, dated 23 Nov. 1642, reveals that Hopton was associated with Basset in sequestrating the estate of the Earl of Salisbury.
[6] Hopton, 23. Clarendon, vi. 245, says that Mohun met the King at Brentford. He hints that the Cornish peer waited until after Edgehill before he committed himself to the royal cause.
[7] Clarendon, vi. 244–6.

gambit of pleading his case at the sessions. But there can be no question that Hopton took upon himself the burden of the King's cause. In a week of rapid riding he had changed the complexion and the prospects of that cause, justified it in legal terms, put its enemies on the defensive, and galvanized the Cornish Royalists into a state of high confidence and *élan*. The sea routes were still open; royal forts still commanded the Cornish coast and the Channel islands; and the Queen's ships were running arms to Falmouth.

The commission and the supplies were his. But where was he to get the men? The answer to that lay with the commanders of the new Cornish army. The troops they recruited and mustered predominantly were their own relations, tenants, neighbours, and retainers. Apart from the voluntary aspect, their recruitment in some cases had certain features of the old feudal levy. Between them and the colonels existed bonds of long association and familiarity. The loyalty of the principal landlords to the King was reflected in the allegiance and attachment of their own dependents. Thus, the success of the army depended, to an extraordinary degree, on the calibre of its ranking field officers, and especially the commanders of the five infantry regiments, whose glory was to become a legend. These were: Lord Mohun, Sir Bevill Grenvile, Sir Nicholas Slanning, John Trevanion, Esq., and Colonel William Godolphin.

Of Godolphin little is known except that he sat in the Short Parliament for Helston with his first cousin, the poet Sidney Godolphin, now a member of Hopton's council of war. Probably he was an officer in the militia. He was active, too, in promoting the tin trade.[1] Warwick, Baron Mohun of Okehampton, born in 1620, was the youngest of the colonels. He sat for Grampound in the Short Parliament and acted for the King in nominating M.P.'s by virtue, largely, of his position as a landlord in the west. For him it is enough to say that, having absented himself from the House of Lords in February after refusing to countenance its agreement with the Commons on the militia, he had been appointed by the King to take a hand in executing the commission of array, which he seems to have done loyally but with no particular ability. Though he raised a regiment and went to great lengths to obtain his commission, he resigned it a year later.[2]

---

[1] Coate, 184, 375; *D.N.B.* viii. 46.

[2] *The Complete Peerage*, ix. 26; Keeler, 8–9, n. 33; *C.S.P.D.* 1641–43 (pp. 386–7), vol. 492 (Sept.–Nov. 1642).

Grenvile, Slanning, and Trevanion were to become the paladins of the Cornish host. Friends for many years, all had served in the Long Parliament and had taken a common position in opposing the attainder of Strafford.[1] Grenvile, born in the same month and year as Hopton (23 March 1596), by all estimates was one of the most influential men in north Cornwall, by virtue of both his landed property and his personal popularity. His character is revealed in a letter to him from Sir Edward Seymour, who longs for his society 'in which ther is soe much cheerfulness as it sweetens all misfortunes, and makes them none where you are'.[2] He proceeded to the B.A. at Oxford from Exeter College, where he 'so fell upon the sweet delights of reading Poetry and History' that he found himself very defective when it came to managing 'occasions of weight'.[3] After going down he had spent some time at court and in 1623 had been granted a pass to travel abroad. His low estimate of his practical aptitudes is accurate only in limning his natural modesty. He gave some attention to the industries of his region, experimenting with the use of coal instead of wood for the melting of tin. He was a member of every Parliament from 1621 until the Civil War.[4] In the early years he was a friend and follower of Sir John Eliot,[5] joining him in opposing the forced loan. But by 1639, the year in which he was knighted, he had become one of the 'King's servants above stairs' and had begun to settle his affairs to devote himself to the King's cause. In 1638 he mortgaged some of his holdings for £20,000 and within the next three years others for perhaps £7,000 more.[6] Such was his zeal to equip a troop for the first Scots war that he jeopardized his domestic felicity by attempting to mortgage some of his wife's property.[7]

By 1640 he thought that he had lost much of his political popularity in his county,[8] but he had no trouble in winning a seat for Launceston in the Short Parliament and for the shire in the Long Parliament. In November, like Hopton, he subscribed his bond for £1,000 to support

---

[1] Coate, 27–28. Bevill Grenvile is not listed as a Straffordian, but allegedly he spoke against the execution.

[2] Granville, 228.

[3] Victoria and Albert Museum, Kensington: MS. letter from Sir Bevill Grenvile to his son Dick (1639). Grenvile's advice on the moderate use of humane authors is reminiscent of Bacon and Montaigne.

[4] Keeler, 195.   [5] D.N.B. viii. 553.   [6] Keeler, loc. cit.

[7] Granville, above. The letters of Sir Bevill and Lady Grace at this time 'reveal the only instance of bitter feeling between husband and wife'.

[8] Coate, 24–25.

the northern war. He was not otherwise active in the House. Though reputedly opposed to the attainder of Strafford, he did not put himself on record to that effect; dismayed by William Waller's defection to Presbyterianism, he nonetheless wrote him a conciliatory letter.[1] It would appear that his genial nature was disturbed by the rise of acrimonious factions. As soon as he could, he left Westminster and returned to Cornwall. As we have seen, he was a key figure in implementing the commission of array. On 17 August 1642 he held a muster at Bodmin racecourse. Attending were 180 men, mostly his servants and tenants, their weapons painted blue and white, his colours.[2]

Slanning was governor of Pendennis castle. The date of his birth was probably 1611.[3] A Devon man, he studied at Exeter College, Oxford and was apparently interested in scientific experiments, being 'able to attend as well the crucible as the gun'. In 1628 he was admitted to the Inner Temple. Afterwards he went to the Netherlands to learn the art of war. Knighted in 1632, he served as a member of the commission on piracy for both Devon and Cornwall and as vice admiral of the southern shore for those counties. He was appointed recorder of Plympton and later chosen to represent that borough in the Short Parliament. In the Long Parliament he was elected for both Plympton and Penryn, officially sitting for the latter borough. In October 1640 he was summoned to attend the King on a secret matter, possibly pertaining to elections.[4] As much as Grenvile, who commended his 'rich stock of worth',[5] he may be regarded as a King's man in the west before the war. It is possible that Hopton, before attending the quarter sessions at Truro, paid him a visit.[6] At any rate Slanning became the chief link between the new

[1] Granville, 235–7.   [2] Coate, 35.
[3] See *Devon, Repts. & Trans.* xix. (1887), 459. Keeler, p. 339 and n. 206, opts for 1606, citing an Inquisition Post Mortem of 1612 which gives Slanning's age as six; also the *D.N.B.* Coate, p. 99, n. 1, points out that Clarendon, vii. 132, does not give the ages of either Slanning or Trevanion correctly. Citing Boase and Courtney, *Bibliotheca Cornubiensis*, ii. 655 and 791, she states that Slanning was born in 1611 and Trevanion in 1613. She corroborates *The Visitation of the County of Devon in the year* 1620, F. T. Colby, ed. (London, 1872: Harl. Soc. vi), 262, which gives Slanning's age as nine in 1620; also the *Complete Baronetage* iii. 270. Coate links Slanning with Sidney Godolphin's group at Exeter College. Godolphin was born in 1610. As a pure hypothesis, we may consider the possibility that Slanning was knighted (1632) in the year of his majority. If twenty-four seems a relatively young age for him to have become governor of Pendennis, we must chew on Coate's assertion that 'in these troubled years men matured early'.
[4] Keeler, 339.   [5] Granville, 237–8.   [2] Hopton, 19–20, n. 2.

Royalist regiments and their continental sources of supply, relaying munitions from the Channel islands to his colleague Francis Basset, vice admiral of the northern shore, for distribution among the various garrisons at Bodmin, Launceston, and Saltash. He also organized a fleet of privateers to seize merchant ships and divert their goods for the King's use, as well as to protect the munitions boats from capture by the navy, now in Parliamentary hands.[1] All in all, Royalist power in the west would hardly have survived without an able and active partisan like Slanning. Between them he and Grenvile strove to augment that power by sea and land.

John Trevanion was the eldest son of Charles Trevanion of Caerhayes and heir apparent to an estate of about £2,000 per annum. His father had been Sheriff of Cornwall and also a deputy lieutenant.[2] John, born 1613, entered Lincoln's Inn in 1633. He was recommended to Secretary Coke by Charles, Lord Lambert, who described him as a proper young gentleman, the 'best seated of any man in Cornwall'. In the Short Parliament he sat for Grampound; in the Long Parliament for Lostwithiel. His political development is harder to determine than that of Grenvile or Slanning. His father Charles had paid an over-assessment to avoid knighthood and had ignored the request for a contribution to the King in 1639. But John, at the age of seventeen, had married Anne, daughter of John Arundell of Trerice, and a few years later attended Lincoln's Inn with her brothers John and Richard, who later became his colleagues in Parliament.[3] These Arundells were staunch Royalists, and John Trevanion showed his inclinations by voting against Strafford's attainder with Richard Arundell, Slanning, and Sidney Godolphin.[4] But though more inclined than Grenvile to associate himself with factions, he was no more active in the House than Sir Bevill and was named to no committees. On 16 June 1642 he was missing at the call.[5]

These were the leaders, as they were the founders, of the Cornish army. Except for Grenvile they were all in their prime: in 1642 Sir Bevill was forty-six, William Godolphin thirty-seven, Slanning

---

[1] Coate, 38–39.

[2] Keeler, 364. John Trevanion's mother, Amye, was the daughter of Sir John Mallet, of Enmore, Somerset. The Cornish were hardly clannish or particular in their marriages. Viewed in this light, the ready reception of an 'outsider' like Hopton is less strange than might be supposed.

[3] Ibid. John Arundell the younger was born the same year (1613) as John Trevanion.

[4] Coate, 27–28.   [5] Keeler, loc. cit.

thirty-one, Trevanion twenty-nine, and Mohun twenty-two. All were men of substance, most of them in their own right, Trevanion potentially as an heir apparent. For the most part they were educated and travelled men: Trevanion and Slanning had attended the Inns of Court. Grenvile and Slanning had showed intellectual aptitude at Oxford—the former in the humanities, the latter in the sciences. Both had been abroad, Slanning studying military science and tactics in the Netherlands, the young Englishmen's school of war. In some ways the earlier careers of these men parallel Hopton's. Except for Slanning, by no criteria could they be called professional soldiers. They were civilians, amateurs, without military mentality, called to arms in a crisis. But their complementary virtues, consolidated by friendship and mutual esteem, would prove decisive in bringing military victories. In great measure the fortunes and success of the Cornish infantry were to depend on Grenvile's cheerful courage, religious spirit, and strict discipline, like Hopton's own; on the shrewd wit, gaiety, and universal courtesy of the slight, well-favoured Slanning; and on the quiet, steadfast, purposeful Trevanion.[1]

Others there were of note. There was John Arundell, Esq. of Trerice, called 'Jack for the King', Trevanion's father-in-law, who in 1643 was to succeed Slanning as governor of Pendennis castle, and his four sons: John, Richard, William, and Francis. In the coming war John and Francis were to lose their lives, while Richard and William continued with the army until it surrendered at Truro.[2] Captain (later Colonel) William Arundell was one of the first two Cornishmen to raise a company for the King, the other being Captain Jonathan Trelawny of Trelawne.[3] Among regimental officers worthy of mention were Sir Peter Courtney, described by a Parliamentarian as lieutenant-colonel to Grenvile and in after years as 'one ready to serve any Insurrection'.[4] Others were Walter Slingsby, major of Mohun's regiment;[5] Major Anthony Brockett; and Sir Francis Hawley, all of whom had joined Hopton in Somerset. As for horse,

[1] Clarendon, vii. 108, 132.
[2] C.R.O.: Tremayne MS. No pagination, but see second sheet in sequence.
[3] Hopton, 23.
[4] Bodleian Library, Oxford: Portland Collection—Nalson MSS. xvi. 72, 10th Paper, p. 1. Courtney is described erroneously as being from Hampshire (see Coate, 31), confusing him with Sir William Courtney, who was.
[5] In the seventeenth century 'Major' was used sometimes as a contracted form of 'Sergeant Major.' Walter Slingsby was a cousin of Colonel Sir Henry Slingsby, the diarist. His accounts of the battles of Lansdown, Roundway, and Cheriton are useful supplements to Hopton's narrative.

Captain Edward Cosoworth increased the Royalist strength in that arm by raising a troop of dragoons.[1]

All told, the new forces numbered about 5,000 foot and, at an estimate, something over 500 horse. The artillery consisted of four brass guns and one of iron, none of any size.[2] The regiments fell somewhat short of full strength, roughly 1,000 men each instead of the theoretical 1,200.[3] But here at least was a nucleus for further recruitment. The forces, however, were not immediately united in one body: early in November they were still scattered between Fowey, Penzance, and Launceston.[4]

Toward the end of October Hopton exchanged correspondence with Hertford. The marquis wrote that he had informed the King of the disasters at Minehead and Dunster castle. Ungraciously he imputed them to the cowardice of the Somersetmen, particularly Sir John Stawell and Captain John Digby, whose prompt action on the Glastonbury road had saved the Royalists at Wells from being surrounded, while giving credit to his own horse and foot for saving the ordnance. Hertford's diatribe displayed a grandee's lack of confidence in the common soldier. He recalled a speech of 'that worthy souldier *Swinden* who was Generall of Ostend in the time of the Infanta, [Isabella], Arch-Duchesse of *Flanders*', to the effect that the English nation 'stood too much upon their owne . . . valour, and that he would with a considerable Army runne through our whole Kingdome, knowing the vulgar sort of our Nation to be faint hearted and unexperienced in martiall discipline . . . '. Hopton replied that at Dunster the odds had been five to one against the Royalists. As for the General of Ostend, his views were hardly pertinent to the present situation. For here and now

Nature at home bindeth filiall affection, and one brother or one nation to fight against another is not warrantable by Gods lawes, and in that respect there might be a faint-heartedness in our Nation, but my Lord let the Generall of *Ostend* or other forraine Princes invade this our land.

[1] Hopton, 23.

[2] Ibid. 24. Called 'drakes', these light artillery were cast in several sizes, running from 3 to 8 feet in length and from $1\frac{1}{4}$ to 3 inches in calibre. They could discharge a 3lb. shot about 15 times an hour. See Young, below, 110.

[3] Brigadier Peter Young and John Adair, *Hastings to Culloden* (London, 1964), 109.

[4] *New Plots Discovered Against the Parliament and the Peace of the Kingdome. In two letters, the one sent from the Marquis of Hartford to Sir Ralph Hopton, the other sent from Sir Ralph Hopton to the said Marquis . . .* etc. (London, 3 Nov. 1642), no pagination.

The marquis at least had the grace to commend Mohun, John Arundell, and Sir Bevill Grenvile, 'who will not wag with every blast of wind'.[1]

Against the manoeuvres of the Cornish army the wind of Parliamentary opposition had already risen, but it blew fitfully and brought mostly rumours exaggerating the strength of both sides. It was bruited that Hopton had 30,000 men and had fortified one castle with fifty pieces of ordnance; but at the same time the 'greatest part' of the county was taking a stand against him, and the Earl of Pembroke was assembling a vast host to crush the Royalists.[2] Fallacious or distorted as they were, such allegations underline the uncertainty of public information and opinion while tending to hide a still-prevailing desire for neutrality.

During this period of jockeying and equipoise the Commons, on 22 October, discussed a report that small ships were available for the transport of men and munitions into some parts of Cornwall 'for the

[1] Ibid., *passim*. The Archduchess Isabella was the daughter of Philip II of Spain and wife of Albert, Archduke of Austria. Together they ruled the Spanish Netherlands as independent sovereigns from 1598 until Albert's death in 1621, after which, these territories reverting to the Spanish Crown, Isabella continued to reign as Regent till her death in 1633. The siege of Ostend was 1601–4. Beyond the fact that General 'Swinden' has a Dutch name, I am unable to identify him.

[2] Coate, 37; *The Declaration and Remonstrance of the Lords, Knights, and Gentry of the Countie of Cornwall. Agreed on by the whole County in generall, October 10, 1642* ... etc. (London, 13 Oct. 1642), 3–5; *A Remonstrance of Declaration of the names of the Knights and Gentlemen that take part with* Sir Ralph Hopton ... etc. (London, 29 Oct. 1642), *passim*; H.M.C., App., 7th Rept., 530: MS. of George Edward Frere, Esq., of Roydon Hall, Norfolk, dated 19 Oct. 1642. According to Frere, Hopton had 'by report' between 6,000 and 7,000 foot, 500 horse, and 12 pieces of ordnance. The first figure is acceptable only if the whole *posse* is considered, and then it is probably too high. Pembroke's great array did not materialize, but a nucleus of 1,000 foot and seven troops of horse was formed under Bedford. See Coate, 40.

According to one Parliamentary report, Hopton's house at Witham, about the middle of October 1642, was the scene of a minor skirmish. Two knights and colonels of the trained bands, Sir Edward Rodney and Sir Edward Berkeley, with one 'Master Dugdale', chaplain to the Marquis of Hertford, fortified themselves with their friends, tenants, and freeholders at the Friary, pursued by a Parliamentary party under Lieutenant Arnold Hyward: 'Immur'd in stone, knit with fast lime and haire', they not only 'washt the AEthiop, but bathed themselves in their owne fruitelesse sweate. . . .' The knights and the priest tried to escape on horseback. Hyward followed. After a short parley and skirmish he made them prisoners.— *Certaine and true News From Somerset-shire; with the besieging of Sir Ralph Hoptons House, together with the valiant and manfully performed courage of Mr.* Arnold Hyward. . . . etc. (London, 15 Oct. 1642), *passim*. This story sounds apocryphal. Rodney had been with Hopton at Sherborne and must have gone with Hertford to Wales. It would have been rash for him to stay in Somerset.

Safety and Defence of that County'. The deputy lieutenants of Devon and Cornwall were empowered to take up such vessels, compensating the owners from the customs of the western ports. Three ships were dispatched to guard the approaches to the peninsula: the *Fellowship* to defend Milford Haven; the *Mary* to patrol from Milford to Land's End to prevent a landing by the Welsh or Irish; and the *Happy Entrance* to lie on the south coast.[1] But the Houses could never carry out, probably they never undertook or even conceived, the strategy of a complete and systematic blockade to cover the landing of their own troops. No flotilla could patrol every cove between St. Ives, Penzance, and Falmouth; and Slanning's privateers were waiting to attack.

Recruiting continued through October. On the whole Hopton's efforts were well received. His reputation at this time appears to have given him the character of a man stern and austere with a tendency to displays of temper, but disinterested and honourable, a man of good will. His sense of justice was rigorous, but impartial. When the Royalists entered Launceston the first time, twenty of them were jailed for arson and plundering.[2]

If one report is to be believed, Sir Ralph was not above plundering himself. Early in November 600 fishermen and their wives came to Bodmin from Mount Edgcumbe armed with clubs and stones. Entering different houses they carried off plate and pewter. Hopton. at Pendennis, marched after them, urging that they go to a 'Mr, Trefuses' at Watford and plunder him. For his advice he got a 'good bang on the neck' and was laid 'gasping on the highway'. His soldiers attacked, two being killed; so he retired. Next day he came back with 500 foot and horse and revenged himself on 'some few stragling fishermen', whom he tied to trees and 'whipped naked with Broom and Furze'. That same day he took six 'light horses' from 'Sir John Vigures's' stable and pillaged him of all his plate and pewter. He was chased by the trained bands and by more fishermen, threatening they would 'whip him . . . to death for his barbarous

---

[1] *C.J.* ii. 822.

[2] For identification of these ships see Edward Peacock, F.S.A., *The Army Lists of the Roundheads and Cavaliers* (London, 1874), 61, 63.

The '*Entrance*': Captain Owen; Master Bowen, Lieutenant; 250 men; burden, 751 tons. 'One of the Kings Majesties Ships set forth for the Guard of the narrow Seas, & for Ireland. 1642.'

The *Mary*: Capt. William Capell, 30 men, 163 tons.

The *Fellowship*: Capt. Thomas Colle, 87 men, 290 tons.

The last two were merchant ships.

F

cruelty to their friends'. He got away with five of the eight horses.[1]

A more general view, however, was expressed by a Parliament-man, one 'Gyles Prescot', writing from Plymouth on 21 October. While declaring that Grenvile was a 'tyrant', and defying all probability by hinting that Hopton had sent to Scilly for seminary priests, this writer had to admit: 'I can no wayes disparage Sir Ralph Hoptons actions, for hee carrieth himselfe nobly without doing any mischief or great spoile.'[2]

[1] *True intelligence from Cornwall: Being a true Relation of the Rising of 600 Fishermen. . . .* ' Sent in a letter from Sir Jonathan Trelawney to Mr. Trelawney, merchant, in London (London, 10 Nov. 1642), *passim.* Not to be confused with Captain Jonathan Trelawny of Trelawne, Royalist. The Trelawn[e]ys of Plymouth, merchants, were to become the prey of Cornish privateers—see Ch. viii, Sect. 2 of this present work.

Coate, 40, only mentions the suppression of the riot. In the same paragraph she notes that Hopton's troopers took £1,700 from a clothier of Tavistock so that he could not pay his spinners. Similar acts of coercion, or accusations thereof, appear from time to time. While it is possible to imagine Sir Ralph ordering a refractory peasant to be flogged, it is hardly typical of him (as his official enemies acknowledged) that he would connive at indiscriminate plunder, much less encourage it. Often his troops acted in his name without his sanction. In any case, he must have seen the folly of such marauding. With the more substantial gentry selling their plate voluntarily, there was little need at this point to alienate the rest. Besides, as any good commander knows, marauding undermines discipline.

[2] *A Remonstrance of Declaration . . .*, dated at Plymouth 21 Oct. 1642, and signed 'Gyles Prescot', 5, 7–8. The Basset MS., 60 (25), mentions two ships to Scilly, but probably for provender rather than priests (C.R.O.).

The Bodmin Mayor's accounts reveal that Hopton at this time was not lacking in good cheer. On 27 Oct. 1642 the borough sent him, Berkeley, Ashburnham, and Killigrew '1 pottle of raw & 1 of burnt sack' (5s.); on 1 Nov. Hopton, Mohun, Grenvile, and two other gentlemen were sent 3 gallons of sack (12s.) 'when they dyned at Mr. Jones his house'.

V

THE KING'S MAN IN DEVON:
The 'Bitter Season of the Year'

(November 1642–April 1643)

MID-NOVEMBER brought the first test. Would the Cornish, with their own homes foremost in mind, march into Devon to join with a *posse* there? They would, reluctantly, and after a bribe or bounty had been paid.[1] Their fears were not entirely groundless, but they had this for their comfort: the Tamar was not easy to ford below Launceston.[2] On the other hand, conjunction with the Devon Royalists was difficult because their main strength was in the southern part of the county, and Plymouth lay between. Undeterred, Hopton, leaving a strong guard on the passes of the river, led his forces to Exeter, about fifty miles east of Launceston, a bold move in view of the distance and the greater number of the enemy. On 21 November he arrived before the chief city of the south-west.[3] The mayor, Christopher Clark, replied that he, not Hopton, was lieutenant in these parts, and furthermore that the Royalist general was a declared disturber of the peace. Hopton wanted to withdraw, but his men assured him the siege could be broken in two or three days. So he gave order for entrenchment.[4]

That night the Royalists made a few approaches on the west side and mounted three iron demi-culverins against the walls.[5] In the morning they began to fire on the ramparts. The besieged played back with their own ordnance, sending the Royalists a 'wholesome present of bullets for their breakfast . . .'. With seven pieces they killed 'at least an hundred in their trenches, the rest wishing themselves againe digging of Tyn, rather than be expos'd to the danger of

---

[1] Coate, 40, citing Basset MS.

[2] Sir Edward Walker, *Historical Discourses upon several occasions*. . . . (London, 1705), 48. Note, p. 123, however, that fording was feasible for horse.

[3] Clarendon, vi. 244–6, n. 1.

[4] *True and Joyfull Newes from Exeter. Shewing how* Sir Ralph Hopton, *Sir* Bevill Grenvile, *with divers of the Cornish Malignants, made their approaches thither* . . . etc. (London, 25 Nov. 1642), 4–5. The Cornishmen, being mostly miners, were good pioneers and 'better indeed with the spade and shovel then with the Pike and Musket'.　　　　　　　　　　　　[5] Ibid. 5.

Iron and Lead . . .'. While Hopton tried for a breach, the citizens
came out of their trenches and killed fifty of his men, losing six
themselves, according to the Parliamentary account. Then, night
coming on, they retired to the city for a council of war. Mayor
Clark advised a night attack. It was agreed upon, and he himself
led it with 3,000 men, wearing white handkerchiefs for identification
in the dark. Surprising 'two or three of the drunken Centinells',
they fell on the centre of the Royalist camp 'like hungry Lyons',
with halberts, pole-axes, and butts of muskets. The men of Exeter
were fresh, and the Dutch engineers did good work with grenades.
But Hopton and Grenvile, though their men are compared with
'wild beasts', were themselves commended as 'men of resolve',
paying no heed to their own safety, defending themselves and their
men in a circle till dawn, finally compelled to flee by sheer opposed
numbers.

The figures are certainly exaggerated: Hopton is reported to have
brought 5,000 men, of whom nearly 2,000 are claimed to have
fallen in the field; while the Parliamentarians, with 8,000 men,
counting militia and auxiliaries, lost only 60.[1] It is reasonable to infer,
however, that the Cornish were outnumbered at least two to one,
though joined by Devon auxiliaries. In taking the offensive, Hopton
had showed considerable daring and initiative. But in falling back to
Tavistock, he decided that he must move with greater caution. It
was necessary to effect a conjunction with the main body of Devon
Royalists, to raise a *posse*, to train and garrison a substantial force
with which to hold the districts of the south coast sympathetic to the
King.

Accordingly, after occupying Tavistock, he marched on 1 December
to Plympton, commanded for Parliament by Colonel William Ruthin,
described as 'a Scotch soldier of fortune'.[2] Ruthin 'dared them on
the sands' with 300 horse and dragoons,[3] but soon was forced to
retreat three miles into Plymouth. The Cornish quartered at
Plympton. The next step was for the new, 'well-affected' sheriff,
Edmund (later Sir Edmund) Fortescue, to summon a *posse*. It was
hoped that a repetition of the procedure followed before in Cornwall would bring the same happy results: new regiments of foot

---

[1] *True and Joyfull Newes from Exceter . . .* , 5–8.
[2] Granville, *The History of the Granville Family*, 245.
[3] Bodleian: Nalson MSS. ii, 105 (213) (H.M.C., 13th Rept., Pt. I, 76): Letter
dated at Plymouth, 2 Dec. 1642, from Philip Francis, Mayor, and John Waddon
to Sir John Young.

for an advance on Plymouth and perhaps for another try at Exeter.

The first week in December was spent negotiating for money and supplies with which to maintain approximately 2,500 men. Funds were needed to pay the quartermaster-general and other officers. The town of Totnes was Royalist in sympathy, or at least acquiescent in the face of force with half of Grenvile's regiment quartered there. The corporation gave the Cornish £250 and twenty barrels of powder; four citizens made a contribution, willing, or persuaded, and agreed to wait a year for security by bond.[1] As the greatest want of the army was dragoons, the clergy about Plympton assisted with a subscription for 140 men and horse.[2] At the same time the commanders were negotiating with Francis Basset to sequestrate the Earl of Salisbury's manor of Trerabo and the tithes of St. Hilary and Clements. Here again they took a legal approach. It was claimed that this estate belonged to Basset's inheritance of St. Michael's Mount, across from Penzance. Basset was given authority to seize the rents and profits for the King's use.[3]

By this time Plymouth was virtually surrounded by Royalist troops. On 5 December Hopton cut off the town's water supply. The Mayor of Dartmouth, Alexander Staplehill, wrote urgently to the Speaker of the House, William Lenthall, reporting that the corporation had solicited the deputy lieutenants to send men and arms, but that the gentry were generally well affected to the commission of array.[4] In the Commons it was resolved that Captain

---

[1] Edward Windeatt, 'Totnes and the Civil War', *Devon, Repts. & Trans.* xlv. 220. This is a printed transcript of an MS. statement by Anthony Goodridge, Mayor of Totnes in 1664 and again in 1682. Presumably he was trying for reimbursement. The monies were collected from the four Totnes citizens on 1 December 1642. On 25 December 1643 security by bond was to be given by Hopton, Berkeley, Grenvile, and others. The receipt is signed by Hopton, but written against it is a notation to the effect that the security was never given nor the money paid. The money was used, by Hopton's orders, to pay certain officers: Quartermaster Fisher, Dr. Clarnell, Sgt.-Maj. Pomeroy, and others.

[2] C.R.O.: Tremayne MS.: Letter dated at Carhyaes 26 Dec. 1642, from Charles Trevanion to his friend Mr. 'Judah May', with mention of a letter from his son Col. John Trevanion.

[3] C.R.O.: Basset MS., 2, 42–44. The first letter, to Francis Basset from Secretary of State Edward Nicholas, is dated 23 November 1642; the next is undated; the last two are dated 1 December 1642. These last three are addressed to Basset from Lord Mohun, Hopton, and Berkeley. Their commission: 'to Commande in Cheife in the West'. In effect, this amounts to an independent, if joint, command. Hertford is now officially out of the picture.

[4] Coate, 40; Nalson MSS. II, 104 (212) (H.M.C., 13th Rept., Pt. I, 77): Letter dated at Dartmouth, 5 Dec. 1642, from Alexander Staplehill, Mayor.

James Chudleigh should levy 1,000 dragoons for employment in the western parts.[1]

On Tuesday 6 December the *posse* gathered at Modbury, nine miles from Plympton. But it was 'rather like a great fayre than a Posse, . . . all the Gentlemen of the Country being so transported with the jollity of the thing, that noe man was capable of the labour and care of discepline'.[2] Only the gentlemen had arms and equipage for war. At this impasse Slanning, on Hopton's instigation, returned to the army at Plympton for consultation with Berkeley and Ashburnham. These officers suggested an advance on Dartmouth, twenty-five miles from Modbury by the coast road. Seizure of this port would have consolidated the Royalist wedge between Plymouth and Exeter. That part of Grenvile's regiment which had remained at Plympton was ordered to Modbury, and two troops of horse were sent toward Plymouth to guard the ways in that direction. That same night, however, Ruthin, now called 'General', marched out of Plymouth with 500 men, making such good time that they were half a mile from Modbury before they were discovered. The detachment from Grenvile's regiment had not arrived yet, and it would seem that the Royalists not only had failed to send out patrols, but had not even posted a main guard.

The *posse* was scattered; Sheriff Fortescue and other notables taken prisoner; and Hopton himself, whose capture alone would have been hailed at Westminster as a victory, avoided it by a hair's breadth. With Slanning, who had returned early that morning, he made a narrow escape, meeting Grenvile's tardy foot half an hour's march out of town. It was too late to follow Ruthin. Receiving money, horses, and arms from some of the gentry at Modbury, he had swept on toward Dartmouth. Among the Parliamentarians there was great hope for uniting the forces of Plymouth, Dartmouth, and Exeter.[3] The Royalist failure was a lack of proper security; a strong and well-placed detachment of guards would have warned them of Ruthin's approach, or even held him off until their main force had had time to rally.

---

[1] *C.J.* ii. 832.   [2] Hopton, 25.
[3] Ibid. 25–26; *Remarkable Passages Newly received of the great overthrow of Sir Ralph Hopton and his forces (sic) At Madburie, 12 miles from Plymouth . . .* etc. (London, 14 Dec. 1642), *passim.; A letter from Exeter sent To the Deputy-Lieutenants of Sommersetshire, subscribed George Chudley* (Sir George Chudleigh, Bart.) *and Nich. Martin. Shewing how Colonell Ruthen sallyed out of Plymouth . . . and surprised the posse comitatus at Modbury,* dated at Exeter 7 Dec. 1642 (London, 1642), *passim.*

Failure or no, Hopton had created a stir in the west that marked him, in the Parliament view, as a dangerous man. On 14 December the House of Lords ordered the deputy lieutenants of Somerset to attach him; the volunteers of that county were joined by others from Bristol, where Parliamentary forces had seized control. At the same time the mayor, common council, and deputy lieutenants of Exeter entered into a covenant against the Cavaliers.[1]

Word reached the Royalists that the garrison at Exeter was weak; and, upon the promise of loyal gentlemen of the county to provide munitions and fresh levies, they resolved to strike at that city again. It was perhaps too soon after their last futile efforts, but the prospect of raising new regiments was inviting. Accordingly, the army moved out in two groups from Totnes and Plympton. From the Exeter district, Hopton sent a detachment of 500 men over forty miles to the north-west to secure Torrington[2] and keep an eye on any threatening action from the quarter of Barnstaple and Bideford. He and Ashburnham, with the main body of troops, quartered at Alphington, two miles south of Exeter, while the regiments of Grenvile and Godolphin took Topsham, a little farther east on the other side of the river Exe. Here again the gallantry and prowess of the Cavaliers was impeded by the difficulty of communication between one contingent and another. It was hard to move as a united force and impossible to watch all the routes into the city. At the same time they were far from their base of supply; munition and victuals were rapidly being diminished.[3] They were faced with the bitter truth that the promise of reinforcements and auxiliaries from the county had been mere bait.

Under these circumstances Hopton's calling on Mayor Clark to surrender can be taken less as an act of assurance than as one of

---

[1] H.M.C., App. to 5th Rept., 60: House of Lords Calendar, 1642; Bristol City Library: *A Letter from Bristol the tenth of* December 1642, *passim; The Covenant entered into by the Mayor of Exceter, Deputy-Lieutenants of that County, and Common-Councell of that City To Defend the City and County against Sir* Ralph Hopton *and his adherents in this their Rebellious Insurrections . . .* etc. (London, 1642), *passim.*

[2] J. J. Alexander and W. R. Hooper, *The History of Great Torrington in the County of Devon* (Sutton, Surrey, 1948), 86, citing *Mercurius Aulicus* for 7 Jan. 1643. The same source cites the Torrington parish register for this succinct and eloquent epitaph: 'Christopher Awberry gent borne at or by mere in Sommett on of Sir Ralphe Hopton's troopers who was kild by the goeing off of a muskett upon the maine gard was buryed the XXVth of December Souldier Like.'

[3] But Cornwall still managed to provide a modicum of Christmas cheer. See the Bodmin mayor's accounts for 16 December 1642: 'Sent the Lord Mohun, Sir Ra: Hopton, etc. 2 gals of wine—6s.'

bravado and bluff. The mayor, knowing the city was well supplied and that Ruthin and the Earl of Stamford were coming to his relief, had only to temporize. To Hopton's first letter he returned no answer, asserting later that the King's commission had no relation to Exeter. A second letter he likewise refused to take seriously: he could not, he said, accept friendly professions, since the cavaliers had invaded Devon and used its inhabitants as enemies. On 30 December Hopton tried again; in reply, Clark accused him of being a partner, 'in the execution at least', of the design to ruin the kingdom through persuading the King 'to bend his Royall face against the Parliament'.[1] The delaying strategy worked. While the Royalists negotiated, Ruthin, about Christmas, was able to slip into Exeter with a party of horse and musketeers from Dartmouth, 'well guided off' from the Cornish quarters.[2] On 31 December Hopton tried a night attack, but the garrison made a sortie and the cavaliers were forced to retreat.[3] This repulse was hailed by the Parliamentarians as a victory.[4] At least the siege had proved the superiority of their scouts and intelligence: Ruthin was well informed as to Hopton's need for powder and match. But his report to the mayor of Barnstaple relating how he planned to follow and seize the Royalist artillery was intercepted by his adversaries, who took the precaution of sending on their guns and carriages a day's march ahead of the rest of the army.

The retreat in that 'bitter season of the year' was efficiently carried out. At Crediton the horse and foot rested one whole day while the cannon, guarded by dragoons, advanced to Bow; having rested, the cavalry and musketeers then caught up with the artillery, and the whole force on the second night (2 January 1643) came safe to Okehampton. From here the guns were advanced to Bridestowe while the horse and foot again rested. This technique was carried off expertly despite the recalcitrance and indiscipline of the infantry, 'through the whole marche so disobedient and mutinous, as little service was expected from them if they should be attempted by the

---

[1] *The true Copie of A Letter sent from Sir Ralph Hopton, Col. Ashburnham, and Sir John Berkeley, To Mr. Christopher Clarke, Mayor of the City of Excester . . . With the Answer which the Mayor returned to them* (London, 1642), *passim.*

[2] Hopton, 27.   [3] Coate, 41.

[4] *A Famous Victory Obtained before the City of* Exeter, *on Sunday* January 1 *by Captaine* Pym, *Against Sir* Ralph Hopton, *and the Cornish Cavaliers . . . Being the Copie of a Letter, sent from Lieutenant* Abell Hyword . . . *Bearing date* January 2, 1643 (London, 6 January 1643), *passim.* Captain Alexander Pym was the son of John Pym, the leader of the Commons.

Enemy . . .'. But when Ruthin suddenly appeared near Bridestowe to make good his word they showed their mettle and fell into line with admirable ardour and aplomb. Ruthin's advance-guard was beaten off; the prudent general drew back, deciding to postpone operations for the time; and on 4 January the Cornish, temporarily reconciled with their commander, marched into Launceston.[1]

It would appear that the Cornish discipline was exemplary in action, but lax otherwise. A few days later Hopton, receiving word that Saltash was being bombarded, set off for that town with Killigrew and Sidney Godolphin, taking with him William Arundell's company and Trevanion's regiment. This last unit proved so untrained that half of it came straggling into Saltash hours after the others had been posted there. The town was under fire from three ships in the estuary.[2] At the same time other Parliamentary forces were advancing out of Somerset, Dorset, and the eastern counties under the general command of Henry Grey, Earl of Stamford. Hopton's plan for resistance, to meet the enemy in an ambuscade, was over-ruled by the council of war at Launceston. Again he retreated: to Liskeard and Lostwithiel and then to Bodmin, where he was joined by the rest of the army. Orders had already been sent out to muster the *posse*.[3]

Thus, after three months of jockeying, of futile marches, skirmishes, wasted sieges, and retreat, the opposed forces were coming to grips at last. Ruthin, after Hopton's withdrawal, came over and took Saltash. Meanwhile, on 13 January, other Parliamentarians had forced a passage at New Bridge, seven miles to the north. Despite strong impediments—a broken arch in the bridge, with heavy earthworks on the other side and vigilant Royalist guards behind them—a party of dragoons and horse managed to cross by a ford, under covering fire from the foot. In the ensuing skirmish two Royalists were killed; the commander, Captain Hartgill, was forced into the river, where he drowned. The Parliament-men captured Lieutenant Greenwaye and forty others, besides forty horses and fifty muskets; for their own casualties, they claimed only one man wounded in the arm. Writing to Lord Stamford of these events, they urged his presence, informing him of their intent to invade Cornwall next day and unite with

---

[1] Hopton, 27–28.

[2] Granville, *The History of the Granville Family*, p. 245, mentions 200 Scots on their way from Ireland to serve the French King and putting in at Saltash from 'stress of weather'.

[3] Hopton, 28–29.

Ruthin.[1] This rendezvous was effected: the united Parliamentary force advanced to Liskeard. When Stamford joined them their preponderance would be overwhleming.

Thirteen miles to the west the Cornish mustered the *posse*, knowing that their best hope of saving the county lay in crushing Ruthin before the earl's contingent arrived. In this time of necessity the indispensable Francis Basset again proved his resourcefulness. Within five days he had supplied Hopton with over £300,[2] a sum considerably augmented when rough weather drove three Parliamentary men-of-war into Falmouth.[3] This windfall turned up both money and weapons; as bruited by Bevill Grenvile the reception of this happy news in the ranks can be imagined as tumultuous. Fuelled by two weeks' pay in advance in addition to all arrears, Cornish morale needed no further incentive than to know that the enemy was on Cornish soil.

On Wednesday 18 January the army with its auxiliaries organized from the *posse* was drawn together on Moilesbarrow Down. Unencumbered by baggage or cannon, the troops marched to Mohun's seat at Boconnoc Park east of Lostwithiel. That night, while the troops slept by fires near the hedges and horse were sent out to get intelligence of the enemy, a council of war was held. Whether Ruthin would move without Stamford, who might be delayed by foul weather and bad roads, was easy to surmise: if he had received orders to wait, he had disregarded them when he left the Tamar. The only conceivable plan was to march toward Liskeard and strike wherever they found him.

Early on the morning of the nineteenth Captain Cosoworth's dragoons, serving as a vanguard as the rest of the army moved out, rode across Braddock Down and on the eastern edge of that open tract encountered twice their own number of Parliamentary horse. A brief fight ensued; the dragoons were reinforced from their own cavalry; and the two mounted bodies skirmished while the Royalist generals hastily devised a plan of battle.

Braddock Down, sloping up from Boconnoc to Braddock Church,

---

[1] Nalson MSS. II, item 136, p. 272: Letter dated at Tavistock 13 January 1642/3 ('10 at night') to Henry, Earl of Stamford, lord general of the Parliamentary forces in the west, signed by Francis Buller, John Pyne, and William Strode. Marginal note by Stamford: he is on the march.

[2] Basset MSS., 55 (17) and 56 (18). On 12 Jan. 1642/3 was received the sum of £100; on 17 Jan. 'by the hands of George Treweske' the sum of £204. 9s. 8d.

[3] Coate, 41.

is today thickly wooded; at the time of the Civil War it consisted of two heaths, a wasteland of low shrubs, connected by a lane, itself flanked by hedges.[1] Ruthin's army had positioned itself on a ridge skirting the northern side of this sector; the Royalists took up their station on a similar hummock of rising ground to the west. The joint commission had been modified in favour of a single command. Public prayers were offered at the head of every regiment. Devotions over, Hopton placed a body of musketeers behind the hedges, with the few remaining horse and dragoons on the wings, next sending back to Mohun's house for two small iron guns or 'drakes', the main artillery having been left at Bodmin. By the time all these preparations had been made it was afternoon, but the skirmishing continued some two hours more. The Parliament-men's preponderance in cavalry was balanced by the Cornish army's advantage in foot; also, Ruthin's heavy artillery had not come up yet. Hopton, who had been con-cealing his own pair of little drakes behind his cavalry, suddenly ordered them to discharge a shot apiece and, leaving a reserve of foot, moved out with the rest.

The Cornish charge—pikes in the middle, with musketeers on either side and horse on the wings—was a feat of *élan* such as only exceptional commanders could have evoked; and here they were the quintessence of an *élite* leadership: the sturdy, broad-faced Grenvile leading the van, closely seconded by the small but dashing Slanning and the other colonels, while Hopton, of the 'sedate countenance and clear eye',[2] must have strained every resource to order the whole.

Grenvile's narrative reveals the pace and impetuosity of the onslaught:

I ledd my part away, who followed me with so good courage, bothe downe the one hill and up the other, it strooke a terror in them, while the second came up gallantly after me, and the winges of horse charged both sides but their courage so faild them, as they stood not out first charge of the

---

[1] Richard Symonds, *Diary of the Marches of the Royal Army During the Civil War*, Charles E. Long, ed. (Printed for the Camden Society, No. 74, in 1859 from B.M., Add. MS. 17,062), 49.

[2] The phrase is used by John E. Bailey in his *Life of Thomas Fuller* (London, 1874), 311. Presumably it pertains to Hopton's portrait, as I can find no physical description of him elsewhere, the seventeenth century being limited in such details. Bailey goes so far as to say that Hopton's nose 'would have gained him the favour of Napoleon'. He also described him as having 'a reddish beard, closely cut'. In the dim light of the National Portrait Gallery, the ginger whiskers are not noticeable; but in my opinion the rest of the description tallies.

foote but fledd in great disorder, and we chast them . . . many were not slaine because of their quick disordering. . . .[1]

The rout was total: the Parliament-men fled back over the narrow and dirty lanes toward Liskeard and on to Saltash. 'But for their horses speed', Grenvile says, '[they] had been all in our hands.' It is probably true that the haste of the retreat, along with Hopton's merciful restraint, reduced the number of deaths to a minimum. The Cornish took 1,250 prisoners and five guns, as well as many small arms and all the enemy's baggage and munitions.[2] With this grand haul they occupied Liskeard that night, resting next day and giving public thanks for their victory.

Ruthin's defeat was decisive, and it was deserved: he had acted not only without but against the order of his lord general, Stamford. A day's delay would have brought him four additional pieces of ordnance and more men.[3] Surely it would have been wiser to wait for Stamford by the Tamar. But wisdom is often a matter of hindsight; it is also possible that General Ruthin wanted to reap a few laurels for himself before the commander-in-chief arrived.[4] Whatever his motives, his strategy necessarily failed to take into account the Cavaliers' recent augmentation of arms and likewise the incalculable factor of morale. The cohesiveness of the Cornish pikes could be explained partly in terms of previous drill and Hopton's tactical leadership. But beyond

---

[1] Victoria and Albert Museum, Kensington: MS. letter of Bevill Grenvile to his wife Grace, dated at Liskeard 19 Jan. 1642/3.

[2] Hopton, 29–30; Nalson MSS. II, 144 (288): Letter dated at Plymouth 20 Jan. 1642/3 from Thomas Wrothe to John Pym: *A True Relation of a late Victorie obtained by Sir Ralph Hopton Against My Lord of Stamford's Forces in Cornwall, which (through the mercifulnesse of the Generall Sir Ralph Hopton) was gotten with little blood-shed* . . . etc. (Oxford, 28 Jan. 1642/3), *passim*; Alfred H. Burne and Peter Young, *The Great Civil War* (London, 1959), 39–40; Sir William Dugdale, *The Life, Diary, and Correspondence of* . . . , W. Hamper, ed. (London 1827), 46; *C.S.P.V.* 1642–43, p. 237.

Miss Coate's account, 41–43, correctly points out the fallacy of the Parliamentary newsbooks which report that Ruthin's force fell into an ambush, but contains one or two errors. On page 42, she states that Hopton had six guns besides the two from Mohun's house, though Hopton says, p. 29, that they marched from Bodmin without cannon. On page 43 she states that 200 Parliamentarians were slain, citing Hopton, p. 30, whereas no mention of numbers slain appears in that context. A minor point: Miss Coate says the Parliament-men were drawn up on the east side of the down; Burne and Young, p. 41. opt for the north. The present author has chosen to abide by professional opinion, but it is a purely academic question: either way, the round-heads had come about three miles out of Liskeard.

[3] Nalson MSS.: Letter of Thomas Wrothe, above.

[4] Burne and Young suggest this, 39.

this and the extra pay in their pockets, there was the solidarity, the community it might truly be called, of a band of brothers. In comparison the Parliamentarian force was motley: a Scottish general, upstart militia colonels from Somerset like Pyne and Strode and from Cornwall like Francis Buller, horse captains like Thomson and Alexander Pym (son of John Pym). It is not too much to say that Ruthin was beaten by Cornish fraternity and the unfailing diligence of Francis Basset, who soon after for his good offices received the accolade of knighthood.

While Ruthin escaped over Saltash passage in a small boat, Stamford, who had reached Launceston,[1] being apprised of the disaster, drew back to Tavistock. The Royalists, having rested, decided to strike two ways at once. Berkeley and Ashburnham, with the regiments of Grenvile, Slanning, and Trevanion and half the horse and dragoons were to go after Stamford; Hopton and Mohun with Mohun's and William Godolphin's regiment, accompanied by Sidney Godolphin and other members of the staff, were to advance to Saltash. Stamford proved elusive and Ruthin resourceful: the former hastening away before the cavaliers came up to him, eventually reaching Plymouth in safety; the latter doing his best to strengthen the town, raising earthworks which he fortified with four pieces of cannon. He also brought a ship with sixteen guns up the estuary to repel the opposing forces. But the Royalists drove the offenders off the works, seized the ordnance and the ship, and drove their enemies to the sea side. Ruthin and the more fortunate of his party escaped in small boats, some of which, however, were swamped by overcrowding. In all, 260 escaped; 100 are said to have drowned; 140 were taken prisoner.[2]

Hopton took Saltash on Sunday 22 January. In terms of ground gained he was hardly better off than he had been two months before. But Cornwall was safe for the time being; Braddock Down was a tonic for the Royalist cause and an irritant to its enemies. On 23 January, at Westminster, it was ordered that the Committee for

[1] According to Wrothe, above, Stamford had spent the preceeding week—that of 20 January 1642/3—viewing fortifications around Plymouth. In that case he must have come from Exeter about the time of the skirmish at New Bridge on 13 January. But this is a highly debatable point. Had he been that close, it is unlikely that Ruthin would have been allowed to manoeuvre independently. Also, if Stamford's aim was to get into Cornwall as quickly as possible, the route from Exeter to Launceston via Okehampton was shorter and handier for getting his army across the river.

[2] Hopton, 30–31; *A True Relation* . . . , above; Coate, 45–46; Burne and Young, 41.

Western Affairs 'do give Order unto the Treasurer for the monies collected by an Ordinance of both Houses of Parliament for the Suppressing of the Rebellion of Sir Ralph Hopton'.[1] The same day the King issued a commission of oyer and terminer, a patent of assize, and six commissions of gaol delivery for the western counties,[2] perhaps a sign of confidence at the way things were going, but more likely just another instance of a remarkable continuity in administration, the procedural forms of which, at least, were adhered to even in the midst of civil tumult.

It was on this basis of a restoration of civil forms that Hopton attempted to negotiate with his opponents. A conference was proposed to discuss a treaty. Hopton, Mohun, and Colonel William Godolphin were to represent the Royalists; Stamford, Sir George Chudleigh, and Francis Buller the Parliament-men. The projected terms were sweeping; Devon and Cornwall were to be 'quarantined', neutralized, sealed off from the general conflict. The old garrisons were to be dismantled; the new ones delivered into the King's hands. Further 'the law should have its due proceedings as in tyme of peace, . . . noe arm'd Troopes should be received into either County of either part, noe contributions exacted to the warr, noe pressing, or leavying of Voluntiers, . . .'.[3] Single persons with their retinues might go out to either party, but should return before the end of the war. On these conditions the Cornish were willing to draw off and pass to the King. Since the bulk of the *posse* had refused to join the voluntary force in the second invasion of Devon, they had given up the idea of trying to destroy Stamford's army, which itself was so depleted in men and supplies that it scarcely dared to venture out of Plymouth. The Parliament party acquiesced in the conference, after some vacillation suggesting it be held near their own command, but as the Royalists might choose. The King's men chose Ham, a mile from Plymouth; the conference met on Sunday 29 January from two till about half-past three 'with reasonable kindness'. But it broke off on the question of restoring the old fortresses to the King, which Stamford adamantly refused. The Royalists were content: they had got what they wanted: a close view of convenient quarters from which to approach the city.

---

[1] *C.J.* ii. 944. 'Hopton' was becoming a by-word. On 11 Feb. 1642/3 Capt. John Hotham at Hull, replying to the Earl of Newcastle, asserts the honesty of his motives and his desire for the King's honour and safety, for 'Sir Ralph Hopton's miracles' are not motives to him.—H.M.C., 13th Rept., Pt. I, 699: Calendar of the Portland MSS., Supp.

[2] Black, *Docquets* . . . , 10 (23 Jan. 1642/3).   [3] Hopton, 32.

Hopton candidly admits they had expected nothing else from the treaty. He and Mohun, drawing up their men, returned to Ham and lay there that night. Berkeley and Ashburnham advanced from Tavistock to Plymouth and then to Modbury, where they guarded the passes eastward from Plymouth and attempted again to rally the county.

To this extent the second siege of Plymouth was virtually a repetition of the first. The difference was that the Parliamentarians now had an effective commander in the person of young James Chudleigh, Sir George Chudleigh's son, who, as major-general of the Parliamentary foot, exerted himself to create diversions in the Royalist rear. At Kingsbridge, nine miles south-east of Modbury, he was checked by Berkeley, who shattered his array, taking 'divers good prisoners', and pursued him through Tavistock as far as Okehampton. From here the Parliament-men dispersed fourteen miles to Chagford over roads covered with snow and 'poor at best'.[1] Berkeley, thinking they had gone on toward Totnes, prepared to follow. Leaving most of his dragoons with Bevill Grenvile to come on after him, he rode out from Okehampton with his main body of horse, accompanied by Sir Francis Hawley and his lieutenant, young Edmund Wyndham, both of whom the previous summer had fought under Sir John Stawell at Marshall's Elm. Also in this flying column was the brilliant Sidney Godolphin, a great mind in a puny body, who, at thirty-three, had added to his reputation as a talented court poet the respect due a sagacious man of affairs as a member, since Sherborne, of Hopton's council of war.

Before dawn on 9 February this party entered Chagford, unaware that a Parliamentary force under Sir John Northcote had occupied it a few hours before. Perhaps sixty miles of hard riding in twenty-four hours in freezing weather had made them less alert than usual. At any rate, with the first shots, Berkeley knew he had advanced too far, too fast: without the dragoons there was no chance of making a stand. Trying to cut their way out before they were surrounded, the cavaliers charged through the town. In the confused skirmish Hawley was wounded by two musket shots. Edmund Wyndham was slain, fulfilling his dying father's injunction: 'I commend you to honour and obey your sovereign, and in all times to adhere to the Crown; and though the Crown shall hang upon a bush, I charge you to

[1] E. H. Young, 'Okehampton During the Civil War', *Devon, Repts. & Trans.* lx. 277.

forsake it not.'[1] Most tragic of all, Godolphin, according to Hopton, 'as perfect, and as absolute peice of vertue as ever our Nation bredd', was struck down by a chance shot above the knee, with only enough time to cry out that he was hurt before he expired. A member of Hopton's troop on the northern border in 1639, he had rendered him invaluable service by guiding him into Cornwall when Sir Ralph had first come down; and though not an officer, he had been linked with Grenvile, Slanning, and Trevanion as a man indispensable to the King's service. Now his brooding speculations on the mutability of life had been rudely confirmed and at the same time closed out forever. In the words of his own verse:

> Ships, which today a storme did find,
> Are since becalm'd, and feele no wind.[2]

After Godolphin had been buried at Okehampton Church, Berkeley and Grenvile rejoined Ashburnham at Plympton. Plymouth was still under close surveillance: on the north in the vicinity of Stoke and Swilly, Hopton kept watch with the regiments of William Godolphin and Mohun. Slanning and Trevanion kept the supply routes open at Modbury. On Tuesday 21 February, about one in the afternoon, James Chudleigh mounted a fierce attack on this post, which continued through the night and into the next day. The Royalists fought stubbornly, taking a heavy toll of lives. But once again lack of munitions forced a retreat; leaving 100 dead, 150 prisoners, 1,100 muskets, and five guns behind them, they pulled back to Plympton, from which the combined force moved on to Rowborough Down. Here they met Hopton and his party, who, attacked by Stamford in their quarters, had retreated about the same time as their friends. The general retreat was well managed: the ordnance was ferried over Saltash passage, while the main part of the army marched on to Tavistock.[3]

The second invasion of Devon had failed. The siege of Plymouth,

---

[1] H. A. Wyndham, *A Family History* (Oxford, 1939), i. 188–9.

[2] Victoria and Albert Museum, Kensington: MS. letter of Bevill Grenvile to his wife, dated at Okehampton 9 Feb. 1642/3; Hopton, 33; Keeler, 188; Coate, 47–53; Burne and Young, 41. The couplet is from Godolphin's 'Chorus'. It is hard to see how a wound in the thigh could kill a man, but Godolphin's constitution was weak, and he may have been wounded before. Fatigue, exposure, and shock all could have contributed to his death. The musket ball may have touched bone or perhaps the great artery near the groin—in which case there would have been a violent haemorrhage with every heart-throb.

[3] *C.J.* ii. 985; Hopton, 33–34; Coate, 54; Burne and Young, 41.

which Bevill Grenvile had 'never expected could have been success-ful', had indeed been futile, since the city continued to be supplied from the sea.[1] The attempt to raise the country, even with the assistance of the high sheriff,[2] had been unsuccessful because of the Devon peasants' innate suspicion of the Cornish and primordial instinct to defend their homes.[3] It was the *posse* mentality all over again, with the shoe on the other foot. It would seem that the cavaliers had chased Chudleigh about the county to no purpose. But since that young officer's star had only begun to rise, they could take some comfort still from the eclipse of Ruthin's.[4]

Both sides needed a respite. The Cornish departure from Devon was made under a treaty of cessation, signed on 28 February and to run for seven days. As explained in a letter to Westminster from two Parliamentary baronets, Sir George Chudleigh and Sir John Bampfyld, the Devon forces consisted largely of trained bands, sufficient to defend the county against a small invasion, but not to follow the enemy into Cornwall.[5] For over a month and a half one truce followed another. On 5 March Slanning led five other Royalist commissioners to Stone House near Plymouth for a conference. All parties swore to uphold the Protestant religion, the prerogative of the King, and the privileges of Parliament;[6] but the only result of their haggling was to extend the treaty twenty days to 26 March. On 8 March Mayor Clark of Exeter wrote to Parliament that Tuesday the 14th had been appointed for a meeting of deputies from Cornwall, Devon, Dorset, and Somerset at Exeter in an attempt to resolve their differences

[1] Victoria and Albert Museum, Kensington: MS. letters of Bevill Grenvile to his wife, one dated at Plympton 20 Feb. and the second written at Tavistock on 25 Feb. 1642-3.

[2] Sir Samuel Luke, *Journal*, I. G. Philip, ed. (Oxfordshire Record Society, 1947, 1950, 1952, 1953), 3. Luke was the Parliamentary scoutmaster. Since his station was in the Midlands to keep an eye on Oxford, his intelligence with respect to events on the western fringe must be received with caution, but in this case there is no reason to doubt it.

[3] Coate, 53-54.

[4] Basset MSS.: Letter of Lord Mohun to (Sir) Francis Basset, dated at Warley House 29 Jan. 1642/3. See also *T.T.*, E. 102/17, undated, in which one 'J. T.', probably Sir Jonathon Trelawney of Plymouth, reports that Lt.-Gen. Ruthin has 'gone from us', mentioning his defeat at Liskeard. But Hopton, p. 34, links him with Stamford in threatening the Royalists at Tavistock. At any rate, we hear of General Ruthin no more.

[5] Nalson MSS. II, 164 (326): Letter dated at Plymouth, 3 March 1642/3.

[6] For the proposed articles of the Cornish, the Devon replies, and the Devon counter-proposals, see a separate MS. among the miscellanea at the C.R.O. For a printed version see *T.T.* 94/21, dated 30 Mar. 1643.

G

through an association based on an agreement not to invade each other but 'mutually to defend each other against all forces whatsoever'.[1] But next day another letter to Westminster from another citizen of Exeter expressed a different view: Thomas Gewen declared that the extension of the treaty had not been approved by Lord General Stamford or the deputy lieutenants and maintained that the meeting of Hopton with the county deputies should be prevented.[2] The same day another correspondent wrote to Pym that he was glad Parliament, to keep factions apart, had forbidden the assizes, scheduled for 16 March. He reported that already two prisons were filled with 'malignants', and expressed fear that the cessation was giving the Royalist cohorts time to rally.[3] The Commons, for whom neutrality virtually meant defeat, forbade the mayor and deputy lieutenants of Exeter to admit Hopton or any of his adherents into the city.[4] Their commissioners arrived to enforce this decree on the 13th; next morning the few Cornish who came were escorted under convoy to an inn in a neighbouring village. There was little support from Dorset and Somerset.[5] On the 17th the Cornish departed, having agreed to a further cessation of ten days. As it was plain that both parties were playing for time, the council of war in Devon resolved to seize the advantage by raising three more regiments.[6]

Meanwhile, as the truce was spun out to midnight of 22 April the Cornish commanders, who well understood such tactics, were busy warning and exhorting their countrymen to make good their defence. It was agreed to assess the county for a contribution of £750 a week; some gentlemen also lent their plate, upon security, to the value of £3,000.[7] On 14 April Grenvile's regiment came to Launceston, marking the third Royalist occupation of that city since October.

[1] Nalson MSS. II, 166 (330).   [2] Ibid. 167 (332).
[3] Ibid. 168 (334); *C.J.* ii. 998.   [4] *C.J.* ii. 99.
[5] Nalson II, 171b.
[6] Ibid. 181 (362). See Exeter City Library: Ancient Letters of the Corporation of Exeter: MS. dated 11 April 1643: 'It is this day ordered by the Mayor and Deputye Lieutenants of the Cittie and County of Exon. that 150 muskets . . . shall be spared to the Deputye Lieutenants of Devon. . . .' On 17 April Sir George Chudleigh and the rest of the Parliamentary committee in Devon wrote to the Committee of Safety at Westminster apologizing for beginning a treaty with the Cornish, but extenuating themselves by urging their desire to spare blood. The treaty had proved ineffectual anyway; both sides were drawing forces to the border. They reported intercepted letters revealing that William Godolphin was in league with the 'Duke d'Espernon' to obtain money for the Royalists. See also Tanner MSS. LXII, 63; *C.J.* iii. 57.
[7] Hopton, 36.

The command picture had changed slightly: since Ashburnham had gone to see the King, his place of major-general had been taken by Francis Basset's brother Thomas, who had ridden with Berkeley in his pursuit of Chudleigh and fought in the skirmish at Chagford. On the morning of the 22nd he and Hopton inspected the approaches to Launceston, placing dragoons within two miles of the city at Polston Bridge. Their position was by no means secure. Parliamentary forces were reported to be at Liston another two miles on, beyond the river. Grenvile's 1,200 men were the only ones at hand; though a general muster had been called for the next morning, the other regiments were still strung out along the Tamar. An enemy advance at this time would have been disastrous; it may be conjectured with what appetite Hopton partook of the mayor's dinner that evening.

At Exeter, meanwhile, Stamford lay sick of the gout; James Chudleigh, only twenty-five but a veteran of the Irish wars, had succeeded to his command. With five troops of horse, 1,500 musketeers, and 200 pikes he had been biding his time at Liston; upon receiving intelligence of the Royalists' slender garrison and lack of artillery, he resolved to attack Launceston next morning. Early on Sunday 23 April his force advanced toward Polston Bridge. The Royalists were in church at prayers; upon being informed of the enemy's move, Hopton waited till devotions were over, then drew out of town with half of Grenvile's regiment, which he posted on Beacon Hill, facing the Tamar and Launceston castle, lining the hedges at the foot with musketeers. He was badly outnumbered, but, luckily, about 9 a.m., as Chudleigh approached the town, Willian Godolphin's regiment arrived. At 10 a.m. Chudleigh attacked Beacon Hill, driving off Grenvile's musketeers. An hour later the tide turned in favour of the Royalists as Mohun's regiment under Major Walter Slingsby came up, along with Berkeley's horse and dragoons.

For six hours Chudleigh's foot stormed the lower slopes of the hill but without gaining ground and with considerable loss. To take advantage of this, Hopton tried the tactic of sending a regiment and three troops of horse to take Polston Bridge from the rear. The Roundheads were saved by reinforcements from Tavistock and Plymouth; 100 of Sir John Northcote's regiment and 700 of Sir John Merrick's London Greycoats, who secured the bridge and kept the Royalist cavalry at bay. About 7 p.m., however, Slanning's and Trevanion's regiments at last arrived so that the Cornish were now in sufficient force to act decisively. The foot were divided into three parts led by Hopton, Berkeley, and Thomas Basset (whose brother James had been killed a short time before), each group charging from a different direction with such effect that the enemy was saved from utter rout only by the darkness and the skill of its commander, who proved to be as much a master of orderly retreat as Hopton himself. Chudleigh led his newly-blooded troops back to Liston and next day on to Okehampton, bested for one battle but hardly discouraged from trying again.[1]

The Cornish were hindered from going after him, partly by darkness, partly by the blowing up of a powder magazine which scorched many officers and men, and partly by the mutinous conduct of the common soldiers, 'according to their usuall custome after a fight', as Hopton sardonically remarks. A day of rest was sufficient to put them in better temper before trying their dispositions in a third invasion of Devon. On Tuesday 25 April the army marched out to Bridestowe: 300 newly levied dragoons, 300 horse, and 3,000 foot, together with volunteers from the Devon gentry under the command of Henry Carey, the new high sheriff. The artillery consisted of four brass guns, two of them 12-pounders taken from the enemy at Braddock Down, commanded by Slanning as general of the ordnance. At Bridestowe in the evening they encountered a party of the enemy's horse and at the same time received word from Okehampton that Parliamentary morale was shaken due to lack of support from the county. Okehampton was a nodal point for roads from Exeter, Barnstaple, Bideford, Torrington, Launceston, Tavistock, and Plymouth.[2] The Cornish commanders determined to attack it next morning. Drawing forth on the west side of Sourton Down as night set in, they ordered themselves for the march as follows: half the dragoons, half the horse, and half the foot in the van; the ordnance in the middle; then the other half of the foot, the left wing of the horse, and the left wing of the dragoons in the rear.

---

[1] *A most true Relation of divers notable passages of Divine Providence in the great deliverance and wonderfull victory obtained by the Parliaments Forces under the command of the Earle of Stamford, in the County of Devon, against the Army of Cavaliers, raised by Sir* Ralph Hopton. . . . (London, 1 May 1643), *passim*; Hopton, 36–37; Coate, 59–61; Burne and Young, 42–43. The Parliamentary pamphlet, stretching a point or two, maintains that Chudleigh lost only twelve 'common men', with thirty or forty 'slightly' wounded, while the Royalists suffered fifty slain, including at least three commanders. The Parliamentary figures, however, refer only to the reatreat and ignore the heavy losses from a day of hot fighting.
[2] E. H. Young, 282.

The weather was hot and sultry, brewing up to a storm.

Chudleigh, five miles away, was beset with problems: some of his troops had deserted; his sergeant-major, contrary to orders, had dismissed the munitions and artillery carriages; and due to the 'foul neglect of the lying Deputy Scout-master', he had not been informed of the Royalists' approach. When this intelligence finally reached him it was 9 p.m.; he was in a position neither to retreat nor to stand still. Sending his infantry, about 1,000 men, to the town's end, he drew out with 108 horse, spreading them over the hillside in many small bodies with great spaces in between. Only an ambuscade would answer against such odds.

The Royalists marched with scouts before and on either hand, 'never as they conceiv'd in better order, nor in better equipage, nor ever (which had like to have spoyled all) in lesser apprehension of the Enemy . . .'. About 11 p.m. Hopton, Mohun, Berkeley, and Basset were 'carelessly enterteyning themselves' at the head of the dragoons; Slanning was in the rear. In the darkness of the night they approached within 100 yards of the ambush before realizing their danger.

Of the Parliamentary forces, Captain Thomas Drake with thirty-six men in two troops charged first, killing his first man and crying, 'Charge on, charge on, they run, they run!' Chudleigh came after, yelling 'Charge all, charge all, kill them all which will not lay downe their Armes!' Captain William Gould charged through a whole regiment of foot in the van of the Royalist infantry; Captain Alexander Pym also 'played a brave part'. Though many troopers, falling to pillage, failed to charge on after their commanders, the first assault carried two or three miles, scattering horse, dragoons, and foot; but Mohun and Grenvile took their stand by the guns, and Slanning brought up the rear to strengthen the line; the enemy was beaten off. The commanders discovered an old trench upon the heath and used it to good advantage, lining it with musketeers on the left and drawing up the remaining horse and dragoons on the right, with the four cannon in front and a palisade of long stakes called 'Swedish feathers'[1] in front of the guns.

The second assault brought up Chudleigh's musketeers, who, however, shaken by the Royalist ordnance and knowing that their own artillery (carriages having come in) was now preceding them in

[1] 'Swine Feathers' (or 'Swedes' Feathers'): pointed stakes, used as weapons of defence against cavalry, being either fixed in the ground as a palisade or carried in a musket rest like a bayonet—*J.S. Army H.R.* iii. 51.

retreat toward Crediton, failed to rally and made off towards the town, but left their matches burning on the bushes as a ruse to make the Cornish think they were still there. Apparently this trick worked till the rain came to put the matches out. The weather was tempestuous: thunder shattering the intervals of the cannonade and lightning exploding the powder in the soldiers' bandoliers. It was too much for Chudleigh's horse, who shortly followed the foot. The brave but unfortunate young general was forced to 'perswade back' a dozen of them with his baton. Besides these there were only a handful of officers: Captains Gould, Pym, Drake, Downing, Fenton, and Lutterell, three lieutenants, and a corporal. Having compelled from prisoners the Royalist password: 'Launceston', they were able to draw off safely, leaving the storm to complete the rout of their foes, who, completely demoralized, crying that 'the militia fought not against them but the Devill', fled, a panic-striken mob, back to Bridestowe, leaving sixty dead on the field.

In tactical terms Sourton Down was a victory for the elements; but with regard to spoils, it was Chudleigh's: twenty prisoners, 1,000 muskets, five barrels of powder, and 100 horses. Much more important was Hopton's portmanteau: his secretary was killed while guarding it, and a Parliamentary trooper picked it up. It contained muster rolls, letters from Devon Royalists and accounts of their contributions, and correspondence from the King, chiefly a letter written in cipher on thin white silk, probably from the hand of Secretary Nicholas or perhaps Sir Edward Walker, the King's Secretary at War. The royal command was for Hopton to draw to Exeter and then to Somerset to effect a rendezvous with the King's horse for mutual support. Sir Ralph was advised to horse all his foot, both musketeers and pikes, as dragoons, to move with more speed and safety.

This valuable trove was brought to Stamford at Exeter. The gouty earl 'leapt out of his chaire for joy', and said it might yield £40,000 if it were well managed, meaning, it is inferred, that he meant to sequester the estates of those listed. Ready for the next round, he ordered his forces to rendezvous at Torrington.[1]

---

[1] *Speciall Passages And certain Informations from severall places, collected for the use of all that desire to be truely Informed* (No. 38): *From* Tuesday *the 25 of* April, to Tuesday *the 2 of* May 1643: *Exploits Discovered, in A Declaration of some proceedings of Serjeant Major Chudley, Generall of the Forces under the Earle of Stamford: Against Sir* Ralph Hopton. *Fully relating the great overthrow given to him.* . . . (2 May 1643); *A Full Relation of the great defeat given to the* Cornish Cavalliers, *by Sergeant Major Generall Chudley, confirmed by divers Letters from those parts to*

At Westminster on 29 April a happy Commons returned thanks to General Chudleigh for the 'great Defeat' given by 'some small Remainder of his Forces to the whole Army of the Cornish Cavaliers'.[1]

And this same army, ready, perhaps, after three tries, to give up Devon as a bad job, humiliated, and yet, it may be surmised more hopefully, inclined to regard Sourton as only a set-back, severe though it was: this volatile but still vigorous force, returned, as always after a relapse, to its refuge at Launceston, taking up again the watch on the Tamar which it had maintained so vigilantly for six months past.

[1] *C.J.* iii. 63.

---

severall Merchants in London (3 May 1643); *Mercurius Aulicus* i. 129 (4 May 1643); Luke, *Journal*, x; Hopton, 38–40; Coate, 62–64; Burne and Young, 43–44.

A Full Relation. . . ., Chudleigh's own account, is none too trustworthy, though it may have been edited in publication. He exaggerates the Royalist losses and says nothing of his troopers who failed to follow their commanders, of the failure of the foot to rally, or the state of the weather. He admits, though, that after the retreat to Okehampton the army 'disperst themselves', leaving 600 foot out of 1,700 and three troops of horse out of five.

VI

TRIUMPH AT STRATTON:
Victory and Loss at Lansdown

(April–July 1643)

PERSONAL prowess and ingenuity redeemed the Royalist reverse at Sourton. Henry Carey, high sheriff of Devon, losing his horse either by being thrown off it or having it killed under him, escaped in the darkness and reached his own home in the southern part of the county clad in woman's clothes, returning to the army a week later with a party of horse. Little Christopher Wray, at fifteen a captain commanding a company in Mohun's regiment, was captured and taken to Okehampton. Since his guards thought him a mere trooper's boy, he was able to elude them and steal away in the night, arriving back in Cornwall three days later with a dozen or so musketeers.[1]

Word came that the enemy was withdrawing in disorder through Okehampton; for the third time the Cornish army marched into Devon and occupied Tavistock. On their way out of that town they received intelligence that the Parliamentarians, far greater in number than the Royalist force, had received fresh supplies from Somerset. Discreetly the Cavaliers withdrew again to Launceston: the fifth time that they had entered that place since the commencement of hostilities. Months of marching and countermarching, it seemed, had led to a stalemate. Plainly the invasion and occupation of enemy territory had its limits as strategy to destroy the enemy's army.

To a great extent the Royalists' floundering tactics were the result of faulty or incomplete intelligence. There appears to have been no scoutmaster to relay and co-ordinate information, the sources of which themselves were often suspect because of the Devonians' inveterate hostility to the Cornish. The Parliamentarians usually managed to pre-empt local scouts; the King's men had to rely almost entirely on their own reconnaissance. This seems to have improved slightly after Sourton, but the Parliament-men's 'retreat'[2] through Okehampton may well have been a ruse to draw attention away

---

[1] Hopton, 40–41.   [2] Ibid. 41.

from Torrington, twenty miles north. Only seven miles south of a
secure base of supply at Bideford, it was the best point from which
to launch an attack on Cornwall. In strategic terms such an attack
amounted to a broad flanking movement, 'going round' the Tamar or
crossing it by shallow fords. This avoided the risk of a direct thrust
at the Royalist 'midriff', Launceston, where it would be easy for the
Cornish to concentrate troops. In addition, between Okehampton
and the river, the steep terrain common to Cornwall and west
Devon, rising from a gritty bed of sandstone and shale, was generally
higher than it was farther north; and the route was further impeded
by three tributaries of the Tamar: the Carey, the Claw, and the
Deer. Torrington, then, was more suitable for the Parliamentarian
rendezvous. Towards the end of the second week in May, 1643 the
cavaliers learned that Stamford, taking the same route Hopton had
followed the previous summer, was marching towards the north
part of Cornwall, threatening Stratton and Stowe, which were just
four miles from the Devon line.

The resources of the Royalists again had reached a nadir. Their
rations were short, their effective strength small, their forces scattered
and still distracted by important but now relatively minor concerns,
such as watching Plymouth. From this city a hostile reporter, the
same 'J. T.' (Sir Jonathan Trelawney) who had reported Hopton's
alleged harassing of poor fishermen the preceding November, com-
mented with satisfaction on the poor prospects of the Cornish cause:
the contribution of £1,000 a week from that county, he said, was
beginning to fail; so that Hopton had sent to 'papists' in Somerset
and Dorset. He reported that munitions for the Cornish had arrived
at Pendennis from Jersey and St. Malo, but that such commerce
could be intercepted from Plymouth and Dartmouth. He concluded by
declaring that Charles Trevanion and his son John would like to leave
their commands and reconcile themselves to Parliament. They were too
involved, however, being the 'two first ring-leaders that raised the rebellion in Cornwall', and besides 'Sir Ralph Hopton by his policy hath
so bewitched their good intentions that they know not where to turn'.[1]
The proposed defection of the Trevanions cannot be proved, but of
Hopton's ability to nip it in the bud there can be little doubt.

---

[1] *A True Relation of the Proceedings of the Cornish Forces under the command of the
Lord Mohune and Sir Ralph Hopton wherein is contained a List of the Sergeant-Majors
and Captains, with the Totall of their Strength, and Garrison-townes, passim,* dated
at Plymouth, 15 May 1643.

Though this correspondent may have been hovering between educated guesses and wishful speculation, his detailed knowledge of the actual composition of the Cornish forces makes it highly probable that he was in communication with Parliamentary sympathizers beyond Tamar, fairly numerous in the north part of the county. At any rate, Westminster was furnished with a full roster of line commanders and staff civilians, down to the rank of captain. The number of foot regiments had been raised from five to seven, with Thomas Basset and Charles Trevanion as additional commanders. There were six to eight companies in each regiment. Only Grenvile's group, near Stratton, on the edge of the danger zone, was at full strength: 1,200 men, some of whom, according to 'J.T.', were a dissipated crew, being captured by Parliamentary trained bands while carousing at a farmer's house, drunk with beer. The Royalist front was fifty miles long. John Trevanion had 700 men at Launceston fifteen miles south of Stratton and Mohun 900 at Liskeard, another sixteen miles to the south-west. Slanning had 1,000 at Saltash eighteen miles down the river from Launceston. Opposing him on the other side of the passage, near Rowborough Down, was Sir John Northcote, with a regiment of 1,200 foot; behind Northcote, about Plymouth and Plympton, was Sir George Chudleigh with 2,000 foot and 500 horse.[1] Chudleigh soon moved north fifty miles to rendezvous at Torrington with Stamford and the levies from Barnstaple and Bideford.

As for horse, there was perhaps one effective regiment out of a possible three or four. The full complement came to 1,400. Hopton's two troops of 150 were considered 'very serviceable', but the rest were deemed no better than plough-horses. With two hundred of the less doubtful mounts Sir Francis Hawley took his post on the river at Bridgerule between Launceston and Stratton, across from a Parliamentary troop and a company of foot.

It is possible that Godolphin, Basset, and Charles Trevanion were recruiting their regiments at Bodmin, where the commissioners, picking over the *posse comitatus*, were conscripting the third man in every hundred. Stamford, detaching 1,200 of his 1,400 horse, sent them under command of Sir George Chudleigh to surprise Bodmin if he could; then on 15 May with his remaining horse and 5,400 foot crossed confidently into Cornwall.

Francis Basset's financial acumen was being tested as never before.

[1] *A True Relation* . . . ; Coate, 65–66.

He came up with £70 on 10 May, and another £500 which he borrowed from a French merchant, a M. Albyn.[1] In addition to the problem of paying the troops the Royalists were further burdened by the presence of many civilians, especially clergymen, including not only Archdeacon William Cotton, a prebendary of Exeter, but, according to the omniscient 'J. T.', ministers 'of all sects of religion'. Indeed there were almost as many 'delinquents' as fighting men.[2]

If Braddock Down had been a prelude, Plymouth an impasse, and Sourton a set-back, the approaching battle was to be a supreme test which was likely to determine the fate of Cornwall and the western parts for the duration of the war. Though the Cornish had the advantage of their own ground, they were strategically in a worse position than they had been in January. At Braddock they had fought only part of the total enemy force, which had been divided by the river. Now this force, led by at least one first-rate commander, young James Chudleigh, was united, freshly supplied, and so poised that once in motion it easily could sweep down the line of the Tamar to the estuary.

There was no time to lose: Stamford had hardly left Torrington before Hopton was on the march north to reinforce Grenvile. Since he could ill afford to strip the garrisons at Saltash and the other passes, he mustered the troops he found at Bodmin and Launceston and advanced, on Saturday 13 May, to North Peterwin. That night they lay in the fields and supped on dry biscuit, the only provisions they had. Next day they met a party of enemy horse and dragoons, but beat them off; the main Parliament army at that time was still marching through Devon. Because of this slight check the Cavaliers came late to Week St. Mary, ten miles from Launceston and five from Stratton. The following day Stamford occupied Stratton, cutting off Grenvile's manor at Stow. If Hopton had delayed any longer, it is possible that the ardent and impetuous Sir Bevill might have dared his regiment against odds of four and a half to one. As it was, his own unit made up close to half of the 2,400 foot which assembled by the evening of 15 May at Efford Mill within the parish of Stratton, a mile from the town. In horse the Royalists, with 500, outnumbered their adversaries, with 200. Although in that hilly terrain they were fit for service chiefly as a reserve, a council of war quickly perceived the advantage

---

[1] Coate, 65–66.
[2] *A True Relation* . . . , above. Cotton was the son of William Cotton, anti-puritan bishop of Exeter (d. 1621).

of striking at Stamford while the main body of his cavalry and dragoons was absent with Sir George Chudleigh. When night fell advance parties were sent out to line the hedges; shortly after dawn the rest of the army drew over the passes towards a high grassy plateau some 200 feet above sea level, where the Parliamentary army was waiting like a suspended avalanche.

A flat-topped peak in this ridge, Stratton Hill (afterwards called Stamford Hill), is today partly rimmed by suburban villas which encroach upon it half-way up the slope, with the Bude golf course flanking it to the west. The village of Stratton lies to the south-east at a distance of less than a mile, beyond it a brook. The ridge, lozenge-shaped, runs north and south and is particularly steep to the south and east. On the west side the slope is more gentle, with a declivity of about 1 in 6 to 10, and here near the summit is an earthwork, which, though placed long before the Civil War, may have served at that time as a powder magazine.[1]

At 5 a.m. on Tuesday 16 May 1643 that earthwork and the whole west slope were covered by a battery of thirteen brass ordnance, probably sakers (with $3\frac{1}{2}$-inch bore) and a mortar piece. Hopton, for the fourth time tactical commander in a major engagement, fell back on the scheme of converging columns he had employed so successfully on a smaller scale three weeks before at Polston Bridge. The Cornish army was divided into four parts, each with about 600 men and two cannon. Hopton and Mohun were to assault the hill from the south; Berkeley and Grenvile from the south-west; Slanning and Trevanion from the west; Godolphin and Basset from the north. Colonel John Digby stood off a little to the west upon a sandy common with the 500 horse and dragoons, ordered to stand firm unless the enemy came his way in a body, then to charge.

Thus, outnumbered more than two to one, with munitions and victuals failing, and with the enemy holding advantage of ground, the Cornish infantry began to advance four ways up Stratton Hill. For ten hours the fight swayed back and forth, the issue doubtful. About three in the afternoon the commanders received word that their powder was down to less than four barrels. This defect, they resolved, could be only supplied with courage. Accordingly, concealing the news from their men, they passed word to each other to mount a general assault without firing until they reached the top of

---

[1] C. R. B. Barrett, *Battles and Battlefields in England* (London, 1896), 262; Burne and Young, 44 and n. 1.

the hill. The stratagem worked: the enemy, amazed at the audacity of men who 'outfaced their shot with their swords',[1] were compelled to quit their posts. Only once did the Royalist charge falter; Grenvile, in the van of his pikes, with Berkeley's musketeers on either side, was met by a countercharge from James Chudleigh so fierce that Sir Bevill was knocked to the ground; but regaining his feet with Berkeley's assistance, he led the files back so hotly as to overwhelm his assailants and take young Chudleigh prisoner. For the Parliament-men, the capture of their best officer betokened that the day was lost.

The four Royalist columns drawing nearer as they ascended, between three and four o'clock they all met near the top of the hill, which the enemy had left in utter rout; after joyful embraces, they continued on to the summit. All told, they had lost no more than 80 men, of whom 46 were common soldiers; of the rest none above the rank of captain. The Parliamentarians, on the other hand, lost 300 men killed; 1,700 were taken prisoner, including over 30 commanders. The Cornish also seized the fourteen pieces of artillery, seventy barrels of powder, over two thousand arms, £300 in ready money, and a great magazine of biscuit and other provisions.[2]

Theirs was a virtually unalloyed triumph. Small wonder that Sir Francis Basset could write to his wife in an almost lyrical outburst of rapture:

Dearest Soule, Oh Deare Soule, prayes God everlastingly. Reede ye inclosed. Ring out your Bells. Rayse Bonefyers, publish these Joyfull Tydings, Beleeve these Truthes. Excuse my writing larger. I have not tyme. We march on to meete our Victoryous frinds, and to sease all ye Rebells left if we can finde such Lyvinge. Your Dutyeous prayers God has heard, and blest us accordingly. Pray Love lett my cosen Harris know these Joyfull Blessings. Send word to the Ports south, and north, to search narrowly for all strangers Travelling for passage and sease them keeping them close and safe, off those Rebells of the West, let it be duly commanded.[3]

Stratton may well be an illustration of the adage that a relatively

---

[1] Clarendon, vii. 89.

[2] *The Round-Heads Remembrancer: or, A true and particular Relation of the great defeat given to the Rebels by His majesties good Subjects of the County of Cornwall, under the command of Sr Ralph Hopton, on* Tuesday May 16. 1643 (Oxford, 1643), *passim*; Hopton, 42–44; Clarendon, vii. 88–90; Thomas Fuller, *Worthies*, 3 vols. (London, 1840), i. 331–2; Sir William Dugdale, *The Life, Diary and Correspondence of Sir William Dugdale . . .*, W. Hamper, ed. (London, 1827), 50; E. H. Young, 268; Coate, 66–69; Burne and Young, 44–46.

[3] Basset MS., cited by Walter H. Tregellas, *Cornish Worthies* (London, 1884), 2 vols., i. 120; and Coate, 69.

small army has an inherent advantage over a much larger army: with less mass it has a greater capacity for action.[1] But to seize the opportunity offered requires tactical skill and boldness of no ordinary sort. There can be little doubt that the plan for an attack with converging columns was Hopton's; he had already employed it at Launceston. The strength of four battalions each advancing from a different direction in three files lay in their flexibility: with sufficient momentum, they could outmanoeuvre and outflank the enemy at the top of the hill and drive them from their place.[2]

Even more, however, the Royalist victory must be ascribed to the nature and quality of the Cornish command. Mary Coate sums up the generalship:

Such a battle in which the force that had the advantage of both ground and numbers was the one defeated, must be explained by factors psychological rather than material. In the Royalist army was not merely the traditional skill of the Cornish pikemen, the Celtic capacity for rising to a sudden emergency, and the courage of desperation, but a unity and common feeling, rooted indeed in racial kinship, and in the personal tie between lord and tenant, but strengthened by the privations which officers and men had shared in the critical days before the battle. Both armies fought with religious fervour but with untrained levies, men given to sudden fear, and frequent mutiny; but the Royalists possessed in Hopton and Grenvile men capable of transmuting this raw material into a finely disciplined and unified army. It is not true, as Clarendon unfairly implies, that the Earl of Stamford deserted the battle at its critical stage, but it is a fact that he possessed neither the steady courage of Hopton nor the fiery enthusiasm of Grenvile. Stratton fight is nothing less than the triumph of forces spiritual and psychological over the brute superiority of numbers and the tactical advantages of position, and this is its chief claim to interest.[3]

Sir George Chudleigh, 'with great jollity', had managed to break up the *posse* at Bodmin; but hearing that Stamford had fled to Exeter, made haste to follow him there. Meanwhile, his son James flourished exceedingly with the Cavaliers, who treated him with the utmost civility: indeed, his prowess at Stratton deserved no less. In return, Chudleigh was generous in praising the Cornish to his father: 'I never saw any army freer from vice, nor more religiously inclined than I perceive the whole genius of this Army to be.'[4]

---

[1] J. de Maistre, *Les Soirées de St. Petersbourg* (Paris, 1850), tome 11, Entretien vii, pp. 44–45, cited by Isaiah Berlin in *The Hedgehog and the Fox* (New York, 1957), 82–83.
[2] Burne and Young, 46.   [3] Coate, 70.   [4] Ibid. 72.

Leaving Grenvile at Stratton to guard the prisoners, the rest of the army on 18 May returned to Launceston. Here the commanders were approached by Dr. William Cox, a prebendary of Exeter,[1] who brought them the great news that a power from Oxford led by the Marquis of Hertford and Prince Maurice was advancing toward the west.

Though it had no real control over the Cornish army, Oxford had not forgotten the western cavaliers. In March or April the King had ordered Hopton to draw into Somerset, less as an offensive thrust against the Parliamentarians than as a defensive ploy to put the Cornish in closer contact with the main Royalist army. Since the fall of Reading to the Earl of Essex on 27 April, Charles had been preoccupied with holding his own. Satisfied, however, that the declining condition of Essex's army would prevent him from striking for the present, and becoming concerned about Parliamentary activity in the west country, he needed only the spur of the victory at Stratton to instigate a plan not only for the co-ordination but for the association of forces from the centre with those of the west. As a grandee of unrivalled stature in those parts, Hertford was still a natural choice to command there; as lieutenant-general, the twenty-three-year-old Maurice, the King's nephew and son of Queen Elizabeth of Bohemia, provided dogged courage and some professional experience. With a substantial array of horse and foot, which, Clarendon implies, in contrast to the Cornish, was actually worthy of the name of an army,[2] the prince and the marquis left Oxford on 19 May 1643.

That same day at Westminster William Strode of Devon's seisin of Hopton's estate was resumed by the Houses, which ordered sequestration to continue.[3] The other William Strode and his fellow members of the Parliamentary committee in Somerset grew apprehensive. On 22 May they wrote to Nathaniel Fiennes, Governor of Bristol, reporting intelligence that a party of enemy horse had advanced to Shaftesbury. They wanted Sir William Waller called back to Bath.[4] Waller, apprised of Hopton's success, had abandoned Hereford on 20 May.[5] An advance against his old friend at this juncture must have proved abortive, especially with Prince Rupert lurking in

[1] *Alumni Cantabrigienses*, John Venn and J. A. Venn, eds. (Cambridge University Press, 1922 ff.), Pt. i, vol. i, p. 409.

[2] Clarendon, vii. 94; Ian Roy, 'The Royalist Army in the First Civil War' (unpub. D.Phil. thesis), 73–74.

[3] *C.J.* ii. 92.   [4] MS. Clarendon XXII, item 1683, sheet 43.

[5] Luke, *Journal*, 82 and n. 2 (Thurs. 25 May 1643).

Gloucestershire. Waller was still strategically placed to threaten the whole Severn valley from Worcester to Shrewsbury, cutting off Oxford from the heart of Royalist strength. An attack on Worcester proving unsuccessful, however, he retreated by quick night marches to Reading. From there he was called to London.[1] Parliamentary intelligence reported that the King's forces were on the march from Salisbury. It was predicted that they would meet Hopton at Dorchester.[2] Waller's triumphs in Wales had proved his worth; he must now save Bristol, the best man for the job—since James Chudleigh had defected.

Chudleigh, without regret, had thrown in his lot with the Royalists. When the Cornish left Launceston on 21 May and advanced to Okehampton he declared himself in a letter to his father Sir George, hoping to win him over. The letter, along with a general summons to surrender, was conveyed to Exeter by Dr. Cox, who, under the safe conduct of a trumpeter and his cloth, might have been considered immune to harassment. Unluckily, being accused of complicity in a plot to blow up the east gate of Exeter, he was detained, strictly examined, and so cruelly used that he fell dangerously ill. James Chudleigh's importunities, however, were not without effect on his father; within a few weeks Sir George also changed sides.[3]

The truth was that young Chudleigh has been disposed to favour the King's cause in the first place. His family's allegiance to Parliament, however, had won him a rebuff at Oxford. Returning to London in a pique he had thrown in his lot with friends who had volunteered for Parliamentary service in the west. After Stratton the Earl of Stamford, to extenuate his own performance, informed Westminster, and spread it abroad in other places, that Chudleigh had betrayed him, going over to the enemy at the height of the battle. Such undeserved censure was more than enough to sour an ardent disposition like Chudleigh's, especially in contrast with the consideration he was shown by the Cornish.[4]

At Okehampton the Royalists encountered no opposition: the Parliamentary commander Sir William Russell had already retired with his regiment, leaving four iron guns. On 25 May, when Grenvile had rejoined them, the Cornish moved on to Crediton. Their marching pace was good: just short of twenty miles a day, and testifies plainly that they encountered no more than token

[1] Clarendon, vii. 30.   [2] Luke, *Journal*, 84 (Wed. 31 May 1643).
[3] Hopton, 45 and n. 1; Coate, 72.   [4] Clarendon, vii. 91–92.

resistance. On Trinity Sunday, 28 May, working around the northern flank of Exeter, they left a small force with Sir John Ackland at Columb-John, and finally reached Tiverton, from which the Parliament-men under Colonel John Weare had fled half an hour before. Remaining there two or three days to 'setle the affeccions of that Countrey', which looked promising, they went on south towards Exeter, but then cut east and, by way of Bradninch, came on 30 May to Cullompton. Enemy horse appeared, but did not approach; there was no challenge from Exeter. Having successfully skirted the danger zone, the army came on 31 May to Honiton, where for a day it rested. On 2 June, as they were marching toward Axminster, they met a Captain Roscarrock, who bore letters advising them that Hertford and Prince Maurice were near Yeovil, twenty-four miles distant.

Next day, 3 June, after an absence of over eight months, Hopton was in Somerset again. The Cornish encamped at Chard in the southernmost tip of Somerset. In the meantime, Hertford and Maurice had reached Crewkerne, eight miles to the east. Here that night Hopton and the other general officers of the Cornish army waited upon them. The following day, Sunday 4 June, the two armies met at Chard.[1]

The Royalists had reason to rejoice, or at least to view their prospects with confidence. Cornwall was solid for the King. Devon was intimidated; only Plymouth, Dartmouth, Exeter, Bideford, and Barnstaple remained in Parliamentary hands. The tin trade with St. Malo still yielded munitions; the Cornish privateers still harassed the merchant ships of London and Plymouth.[2] The western peninsula, in a word, was virtually secure. Elsewhere, the King held all of Wales except for the south-western fringe in Pembrokeshire; since Waller's pull-back from Hereford and repulse from Worcester, the passage from Oxford into the Severn valley and the western marches had remained open and safe. In the north the Earl of Newcastle, with a virtually independent command, held most of the six counties above Trent and a long tongue of territory reaching from the confluence of Trent, Humber, and Ouse south to the Wellard and the line of the Wash, within thrusting reach of the puritan core.

At the same time the Parliamentary cause was beginning to founder. On 1 June John Ashe, 'in the midst of a passionate debate amongst the necligent Counstables', wrote to Governor Fiennes at

[1] Hopton, 45–46. [2] Barrett, 275; Coate, 73.

H

Bristol and complained about the slowness of the Somerset hundreds to bring in their contributions.[1] Two days later the committee at Gloucester issued a plea for money: the Parliament-men were not only too few to meet the Royalists but too many to be properly paid.[2] From Plymouth, now pushed to the far periphery of events, and impinged upon by one completely hostile county and the hostile half of another, came a nearly frantic declaration: the city was 'in deplorable condition, our whole county being harrowed by Sir Ralph Hopton lately in their going forth, leaving forces behind to join those raised by the sheriff [Henry Carey], which have cut off intelligence between Plymouth and Exeter'. The loss of Plymouth would mean the loss of the whole county.[3]

Parliamentary intelligence was extremely confused. On 2 June when Hopton was marching toward Axminster he was reported to have already met Hertford and Maurice within seven miles of Exeter, the combined forces 'coming towards Oxford'.[4] Another scout reported that Hopton was still in Cornwall, 'likely there to continue for the country doe dayly rise against him'. Hertford was at Blandford, '30 miles distant from Sir Ralph Hopton'.[5] The scout's vagueness in reckoning distance and his casual placing of Blandford in Somerset instead of in Dorset—it was sixteen miles from the Somerset line— indicates that a long-range and well-coordinated intelligence system, something more reliable than compounded local rumours, had yet to be developed.

On the Royalist side perhaps the most extraordinary accomplishment was Hopton's feat of leading his Cornish out of their native county into Somerset:[6] several months before it had been hard enough to persuade them to enter Devon. Stratton Down, of course, had done wonders for the army's morale; it had sealed irrevocably the already strong ties of mutuality with the commanders and had set Hopton even higher in the esteem of the rank-and-file. Building upon this personal respect he had laboured to infuse the troops with his own spirit of piety united to rigorous discipline. Vice was severely punished; the Sabbath was strictly kept.[7] Hopton, a puritan Cavalier, had succeeded partly due to a policy worthy of a Cromwell.

The meeting at Chard, however, marked a transition of utmost

---

[1] MS. Clarendon XXII (S.P.), item 1704 (sheet 85), dated at Bath; Hopton, 88.
[2] Nalson MS. XI, 272.   [3] Ibid. 276, letter dated 15 June 1643.
[4] Luke, *Journal*, 12. The report had circulated in Wallingford.
[5] Ibid. 95.   [6] Burne and Young, 77.   [7] Coate, 73, 75.

consequence in the history of the Cornish army, though with less effect on its immediate fortunes than on the slower process of erosion and deterioration which, in less than three years, was to reduce it to a mere shell, or shadow, of its former strength. It was the beginning of a series of metamorphoses in the course of which the original structure, and with it the animating spirit, of those regiments was vitiated by merger with other—to the Cornish, alien—units, by different forms of organization, and above all by unfamiliar commands.

Not that the men from Oxford were necessarily inferior to the Cornish. Some of the ranking officers—such as Prince Maurice, Henry, Lord Wilmot, and Robert Dormer, Earl of Carnarvon—had rendered good service with the Royalist horse at Edgehill in October.[1] But the increased number of colonels in the new, united western army meant diminished authority for those from beyond Tamar. Hopton himself, from being lieutenant-general of the horse and the dominant voice on the council of war, was relegated officially to the rank of a horse colonel,[2] though he seems to have retained the post of marshal of the field. To make his will felt he might perhaps have to force it now and then on his superiors. This was something more than applying the rules in a tactical situation: it involved whole concepts of strategy, the divination on which strategy rests, and the sort of suasion, ruthless if need be, on which the answers to great questions of state depend. In assessing Sir Ralph's role, the following supposition must be kept in mind: 'Had Hopton been able to impose on the Royalist forces as a whole his own standards of loyalty, discipline, and piety, the fate of the monarchy might have been different.'[3]

Together the two armies, with nine regiments of horse and nine of foot, were a formidable host. The Cornish had about 3,000 foot, 500 horse, and 300 dragoons, 'all old souldyers', with five field pieces. The men from Oxford came with 1,000 'new-leavyed' foot, 1,500 horse, and eleven field pieces.[4] That Sunday, 4 June, they marched to within two miles of Taunton; next day they advanced upon the town and took it, the enemy having retreated toward Bridgwater. At ten that night, 5 June, Colonel Edward Popham wrote to Fiennes from Glastonbury complaining of the difficulty in relaying letters from Essex to Stamford, since, with the taking of Taunton, the

[1] *J.S. Army H.R.* xvii. 105.
[2] 'The Praying Captain . . .', Peter Young ed., *J.S. Army H.R.* xxxv. 69–70, App. D.
[3] Coate, 75.   [4] Hopton, 47.

passage to Exeter was nearly blocked. He said that his plan to throw the ordnance and carriages into the moat of Taunton castle and to evacuate the guards had been impeded by the rising of the townsmen. Consequently the Royalists had been able to impose a treaty and seize the 1,000 arms, twenty-two barrels of powder, and perhaps as many as eight pieces of ordnance. When the news came to Bridgwater, the Royalist 'malignants', being strong in that town, caused a mutiny among the soldiers, who, in deserting their posts, broke through the Parliamentary guards at the town gates, of which the King's men in a short time took easy possession.[1]

Taunton agreed on a composition of £8,000, sufficient to pay the whole army for several weeks. The district was prosperous and had no objection to free quarter 'soberly taken'. But then 'began the disorder of the horse visibly to breake in upon the prosperity of the publique proceedings'. Their 'extravagant disorder' overran the line between free quarter and freebooting. The generals, impressed with the need for discipline,[2] were never able to impose it as stringently on the horse as they could on the foot; and, unfortunately, the infantry was too often amenable to the demoralizing influence of the mounted arm. It boded ill: plainly the Oxford troopers, for all their dash, stood in great need of seasoning. The 'four wheels of Charles's wain', as a later lament put it, were still Grenvile, Slanning, and Trevanion, with Hopton, back on his home ground, stepping into Sidney Godolphin's place as chief guide, while retaining the driver's seat.

The Royalist star was clearly in the ascendant. Through the good offices of Mr. Francis Windham, Dunster castle was surrendered; the west part of Somerset was again in the King's hands.[3] Meanwhile, the vanguard of the Parliamentary horse, under Colonel Edward Popham, had reached Glastonbury on the road to Somerton, some twenty-five miles north-east of Taunton. Though they underestimated the Royalist numbers, they were none too sure of their own. Major Hercules Langrishe, second-in-command of Colonel Nathaniel Fiennes's regiment of horse, wrote to the governor from Wells on 6 June reporting that, of 2,000 horse and dragoons from Somerset and Devon, there were only 1,000 left: apparently half of them had deserted within four days. He also said that, the night before, eight troops of Royalist horse had come 'to the village where

---

[1] MS. Clarendon XXII, item 1696 (sheet 69); Hopton 47, 85–86 (inc. Col. Slingsby's narrative).
[2] Hopton, 47. [3] Ibid. 47–48.

wee should have quartered', but, not finding the Parliament-men, had stayed to plunder. Around midnight on 7 June at Bath, Anthony Nicoll and William Gould, both survivors of Stamford's army (Gould had distinguished himself at Sourton Down), were petitioning Fiennes for £500 and 500 foot. They were anxious for a speedy rendezvous of the local forces with Sir William Waller.[1]

'William the Conqueror', as he had been called by a grateful city and Parliament since his reduction of Portsmouth and his taking of 1,200 Royalist prisoners near Gloucester, came to Bath full of the reputation he had gained by victories in Monmouth and Wales. Easily outshining Essex, his nominal commander-in-chief, he had attained high stature in the eyes of those who doubted that the lethargic, pipe-smoking earl would 'keep them company to the end of their journey'. In his youth, like Hopton, he had held a commission in the regiment of Sir Charles Rich; he had served in the Palatinate wars; he had fought in Bohemia. Married to Jane Reynell, an heiress of Devon, he had brawled with one of her kinsmen near the gate of Westminster Hall—a serious offence, since the courts were sitting—and had been heavily fined. Clarendon describes this incident as the basis of Waller's anti-Royalism.[2] Up to this point his career had paralleled Sir Ralph Hopton's. He was born in 1597, matriculated at Magdalen Hall, Oxford in 1612 without proceeding to a degree, was knighted in 1622, and married the same year as Hopton (1623) between campaigns.[3] His military experience and capacity also were similar to Sir Ralph's: he was a 'good trainer of troops, a good organizer',[4] and generally a good chooser of ground. The two men were well matched; they had been friends since the Palatinate days; and they were to face each other as antagonists in the field in three major battles of the Civil War (Lansdown, Alresford, and Second Newbury).

The Royalists' next move requires some explanation. Hopton's *Bellum Civile* does not reveal that on Friday 9 June the King's men began a march from Taunton back to Exeter. It seems implausible, since there is no evidence of an immediate threat from that quarter. On the contrary, Exeter, surrounded by the Royalist sympathizers of rural Devon, had little choice but to hang on. At the same time it was bad strategy for the Royalist western army to leave threatening powers from Bath and Bristol at their backs.

[1] Ibid. 86–87 (Slingsby).
[3] *D.N.B.* xx. 588.
[2] Clarendon, vii. 100.
[4] Burne and Young, 231.

Yet the record is clear. On Tuesday 13 June a letter to Sir Francis Basset, John Arundell, and others, written at Wells and signed by Mohun, Hopton, and Berkeley, expressed the intention of retracing their steps:

On Fryday last [9 June] being in our march from Taunton towarde Exeter upon certaine intelligence of Sir Wm. Wallers beinge at Bath, and his intentions towarde us, wee returned to Taunton, wherre (our men being refreshed) on Sundaye [11 June] wee advanced to Somerton, having notice of the Enemyes being at Glastonbury and this Towne [Wells], which were found accordingly.[1]

The motivation behind this move is obscure, but it may be connected with the dispatch a few days later of Sir John Berkeley with Colonel Thomas Howard's regiment of horse to reinforce and command the troop of dragoons and two companies of foot left at Columb-John three miles east of Exeter. The Earl of Warwick was prowling the seas near the Exe estuary;[2] probably Basset needed reassurance that he was not forgotten. This seems clear from the conclusion of the letter: 'wee hope shortly [to] returne towardes Exeter, and secure the rest, which is, and shall be, our speciall care, our advancinge hither having most of all conduced thereunto'. Or was this action perhaps a feint designed to distract attention from movements northwards?[3] At any rate it strikes one as absurd that Hopton, having succeeded in leading his Cornish into Somerset, should so quickly lead them back again.

He did lead them to Somerton. Here, early in the morning on Monday 12 June, as he was making the rounds 'according to his custome in times of necessity about an hower before day', he met some of the dragoons, who had been quartered outside Somerton toward Glastonbury, 'unhorst and hurt', having been set upon by a party of enemy horse. One man had been killed and two or three wounded on each side. Upon this challenge, the whole Royalist army moved out, gradually forcing the opposed numbers back into Wells and through that town into the Mendip Hills, that uninviting plateau given over to coal-mining and sheep-raising—twenty miles long, fifteen miles wide, and with a maximum altitude of over 1,000 feet, an

---

[1] Basset MS., 11. [2] Hopton, 50.
[3] Possibly. Luke's *Journal*, 104, reports Hopton 'against Exeter' (he was then at Wells). Other reports hazard that he is marching towards Oxford. Col. Alfred Burne declares, *More Battlefields of England* (London, 1952), 164, that Oxford was one of Hopton's objectives, though the reason is not clear.

effective barrier between the central part of Somerset and the valley of the Avon to the north.[1] A thrust by Prince Maurice went unchecked; the Parliamentary horse faced him with a large front, giving the foot and baggage time to retreat, and then followed. Maurice, seconded by Hopton and the Earl of Carnarvon, went after in pursuit. Carnarvon could not be stayed; he pressed forward and, routing the whole body, harried them for over two miles. Hopton, speaking as a countryman, warned the prince against pursuing too far: there was no telling what mischief would ensue if Fiennes and Waller sent aid from Bristol and Bath. The prince sent a messenger after Carnarvon to call him back, but the impetuous earl was rather incited to go on forward when he learned that Sir William had already drawn out. His direction changed, however, when Waller advanced under cover of a thick fog and chased him back towards Chewton, on top of Mendip between Wells and Bristol.

Richard Atkyns, a captain of dragoons, went forward to help Carnarvon with 'not above 100 men'. He described the rout later as one of utter panic. The Roundheads' array descended upon Chewton: 200 dragoons, with a regiment of horse 200 yards behind them, and over 300 dragoons more lining the hedges on either side of the horse. Maurice, on the advice of Sir John Berkeley, drew back from the hedges to an open heath. He had only part of his regiment with him, and Carnarvon's coming up broken and panting, the young prince showed his courage by presenting a charge which routed half the enemy's horse. The unbroken remainder, however, wheeled about and charged the prince's rear. Maurice, slightly wounded by two sword-cuts in the head, was thrown from his horse and briefly captured, being rescued when Carnarvon, having had time to rally and catch breath, hurled his regiment against the Parliamentary rear, beginning a second chase which lasted through the twilight. With the enemy running, the Royalists retired to Wells, the gallant, but foolhardy, earl himself not returning until ten that night.[2]

For ten or twelve days thereafter all was quiet. The Royalists refreshed themselves at Wells and remounted their ordnance; the Parliamentarians held quarter at Bath. The exact size of their force

---

[1] Barnes, 1–3; *Bartholomew's Survey Gazetteer of the British Isles*, 7th ed. (Edinburgh, 1927), 470.

[2] Basset MS. 11; Hopton, 48–50, 90–91 (Slingsby); Richard Atkyns, *The Vindication of Richard Atkyns, Esquire as also a Relation of Several Passages in the Western War* (London, 1669), 25–27; Coate, 76–77.

is hard to ascertain. The Royalist commanders estimated 3,000 of
the enemy at Glastonbury and Wells, mostly horse, of which 1,200
had been sent by Stamford out of Devon. They guessed 2,300 to be at
Bath, including a regiment of 900 Welsh foot under Colonel Edward
Cooke.[1] These were strengthened by 1,200 armoured horse and
dragoons under Sir Arthur Hazelrig: the famous 'Lobsters', so called
by the Royalists 'because of the bright iron-shell with which they were
all couvered'.[2] The two armies were of roughly equal strength, but
the Parliamentarians were top-heavy in horse. This may have been
genuinely, if only partly, the reason for their failure to launch an
offensive. On 24 June Colonel Cooke, on Waller's behalf, wrote to
Fiennes imploring 500 additional foot—and to save time he wanted
them sent mounted.[3] Two days earlier Waller and Hazelrig had
written to Speaker William Lenthall in a tone of supplication not
unmixed with irony:

Sir,
    Wee as your servants cannot but acquaint you with our condicion. Wee
have a bodie of horse by Gods blessinge able to doe the Kingdome good
service. The enimie lies still att Wells. That part of the cuntrie is altogeather
unfitt for horse. It greeuves our soules wee dare not attempt what wee desire.
Wee must not hazard your trust like fooles, Nether can wee stay heare and
starve. Wee have longe and often supplycated you for mony. Find us but a
way to live without it, or else wee humblie begge a present supply, if not,
this horse will certeinly disband, which thought makes our harts to bleed.
We doubt not of your well wishes, but if you rest there, hold blameles,

                                    Sir,
                                    Your humblest servants,
                                    William Waller
                                    Art. Hesilrige[4]

The need for additional foot and funds, however, conceals the
deeper significance of this fortnight of relative calm between Bath
and Wells. Hopton had written to Waller asking for an interview.
Whatever his pleas or proposals might have been, there is little
reason to expect that an accommodation could have been found even
on a broader basis than the personal friendship of these two men.
Waller affirmed as much in his reply, one of the most moving docu-
ments of the war:

[1] Basset MS. 11.   [2] Hopton, 51.   [3] Ibid., 89.
[4] Tanner MS., No. 62, f. 128.

To my Noble frend Sir Ralphe Hopton at Wells

Sr

The experience I have had of your Worth, and the happinesse I have enjoyed in your friendship are woundinge considerations when I look upon this present distance between us, Certainely my affections to you are so unchangeable, that hostility itselfe cannot violate my friendship in your person, but I must be true to the cause wherein I serve; The ould limitation *usque ad aras* holds still, and where my conscience is interested, all other obligations are swallowed up. I should most gladly waite on you according to your desire, but that I looke upon you as you are ingaged in that partie, beyond a possibilitie of retraite and consequentlie uncapable of being wrought upon with any persuasion. And I know the conference could never be so close betweene us, but that it would take wind and receive a construction to my dishonour; That great God, which is the searcher of my heart, knows with what a sad sence I goe upon this service, and with what a perfect hatred I detest this warr without an Enemie, but I looke upon it as *Opus Domini*, which is enough to silence all passion in mee. The God of peace in his good time send us peace, and in the meane time fitt us to receive it: Wee are both upon the stage and must act those parts that are assigned us in this Tragedy: Lett us do it in a way of honor, and without personall animosities, whatsoever the issue be, I shall never willingly relinquish the dear title of

Your most affectionated friend
and faithfull servant,
Wm. Waller[1]

Bath, 16 June 1643

The word '*aras*' ('altars') is revealing here as the metaphorical and moral equivalent of 'conscience': obligations of friendship can be maintained only as far as conscience allows. Waller's detestation of his duty expresses the tragic truth about civil wars: that they often appear as 'just wars' in comparison with the apparent vulgarity of national wars.[2] It would be hard to deny that his thoughts must have gone back twenty years to the time when he and Hopton had been young officers together in Rich's regiment, defending the Protestant cause in the Palatinate. Soldierly sentiment cannot be ruled out

---

[1] Coate, 77. The Latin reads 'as far as' (or, 'up to the limits of') 'the altars', i.e. *conscience permitting*. Miss Coate transcribed from the original in the possession of Colonel Prideaux-Brune of Prideaux Palace, Padstow. There is a rough draft among the Clarendon papers at the Bodleian, part of which was printed in the Clarendon State Papers in 1773. Another copy is extant among the Somerset MSS. and is transcribed in the H.M.C.'s 15th Report, p. 65, where the noun in the Latin motto is printed as '*alias*', not inappropriately, perhaps: since the translation then might read: 'wait on other times' (or, 'better days').

[2] Hugh Thomas, *The Spanish Civil War* (New York, 1961), 616.

altogether as a possible reason for his lingering at Bath instead of taking the offensive at once.

Growing impatient of distance and delay, the Royalist commanders decided on an advance to Frome, seventeen miles east of Wells. From here, on Sunday 2 July, the army continued to Bradford-on-Avon in Wiltshire, some five miles south-east of Bath. The Avon, a sluggish stream, but deep, bounding Bath on the south, made it hazardous to attack from that side. Waller had already taken advantage of the ground to move a good part of his force across the river, planting infantry in an ambuscade north of Bradford at the foot of Monkton Farleigh Hill. On the morning of 3 July, Edward Popham's regiment having come in, he was able to advance strong parties of horse toward the Royalist outguards. Met by Major George Lower of Thomas Howard's regiment, they were held until the whole Royalist army drew forth. In the resulting skirmish the Cornish foot led by Grenvile, Godolphin, and Trevanion broke up the enemy ambuscade, and Maurice was able to dislodge Waller's main body from the Avon ford. Sir William retreated into Bath. At the same time, some of the Parliamentary horse having fled in a more northerly direction, they were pursued by Royalist cavalry under Carnarvon, Mohun, Hopton, and Slanning. This manoeuvre implemented and accelerated the Royalist strategy of avoiding the Avon by outflanking Bath to the east. The chase brought them into the vicinity of Lansdown Hill, five miles north of Bath, an admirable position from which to assault the city. At midnight, however, a council of officers decided against seizing it at once, since the army was still divided and weary with the chase.[1] Perhaps they were too cautious.

Except for greater growth in the coppices covering both sides of the road, Lansdown appears to have changed little since the Civil War. It is still as a lady traveller described it in 1698: 'a very pleasant hill for to ride on for aire and prospect', and the way down to Bath is still 'a vast steep descent of a stony narrow way'.[2] With an average slope of between twelve and fifteen degrees,[3] and reaching a height of 769 feet,[4] it is a toilsome climb to the top. Four or five miles from

---

[1] Hopton, 51–52; Burne, 161–2; Coate, 78–79.

[2] *The Journeys of Celia Fiennes*, Christopher Morris, ed. (London, 1947), 236. Celia Fiennes (1662–1741) was a daughter of Nathaniel Fiennes, Parliamentary governor of Bristol.

[3] This is Col. Burne's calculation. See *More Battlefields . . .* , 170.

[4] Coate, 79.

Bath it ends in an escarpment with a drop of 150 or 200 feet. Here
by the morning of 4 July Waller had raised breastworks and set up his
artillery: seven drakes, relatively small field pieces, no bigger than
heavy machine guns today, but in that position calculated to wreak
real carnage.[1] Facing north, the Parliamentarians could watch the
two lanes from Marshfield and, a little more than a mile away, the
adjacent ridge of Tog Hill.

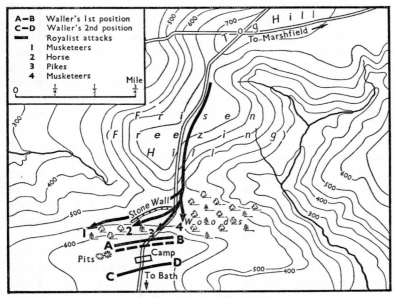

Map 2. Battle of Lansdown
5 July 1643

When the whole Royalist army—nearly 7,000, counting staff and
artillery—appeared on Frisen Hill, which made up the lower slope
of Tog Hill, and pushed on through the narrow valley to ascend
Lansdown, they found their enemies so firmly placed as to give them
the almost insurmountable advantage of the field, out of which, from
the Royalist standpoint, 'there were verie onconvenient wayes to
retreate, to advance noe possibility, and to stay there least of all, for
the Enimye's cannon played in to them . . .'.[2] Having lost that 'high

---

[1] Col. Burne, above, 179–81, discusses the guns in some detail: weight of shot—
6 lb.; diameter of shot—3.5″; muzzle velocity—400′ per second; range—180 yds.
[2] Hopton, 52.

ground of advantage', the Cavalier commanders, about one in the afternoon, resolved to withdraw. Hopton, after dispatching the cannon and carriages, sent 1,000 musketeers to guard the hedges; the rest of the army withdrawing in sections, he held the enemy at bay with a 'forlorn hope' of horse, finally marching off himself without loss.

Pulling back five miles to Marshfield, the Royalists knew that next day a fierce battle was likely to be joined. Who was to command it? The records are not explicit; but nothing is noted of the lord general, Hertford, and Prince Maurice appears only as lieutenant-general of the horse, while Hopton, more experienced than either and with the laurels of Stratton still fresh, again ranked as marshal of the field.[1] Stratton, however, a lower rise by several hundred feet and exposed to attack on three sides, had been more vulnerable than Lansdown. Such flexibility of manoeuvre was now out of the question. The Cavaliers perforce had to accept the prospect of a direct frontal attack in the face of murderous artillery fire, enough to dishearten the strongest. Why bother? Bath was a minor object. But a dozen miles beyond Bath lay Bristol, the second port in the kingdom and capital of the west. It required no profound strategist to see that Bristol in the King's hands, no longer a threat at his back, would become the link and gateway between the Royalist armies of the south-west and those in the Severn valley and Wales.

Next morning, 5 July, about 8 o'clock, the whole Royalist army drew out and faced Lansdown again. 'Thus fortyfied stood the foxe gazing at us when our whole Army was raung'd in order of battle upon the large corne field neare Tughill.'[2] The mutual observation of Parliamentary foxes and Royalist hounds continued with some petty skirmishing about two hours, with little profit or credit for either side.

There were four tactical alternatives open to the Royalists: to assault Lansdown ridge at once; to try to lure the main body of the enemy from the heights into the valley; to hold the present ground and deal with them piecemeal as they came; or to yield the encounter and withdraw towards Oxford. The first might have been suicidal, considering the vulnerability of their position and the relative small-ness of their effective numbers: the homogeneity and discipline of the Cornish was balanced, if not outweighed, by Waller's greater strength in cavalry. The second choice was the most doubtful: it

[1] Burne, 162-3.　　　　　　　　　　[2] Hopton, 94 (Slingsby).

might take time, and time was pressing. As for the third, that was leaving the initiative to the enemy. The last plan, considering the shortage of rations, had its attractions: though less perfect, it was less costly and more rapid, and provided the prospect of a richer county for feeding troops.

Early in the afternoon, with munitions running low, they decided to retreat.

They moved out, however, still in battle ranks, which the openness of the plain allowed. When they had marched about a mile away from Tog Hill, Sir Arthur Hazelrig, seconded by a Major Dowet and a Captain Butler, with a party of 400 horse and 600 dragoons, descended upon them: the cavalry charging their rear, the dragoons standing by the hedges to harass their flanks. It was a bold, perhaps a foolhardy, stroke, which routed two bodies of Royalist horse; 'so that had not our foote bin excellent wee had certainly suffer'd'.[1] Maurice, repeating a tactic he must have learned from his brother Rupert, had advised Hopton to place contingents of Cornish musketeers along the wings of the horse; and these held fast when the cavalry was broken, maintaining their ground until the Earl of Carnarvon's regiment came up to fill the gap. Carnarvon's charge and the volleys of the Cornish shot drove the Parliamentary horse from the field into the narrow land. At the same time Sir Nicholas Slanning with two or three hundred musketeers fell upon the enemy's reserve of dragoons and beat them off. The Parliament-men rallied once more and tried another advance toward the Royalist flank. Maurice countered this by bringing all his horse together in the lane and ringing them again with musketeers inside the hedges. It was prelude to the first wave of an assault that was nearly to eclipse Stratton, signalized by the ferocity of the Cornish foot, who beat the enemy all the way down Tog Hill.

On the far flanks, left and right, musketeers were sent under cover of the enclosures to penetrate the woods fringing the summit. Maurice's horse were placed just off the lane on the immediate right of the pikemen. This deployment was unusual, reversing the normal battle pattern of musketeers in the centre and cavalry on the flanks; but here peripheral movements were restricted by the hedges and a wall. Possibly also Hopton had a low opinion of the capacities of the mounted arm. At any rate the main burden of the attack was borne by the pikes, whose *élan* had now reached a zenith. Raked by artillery beyond the range of their muskets, but convinced, not without

[1] Ibid. 95 (Slingsby).

reason, that no men were their equals, these fully tempered and triumphant veterans cried out to fall on, and shouted that they would take those cannon! With Bevill Grenvile at their head they charged across the remaining mile of level ground and stormed up the lane and ridge towards Lansdown Hill. In the face of small shot and cannon and five charges of Hazelrig's horse they gained the brow— but in the third charge Grenvile was struck on the head with a pole- axe and wounded mortally.

There was no time to measure the loss: the musketeers had gained the woods. The cavalry, however, as the fight grew hotter, became discouraged and began to melt away, some not stopping till they reached Oxford; so that of 2,000 horse, subtracting runaways and casualties, only 600 actually reached the summit. One of them, Captain Richard Atkyns, as he approached the crest, saw

Sir Bevill Grinvill's stand of Pikes, which certainly preserv'd our Army from a Total rout, with the loss of His most pretious life: They stood as upon the Eaves of an House for steepness, but as unmovable as a rock; on which side of the stand of Pikes our Horse were, I could not discover; for the Air was so drakened by the smoak of the Powder, that for a quarter of an Hour together (I dare say) there was no light seen, but what the fire of the Volleys of Shot gave.[1]

These volleys took a dreadful toll. 200 Cornish foot were slain and 300 badly wounded. But the Royalists had gained the breastworks, the enemy pulling back 400 yards to the second line of defence behind a stone wall. The remnant of Royalist horse and the two wings of musketeers from the woods converging on that ground about the same time, with cannon coming up, the King's men spread themselves, and played back furiously at the foe, the duel continuing into the night, being heard as far as Bristol, a dozen miles away.

Their position was as untenable as it could be. With their backs to the declivity, a strong push would have been disastrous. They had lost more than two-thirds of their horse and were nearly out of munitions. The last days on the march had been gruelling. Maurice, Hopton, Sir James Hamilton, and Major Thomas Sheldon in a council of war resolved that if the enemy fell on them every man was to shift for himself. Yet they hung on. About one in the morning they heard a stealthy advance of horse and foot and received a volley from the enemy's musketeers. Then all was quiet again. At two

---

[1] Atkyns, 32.

Hopton sent a soldier to investigate. The Roundheads were gone; Waller had retreated to Bath, leaving, as they discovered at dawn, 350 arms and ten barrels of powder.[1]

Steadfastness had turned the tide at Lansdown, a tactical victory in the sense of gaining an immediate objective. In the opinion of Colonel Alfred Burne (1952) it was Hopton's decision to remain (a decision which Burne compares with Robert E. Lee's on the evening of Sharpsburg) which marks him as a great general.[2] Going beyond this professional view, it is reasonable to infer that the choice, informed by ripe experience and personal knowledge of his opponent, was based on a calculated hunch as to what Waller would do. It is true that civil war does spawn much tactical action based on mutual personal knowledge among the commanders of the contending forces. Hopton's ploy was a gamble, and it paid off. If we accept this as probable, it is legitimate to assert that this phase of his career illustrates two supreme qualities of generalship: the ability to 'stick it out' and the ability to 'see the other side of the hill'.

Lansdown, however, was by no means an absolute victory. The Royalists' strategic objective, Bath, was still in the hands of the enemy, and the enemy's main army was still intact. Waller himself, with reinforcements coming in from Portsmouth, Dorchester, and adjacent counties, claimed a 'success', if not a victory.[3] This claim had some justification. The defection of Maurice's horse was ignominious enough. There is a note of pardonable glee in the mayor of Bristol's report that 'Master John Ashe had his ground well-stocked with 60 cavaliers horses, who fled from the Army the night after the battell', horse which might have been used to destroy Waller's army. The same authority asserts that the Royalists 'wanted Chirurgeons much', going so far as to declare that 'seven cart loads of dead men were carried from the place . . .'.[4] Indeed, the losses had been terrible, with a high rate of casualties among commanders. Among those besides Grenvile who were killed or who died later of their wounds were Major George Lower, who had fallen near him, and Lieutenant-Colonel Joseph Wall of Sir Humphrey Bennet's

[1] Hopton, 53–55; 94–96 (Slingsby); Burne, 164–7; Burne and Young, 78–83; Coate, 79–82; Samuel Seyer, Jr., *Memoirs historical and topographical of Bristol . . .*, 2 vols. (Bristol, 1821–3), ii. 401; *J.S. Army H.R.* xxxi. 129.
[2] Burne, 168.   [3] *C.J.* iii. 163.
[4] *The Copie of a Letter Sent from the Mayor of Bristoll unto a Gentleman . . . in London, relating The great defeat given to the Cavaliers in those parts by Sir William Waller, and Sir Arthur Haslerig . . .* etc. (London, 8 July 1643), *passim.*

regiment. The Earl of Carnarvon was wounded, as were Colonel
Sir George Vaughan and Lord Mohun. Slanning had escaped with
having his horse killed under him; Hopton had been shot in the
arm,[1] a minor injury, however, compared with what was soon to
follow.

At 8 a.m., 6 July, the battered Royalists moved off towards
Marshfield. On Tog Hill Captain Atkyns, who had just been made
adjutant-general of the army, approached Hopton, then by a munitions cart with Major Thomas Sheldon interrogating some prisoners,
who had been allowed to retain some match to light their tobacco.
The major desired Atkyns to return to his regiment while he,
Sheldon, received Hopton's orders. Atkyns then relates:

> I had no sooner turn'd my Horse, and was gone 3 Horse lengths from him,
> but the Ammunition was blown up, and the Prisoners in the Cart with it;
> together with the Lord *Hopton*, on Horseback and several others: It made
> a very great noise and darkened the Air for a time, and the Hurt men made
> lamentable Screeches. As soon as the Air was clear, I went to see what the
> matter was; there I found his Lordship miserably burnt, his Horse sing'd
> like parch'd leather, and *Thomas Cheldon* (that was 2 Horse lengths further
> from the blast) complaining that the fire was got within his Breeches, which I
> tore off as soon as I could, and from as long a Flaxen head of hair as ever I
> saw, in the twinckling of an eye, his head was like a *Black-Moor*, his Horse
> was hurt, and run away like mad, so that I put him upon my Horse, and
> got two Troopers to hold him up on both sides, and bring him to the head
> Quarters. . . .[2]

The cart had contained eight barrels of gunpowder. How Hopton,
the closest to it, survived is a miracle—for Sheldon died the next day.
As it was, Sir Ralph, blinded and maimed, was unfit to be moved,
though Waller had come out again from Bath to reoccupy the old
ground. Sick at heart, the army quartered at Marshfield, with only
one day of respite before the retreat. The grim epilogue to their
qualified victory was also an omen that filled them with apprehension.
'Charles's wain' had now lost two wheels: Sidney Godolphin the
guide and Bevill Grenvile the pivot. And Hopton the driver could
no longer see his way. Colonel Walter Slingsby's lament almost
attains the elegiac note of *Lycidas:* 'Our horse were bad before but
now worse, our ffoote drooped for theire Lord whom they lov'd, and
that they had no powder left to defend him.'[3]

---

[1] 'The Praying Captain . . .', Peter Young, ed. *J.S. Army H.R.* xxxv. 68;
Hopton, 54–55.
[2] Atkyns, 33–34.   [3] Hopton, 97 (Slingsby).

VII

ROUNDWAY: WALLER ROUTED;
BRISTOL:
'Gone the Four Wheels of Charles's Wain'

(July 1643)

THOUGH slighting their own losses,[1] Waller and Hazelrig remained
at Bath until reinforcements arrived from Bristol. Despite a
technical defeat, the advantage was still theirs: superior cavalry and
the resources of the county at their command. With this edge they
could push a continuous, harrying offensive. Spending the night of
6 to 7 July 1643 on Lansdown, they descended next morning into
Gloucestershire, reasonably sure that the weakened state of the
Royalists, along with the weight of their 'plunder',[2] would so retard
them that their piecemeal reduction must be a matter of time.

Yet Waller seems to have been in no special hurry. He has been
accused of often lacking resolution,[3] and it is fairly clear that throughout the encounters and skirmishes of those July days Hazelrig's horse
did a disproportionate share of the fighting. While their 'excellent
service' is commended, however, it appears to have been held in
check; for, when the Royalists left Marshfield and moved on nine
miles eastward to Chippenham, the Roundheads occupied Marshfield,
'yett came not so neere as to incommode att all that daye's march'.[4]

The King's men, whatever they possessed of 'plunder', had little
to exult about: once more they had reached an extremity, if not an
impasse, where victuals, munitions, and intelligence were all equally
scarce. The Wiltshire peasants, as froward as those of Devon had
been, even if they had not been hostile to begin with, were hardly
inclined to abet a force so closely pursued and already diminished.
The Royalists stayed, however, two nights in Chippenham, no
doubt for the greater comfort of Sir Ralph, still blind and physically

---

[1] Tanner LXII, 164: Waller and Hazelrig to Speaker Lenthall, dated at Roundway 12 July 1643: 'Many of there [the Royalists'] cheife Commanders and officers
were slayne or hurt we lost only one serieant maior of the Dragoons and two Cor-
netts and not twentie common souldiers.'

[2] Ibid.   [3] Burne and Young, 231.   [4] Hopton, 55.

immobilized, and perhaps also for the purpose of an appeal to local worthies, of whom Hopton, seised of nearby Fitzurse farm,[1] must have known a few.

Next day, Sunday 9 July, as the Royalists turned south toward Devizes, Waller's strategy became clear. He sent a trumpeter to offer Hertford the chance of a pitched battle. The marquis, probably knowing his opponent to be an experienced 'shifter' of ground and 'smelling a rat', with great cunning managed to keep the trumpeter with him for two or three miles and then sent him back 'with an answeare fitt for the question'.[2] Waller, wise in hoarding his time, waited till his quarry came to within two or three miles of Devizes and then fell on.

But the prowess of the Cornish, heightened by sorrow for their lost leader, was superb. Under Slanning they disputed every step of the way, repulsing a heavy attack and saving the guns from capture.[3] Maurice's horse showed equal spirit; indeed, the whole episode for a time reconciled the differences of the two forces in terms of mutual amity and admiration. The Cornish had never ceased to jeer at the horse for their pusillanimous conduct at Lansdown; though some of them may have realized that taking such a height by storm was eminently a work for infantry, they had never ceased to deprecate the cavalry's bad showing on that occasion and referred to them scathingly as 'run away Horse'. Now, acknowledging the bravery of Lieutenant-Colonel Neville's troopers in covering their rear, they changed tune and called them 'gallant Horse'; for, as Richard Atkyns explains, 'the Cornish Foot knew not till then the service of Horse'. In truth, there had been little recruiting for cavalry in Cornwall.[4]

With Mohun's regiment under Lieutenant-Colonel Walter Slingsby holding the pass at Rowde Ford and losing forty men, the Cavaliers deployed on Roundway Hill; darkness preserved them from an enemy advance. Next day, 10 July, they descended into Devizes, Waller's force occupying Roundway. Sir William advanced no farther for that time; but in the afternoon the Parliamentary army came down into the valley between the hill and the town. For the exhausted Royalists the margin of safety was minimal; never had their defences

---

[1] The Ven. Archdeacon E. J. Bodington, 'The Church Survey in Wiltshire, 1649–50', *Wilts. Arch. & Nat. Hist.* xxiv. 82–83. Hopton also held in Wilts. the rectory of Tilshead at a rent-charge to one William Mewe. In 1642 he stopped payment to Mewe's heir. The inference is that Mewe was a Parliamentarian. See ibid. xl. 395.

[2] Hopton, 55–56.   [3] Barrett, 1, 2, 3.   [4] Atkyns, 34–35.

been weaker than at Devizes: barricades across the roads and a few
loop-holed houses and walls had to suffice.[1] In the evening the
commanders held a council of war at Hopton's quarters. Sir Ralph—
who on the march had been 'carryed in a chaire', presumably a litter
or palanquin—was still immobile, though articulate and alert. It was
decided by all present that horse and foot should separate: that Hertford,
Maurice, and Carnarvon should break out to Oxford that night;
while Hopton 'held the fort', assisted by James Ley, Earl of Marlborough (a Wiltshireman, whose seat was nearby), Mohun, Slanning,
Sir Arthur Basset, and Colonel Brutus Buck. If the town were
invested, some of them at least would be saved; it is suggested also
that the decision was a hasty one due to lingering ill-will between
the Cornish and the cavaliers from Oxford.[2]

The plan was carried out with success. The Royalists made a feint
to draw the Parliamentary horse south-east towards Salisbury Plain,
with the hope of losing them there before swinging back towards
the north-east and the Oxford road. The cavaliers 'rid very fast yet
all cried halt halt but no man stood'.[3] Maurice was at Oxford—
forty-four miles distant—by next morning. His escape, however,
was partly balanced that same night by the capture at Beckhampton,
seven or eight miles from Devizes, of a convoy under Ludovic
Lindsay, Earl of Crawford, coming to the Royalists' aid with five
wain-loads of munitions.[4]

Here was a blow: from nine barrels of powder at Marshfield the
Cornish were now reduced to two. To make matters worse, on the
morning of 11 July the comptroller of the ordnance, Captain Pope,
'being a carefull man', came pensively to Hopton and told him the
match was giving out: there were only 150 lb. left. Sir Ralph, un-
dismayed, ordered him to go from house to house with a guard and
collect all the bed-cords he could find; these, beaten and boiled in
resin, yielded fifteen hundredweight of match.[5]

From 10 to 12 July, Waller bombarded the town and tried to
storm it, but the siege was a stalemate: all depended on the speedy
return of Maurice with reinforcements. On the 12th an exchange of
trumpeters was arranged to allow free passage for Bevill Grenvile's
body. Waller took occasion to inform the cavaliers of the capture of

---

[1] Barrett, above.
[2] J. M. Prest, 'The Campaign of Roundway Down', *Wilts. Arch & Nat. Hist.*
liii. 277–93 (June 1959), 285.
[3] Tanner LXII, 164.   [4] Barrett, 287.   [5] Hopton, 56, 98.

Crawford's convoy and offer terms of surrender. Cannily, Hopton
spun out the negotiations for seven or eight hours, saving powder
and giving his men a much-needed rest. Acting through Colonel
Buck he professed a desire to prevent further shedding of blood. By
the time this ploy was recognized as a stratagem it was six in the
evening. Waller fell on again, but it was too late to make headway.
The Parliamentary commanders were generous to their foes,
admitting in a letter to Speaker Lenthall that 'The Cornish defend
it bravely'; and adding, along with a prayer that 'this mightie armie
of the west' would be scattered by the God that had wrought it, the
hope that they might give 'A good account of Sir Ra. Hopton for
the present he is miserably burned with powder'.[1] Though the 'good
account' may refer to an anticipated victory, there is some reason to
believe that Waller had delayed making a direct assault on Devizes
because he knew that his friend Hopton lay there wounded,[2] though
there is no evidence to support such a surmise.

Sir William withdrew to his headquarters in a farmhouse at the
foot of Roundway Down. Knowing that Oxford would try to relieve
Hopton, he kept 500 dragoons at Potterne, less than two miles south
of Devizes, and an outpost of horse on the plateau of Roundway.[3]
His hope that Essex would intercept the relieving forces was not to
be realized; the earl remained in the valley of the Thames. The
weather continued inclement: 'that day and night being extreame
wet, hindered us much'.[4]

Next morning—Thursday 13 July—Hopton received word that
the enemy had drawn off, pulling back to the downs. Certain that the
relief was approaching, Hopton called a council and proposed that the
foot prepare to march out. A majority of the officers, however,
demurred. They thought the enemy's withdrawal might be a ruse,
perhaps considering it too early for succour to arrive from Oxford,
or possibly retaining a few doubts concerning 'runaway horse'. At
any rate Hopton, from his sick-bed, was unable to persuade them.

Maurice had made good time.[5] Arriving at Oxford about noon on

---

[1] Tanner, above (dorse).   [2] This is Colonel Burne's opinion, 163.

[3] Barrett, 4–5. A highly-coloured personal account of Waller's sojourn, printed
as an appendix to *The Poetry of Anna Matilda* (J. Bell, 1788), 110–12, is of little
historical value.

[4] *A True Relation of the late Fight between Sir William Waller's Forces and those
sent from Oxford* . . . , etc.

[5] A good cavalryman on a fresh mount could cover five miles an hour, up to
forty or fifty miles a day, weather and terrain permitting—Prest, 286.

11 July, he left the exhausted Hertford there to recuperate, along with the greater part of the troops; and on the 12th started back toward Devizes with Sir John Byron's brigade of horse and 300 of his own who were still fit to fight. At Marlborough they rendezvous'd with Lord Crawford's brigade of 600, which had lost its munitions in the skirmish at Beckhampton two days before; and the brigade of Henry, Lord Wilmot,[1] who had been appointed commander of the united relief of 1,800 men. They had no foot at all and only two light guns.

About 3 p.m. on 13 July this tiny force, some of it straggling far to the rear, approached Devizes along the Bath road. In the town, four miles away, lay Hopton, with between 2,000 and 3,000 foot and sixteen field pieces. Half-way between waited Waller with five regiments of 2,500 foot, six regiments of at least 2,000 horse, a regiment of 500 dragoons, and eight field guns.

Some two miles north-east of Devizes, Roundway Down begins as a chalk hill which levels out as a wide plain. Skirting its north edge are two sections of Waynsdyke, the old Roman road; at their junction is a tumulus, a Celtic barrow-tomb. To stand south of this mound and watch the ancient highway flowing over the skyline towards Bath and Bristol is to assume the perspective of the Royalist cavalry on the morning of 13 July 1643. Fringed by woods on the west, Roundway is otherwise open ground; in the seventeenth century it was unenclosed. This lack of obstructions, along with its breadth of about 1,500 yards, made it a choice field of battle. Its boundaries might be drawn roughly from four hills: to the south, Bagdon Hill (today called Roundway Hill); to the north, King's Play Hill; and, proceeding about two miles to the east, Morgan's Hill and Roughridge Hill, straddling Waynsdyke.[2] The old road from Oxford may be taken as the bar of a letter H, bisecting the shallow valley between these slopes and running south-west. Two thousand yards beyond Waynsdyke, while the main branch continues towards Bristol, the left fork bends sharply and runs straight to Devizes.[3]

The Royalists left the road at Waynsdyke and advanced toward Roughridge Hill, the dip between that rise and Morgan's affording

<hr>

[1] Patent of the honour of Baron, 29 June 1643, *Black's Docquets* . . . , 53.

[2] The Roman foundations may still be seen, though reduced to a stony track in a grassy embankment.

[3] For these dispositions see map in *J.S. Army H.R.* xxxi. 130, with notes by Lt.-Col. P. Young; Burne and Young, 88.

them a sweeping view of the enemy being drawn up between King's Play and Bagdon Hills. From Roughridge Wilmot had the guns shot off to let Hopton know they were there. The two armies

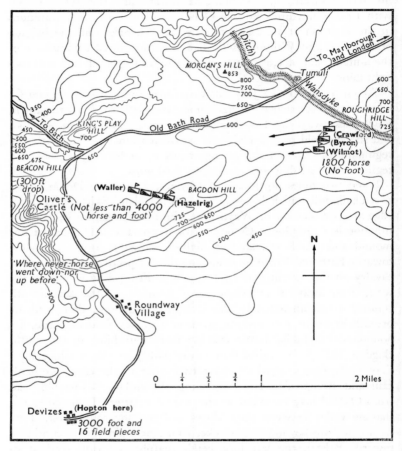

Map 3. Battle of Roundway Down
13 July 1643

deployed half a mile apart: the Roundheads with their foot in the centre, Hazelrig's horse on the right flank and Waller's on the left; the Royalists, who had only cavalry, aligning them in three brigades, an echelon formation with Wilmot in the forward position to the left, Byron covering him to the right, and Crawford covering Byron. These manoeuvres took nearly an hour; Wilmot, badly out-numbered and assuming Hopton's foot were being marshalled to join him, was in no hurry to engage. Having little confidence in Crawford, he ordered that only he and Byron should charge, with not above 1,200 horse. In advance of this main body rode Sergeant-Major Paul Smith, leading a forlorn hope of 300 men. As the roundhead troopers moved forward, Smith met them and forced them back. From the Roundhead right flank, near Bagdon Hill, Hazelrig sent in his 'Lobsters'; the armoured men were a tough nut to crack, but Wilmot hit them hard and drove them back. Another Parliamentary charge was likewise repulsed, as Byron moved up to second Wilmot. Then Waller drew out his whole army and descended the slope with his own brigade of horse, covered by musketeers and artillery. Byron charged them all in the face of their fire, not letting his own men fire till the enemy had expended their shot. Meanwhile, Crawford's horse, who had been protecting the flanks, got their second wind and came on for the last push. The Roundheads fell back on their own reserve, and the whole mass was swept a mile towards the woods on the west side of the downs. Suddenly, to their horror, the ground seemed to drop away; between the woods and the Bath road was a semi-precipitous slope with a drop of 300 feet. Over they went, man and horse, 'where never horse went downe nor up before'.[1] In that harrowing plunge Waller's cavalry was annihilated.

His infantry stood fast, gaping, with nothing to do, though the battle swirled around them. On their north flank Wilmot was preparing to regroup; he had sent word to Hopton, and the Cornish were on their way up the hill from the south. The combined Royalist attack finished Waller's foot: the Roundhead formations broke up and dissolved; 600 were slain, 800 wounded and captured, thirty-six colours taken, with numerous arms and seven pieces of cannon.[2] Waller himself, with a few horse, fled to Bristol.

Roundway has been called the 'most sweeping victory the Royalists ever won'.[3] The Parliamentarians deplored it as 'a great losse to us,

---

[1] Hopton, 98 (Slingsby).
[2] *Sir John Byron's Relation to the Secretary of the last Western Action between the Lord Wilmot and Sir William Waller*, dated 14 July 1643 and reprinted in *J.S. Army H.R.* xxxi, above, 130–1; J. M. Prest, 'The Campaign of Roundway Down', *Wilts. Arch. & Nat. Hist.* lviii (June 1950), 227–93, 426–9 (useful for photoplates and Ordnance Survey sketch maps); Burne and Young, 86–91; Coate, 91–93.
[3] Burne, 178.

so likely to all the West'.[1] Who cannot sympathize with Hopton, lying within earshot of the battle, unable to command his Cornish in person?

After Roundway Hopton remained at Devizes to recover his health,[2] while the army moved on for several days' rest at Bath, now open to the Royalists. From here they marched to Keynsham, five miles south-east of Bristol. On 18 July Rupert left Oxford to link up with the western army. With him were three brigades of infantry, two wings of cavalry, and nine troops of dragoons. On 22 July he appeared on the north, or Gloucestershire, side of the city; at the same time an advance-guard of Cornish appeared at the south, or Somerset, end. Waller, bitter that Essex had left him in the lurch, showed no compunction at leaving Fiennes to face the music, and retired first to Gloucester and then to Evesham, putting fifty miles between himself and Bristol.

On 23 July Rupert carried out a reconnaissance; next day the main body of the Cornish advanced over the Avon at Keynsham Bridge and deployed along the south-eastern purlieus of the city, seizing Pine Hill against Temple Gate, setting up their artillery on the highway, and cutting gaps for passage through the hedges.

With such a mixed body the problem of the Royalist command could hardly have been settled on any basis other than precedence. By this time Hertford had reappeared as lord general of the western army; Maurice, far more active, was still lieutenant-general for the King. Despite the allegation that Hopton, as field marshal, was *de facto* commander,[3] a strong doubt remains as to whether he was actually at the battle of Bristol. His own narrative of that event is restricted to two short paragraphs,[4] and he is nowhere specifically named in more detailed accounts. Even assuming that he possessed a primordial toughness of physique, it is fair to suppose that any man rendered blind and immobile by eight exploding kegs of gunpowder would take slightly longer than a fortnight to recover. Sir Ralph, even if present in the Royalist camp, must have been *hors de combat*.

---

[1] *A True Relation of the late Fight between Sir William Waller's Forces, and those sent from Oxford, with the manner of Sir Will. Waller's Retreat to Bristoll . . .*, etc. (London, 1643).

[2] Barrett, 8.

[3] Sir Bernard De Gomme, 'Bristol taken by Prince Rupert: Julye 26, 1643', *J.S. Army H.R.* iv (1625), Sir Charles Firth and Lt.-Col. J. H. Leslie, eds., 194 ff.

[4] Hopton, 58. He relates, p. 59, that he was 'noet yett recovered of his hurts' by the end of July.

The ordering of the Cornish army, then, devolved on the field commanders; their forces were consolidated in three brigades called 'tertias': the first led by Colonel Brutus Buck, commanding his own, Hertford's, and Maurice's regiments; the second by Slanning, commanding his own, Mohun's, and Trevanion's; the third by Thomas Basset, major-general of the foot, commanding his own, Grenvile's, and Godolphin's. Grenvile's regiment was now commanded by his fifteen-year-old son, John Grenvile (the future Earl of Bath); Hertford's was led by Colonel Bernard Astley, and Mohun's by Lieutenant-Colonel Walter Slingsby. Buck's tertia took the right wing, Slanning's the centre, and Basset's the left, the first two remaining on Pine Hill behind the battery; Basset farther down and closer to the city.

Against the nine regiments of the western army (of which six were Cornish) and the fourteen regiments of Rupert, Colonel Fiennes had only 300 horse and 1,500 foot, besides townsmen, the garrison being weakened by the 1,200 foot who had followed Waller to Roundway. Yet Bristol, if not impregnable, was remarkably well fortified, considering that it had spread out far beyond its medieval walls. The city proper was almost completely girded by the rivers Frome and Avon; the castle, built on a lofty summit of rock that could not be mined, had been repaired with fortifications along the walls and planted with cannon, prompting the observation from an inspecting sergeant-major, Edward Wood, that, assuming sufficient arms, men, and victuals, Bristol could have held out till November.[1] To defend the suburbs on the north and west five forts had been constructed, strengthened by dry ditches and palisades and connected by earthworks. The stoniness of the ground, however, made it necessary in many places to leave the ditches shallow and the earthen ramparts low;[2] at the same time it was impossible to protect the parapets with an artificial mound or glacis against bombardment. On the Somerset side, however, no new works were considered necessary, 'the old walls, ditches and gates being uncommonly strong'.[3]

On 25 July Rupert crossed the Avon to the Somerset side to confer with the commanders of the western army. They finally agreed to

[1] Samuel Seyer, Jr., *Memoirs historical and topographical of Bristol and its neighbourhood* . . . 2 vols. (Bristol, 1821–3), ii. 301.

[2] The Council House, Bristol, Archives Dept.: *Brandon Hill Earthworks* (brochure, XI/9).

[3] Seyer, ii. 306.

his plan of a general assault by both armies, the attack to begin next day—Wednesday 26 July—at dawn. The password was 'Oxford'; the sign was to be green colours—boughs, or the like. The firing of two demi-cannon from Lord Grandison's battery would be the signal for the attack.

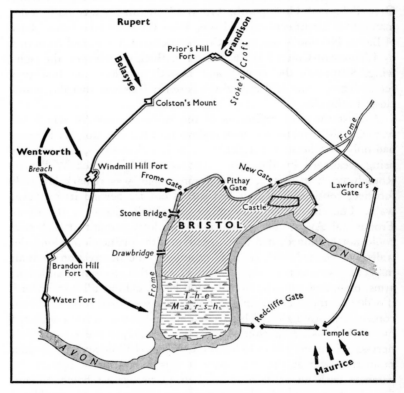

Map 4. The Storming of Bristol
26 July 1643

The Cornish, however, could not be restrained; at 3 a.m., they fell on, and the sound of the signal-gun followed their assault. Slanning, in the centre, moved out first, Buck and Basset close behind him, to right and left. An attempt to bridge the ditch before Temple Gate with carts, or to give it a dry floor by filling it with faggots, proved abortive: the trench was too deep and full of water even for 'as gallant men as ever drew sword'.[1] After half an hour's fight, they were beaten off with stones as well as bullets. Retreating to the hedges they continued to skirmish, Maurice going from regiment to regiment, encouraging the soldiers, urging the officers to keep their companies by their colours, and asserting the belief that his brother had already entered on the other side. Between six and seven in the morning, Rupert did make a breach and sent over the water, exhorting Maurice to dispatch 1,000 Cornish foot to help him hold it. 200 went first, Maurice following later with 500 more, but by then the outer ramparts had been levelled and the enemy beaten into the town.

The Royalists advanced through the suburbs toward Frome Gate, under heavy fire from walls and windows. Some 500 were killed, among them Colonel Henry Lunsford, shot through the heart: he who nearly a year before had shown his skill at Marshall's Elm. Back on the Somerset side the toll of commanders had been fearful. Basset escaped with light hurts, but Astley was carried off shot through the thigh; and Walter Slingsby, falling into a cart that he was trying to thrust into the ditch, wearing his armour, was knocked unconscious. Brutus Buck was killed; Trevanion's sergeant-major, Nicholas Kendall, was killed. Trevanion himself was wounded in the thigh: 'it swelled, grew black and stanck: whereof he dyed about midnight'.[2] Slanning had his thigh broken with case-shot: with him gangrene worked more slowly; he survived three weeks.[3] Upwards of seventy others were killed or badly wounded, most of them in that first half hour's fight under the walls and in or about the ditch. When Slingsby regained consciousness that evening he saw a hecatomb: of the three tertias, Slanning's had borne the brunt of the slaughter, there being 'five times more dead bodyes on the place where wee were then on both theire grounds'.[4]

He revived about the time that a parley between Rupert and Fiennes drew to a close. The governor, under pressure from the

---

[1] Atkyns, 43.   [2] De Gomme, loc. cit.
[3] The Cornish paladins—Trevanion, Slanning, and Sidney Godolphin—appear to have been as vulnerable in the thigh as Achilles was in the heel. Sidney Godolphin's death from a chance shot above the knee is still inexplicable, unless it is assumed that he had been wounded before or that his delicate frame, worn down by privations, succumbed to shock. In considering the high rate of mortality from flesh-wounds, the lack of competent surgeons cannot be ignored. The assumption is, however, that in some of these cases the shot must have touched bone.
[4] Hopton, 92–93; De Gomme, loc. cit.; Atkyns, 43; Seyer, 402; Burne and Young, 92–96; Coate, 94–98.

mayor and sheriff, and with powder failing, had agreed to surrender the city. Bristol was again in the King's hands. It had been dearly bought.

> Gone the four wheels of Charles's wain—
> Grenvile, Godolphin, Trevanion, Slanning slain.[1]

[1] Walter H. Tregellas, *Cornish Worthies*, 2 vols. (London, 1884), ii. 3.

VIII

THE CORNISH ARMY IN REVIEW

(October 1642–July 1643)

'I T is not given to any narrator, however conscientious he may be, to absolutely fix the form of that horrible cloud which is called a battle.'[1] To describe its components before they take the field is often hard enough. The exact structure and organization of the Cornish army is unknown.[2] Nonetheless, with the memory of its greatest exploits still fresh, it is essential to attempt a more systematic description of how it was formed and led: how problems of intelligence, administration and supply, morale, discipline and command impinged on each other to influence action in the field.

1. Organization and Recruiting

The original nucleus of volunteers supplanting the old *posse* may have consisted of about 1,500 foot[3] in the five regiments of Mohun, Grenvile, Slanning, Trevanion, and William Godolphin. These were cadres only. By November 1642 they possibly numbered 1,000 men each; for most of them this may have been the maximum strength, though Bevill Grenvile had 1,200 men just before Stratton. Not all the companies, however, took the field at once. Some were assigned garrison duty to guard the ports and collect supplies. The number employed at one time in combat may have been no more than six or eight in each regiment, instead of the usual ten. There was also a 'free company' of younger sons called the 'Reformado Captains'.[4] Early in May additional regiments were formed by Thomas Basset and Charles Trevanion, though the latter unit seems to have been kept within Cornwall. The need to disperse the troops to protect the coasts and keep a watch on the Tamar naturally reduced the prospect of concentrating an effective force at one spot; hence the need in a

---

[1] Victor Hugo, *Les Misérables*, 2 vols. (New York and Boston, n.d.), i, 'Cosette', 14.
[2] Young and Adair, 158.   [3] Coate, 38.
[4] *A True Relation of the Proceedings of the Cornish Forces* . . . , dated at Plymouth, 15 May 1643.

pinch, as before Braddock, to conscript auxiliary forces from the *posse*. Statistics on the early battles are scanty, but the number engaged in the field appears to have fluctuated between three and four thousand. There were 3,000 at Sourton, 2,400 at Stratton (drawing from a total of 3,800 stationed along the Tamar), 3,000 again at Lansdown, reinforced by the 1,000 conscripts that came with Maurice.

Until Lansdown the Cornish infantry, partly because of effective deployment and well-managed retreats, sustained relatively light losses. Over 100 were killed before Exeter in November 1642 and nearly as many at Modbury in February 1643; sixty died at Sourton and eighty at Stratton. The toll at Lansdown was at least 200, not counting those who died later of wounds; the skirmishing into Devizes added more casualties, so that little more than 3,000 were ready for combat at Roundway. Here few losses were borne, but the battle of Bristol reaped a grim harvest: upwards of 200 killed on the spot, with many others mortally hurt.

So much for the foot. The horse are somewhat easier to account for. To Hopton's 160 cavalry and dragoons was added Captain Edward Cosoworth's troop of horse; additional volunteers brought the mounted arm to 500. It seems to have borne proportionately fewer losses than the infantry: the principal battles, after all, involved uphill assaults, best suited to be carried out by foot, who consequently bore the main burden of the offensive and the brunt of the counter-attack. As for dragoons, a small regiment of 300 finally emerged, but the initial deficiency was never fully overcome.

The Cornish army, then, before its meeting with Hertford and Maurice at Chard, numbered about 3,800 in its regimented fighting arms: this tally did not include officers. These, with the civilian staff, artillerymen, and gentlemen-volunteers like Sidney Godolphin would have brought the total field force to something well over 4,000, and when joined by the 1,500 horse and 1,000 foot from Oxford with their train the united western army must have approached 7,000.[1]

The responsibility for recruiting seems to have devolved on the colonels. Grenvile enlisted his tenants; Slanning from his base at Pendennis could exercise persuasion on likely volunteers from the castle guard or from the purveyors of tin. Lines of authority were never distinct. Hertford's commission of array and the joint commission of Mohun, Hopton, Berkeley, and Ashburnham were

[1] Hopton, 47; Burne and Young, 77.

supplemented from time to time by colonels' commissions. These were first issued in the summer of 1642 as a move to transfer the leadership of the militia into loyal hands. On 5 August, for example, Arthur Bassett of Devon, a brother of Francis and Thomas Bassett, was appointed colonel of the regiment of trained bands formerly commanded by Sir Samuel Rolle, a Parliamentarian, and given the power of appointing captains.[1] The difficulty of communicating with Oxford left much to personal initiative and discretion, even while the formalities of a chain of command were observed. On 22 March 1643 a royal warrant was given at Oxford to Hopton's friend George Trevillian, Esq., of Nettlecombe, Somerset, authorizing him to raise one regiment of 1,200 foot. He was to command as colonel under orders from the King, his lieutenant-general, or other superior officers.[2]

Hopton himself, the evidence would indicate, pushed recruiting through the spring and early summer of 1643, being commissioned for one regiment of horse and one of foot, though the commissions were not officially engrossed till August.[3] His activities are shown by correspondence he held in June with Colonel Trevillian. Writing from Wells on the 20th, Hopton introduced the bearer of the letter, a captain of his regiment, as his kinsman, Charles Mathewe, who wished to raise a company of foot near Nettlecombe. He must have been recruiting musketeers: among other things, bandoleers were needed. Hopton requested that Trevillian, as a friend, do what he could to supply Mathewe.[4] Apparently he did his best: ten days later Hopton, hearing that Trevillian was levying a troop of horse and needed a lieutenant, sent him one Roger Grifith, a man 'that understands horse well'.[5]

Sir Ralph at this time ranked officially as a horse colonel and probably was in charge of the Cornish and Somerset horse, since Berkeley had gone back towards Exeter; functionally, of course, he

[1] Tanner, LXIII, 124.

[2] Royal warrant given at Oxford, 1643, 19 Charles I, Mar. 22, Nettlecombe Court MSS., S.R.O., document No. 9 (1).

[3] Harl. MS. 6852: 171. The endorsement is dated 5 August 1643: signed by Sir Edward Nicholas, Secretary of State, and directed to Edward Walker, Secretary at War. The commission for horse is retroactive to April; the commission for foot, to June. Post-dating may have been the necessary consequence of bad communications.

[4] Nettlecombe Court MSS. S.R.O., doc. No. 9 (2) 2a, printed in *N. & Q., Som. & Dor.*, Rev. G. W. Saunders and R. G. Bartelot, eds., xviii (Sherborne, 1926), 269.

[5] Ibid., doc. No. 9 (2) 2b, printed in *N. & Q., Som. & Dor.*, above, 270.

ranked as marshal of the field. In the relatively quiet weeks before Lansdown he seems to have aided Royalist recruiting almost in terms of private transactions on his home ground, although of the proposed foot regiment, beyond Mathewe's embryo company, nothing more is recorded. Apparently transfers of officers took place without formal procedures. At some time before the battle of Bristol Henry Lunsford and Thomas Shirley wrote to the King and council of war, ostensibly on behalf of the other colonels, to complain against the practice of granting commissions to regimental officers in other commands without the consent of their colonels. They also suggested that, instead of raising entirely new regiments, new recruits should be added to old ones, weakened by continual service.[1]

2. Finance and Supply

To supply these units—to provide even the minimal requirements of pay, arms, munitions, billeting, and victuals—was a formidable task. Francis Bassett, sheriff of Cornwall, was the Royalists' financial mainstay. His papers contain accounts and receipts, a few reckoned up after his death (1645), which reveal the extent of the Cornish army's dependence on him. Ten days after the battle of Braddock Down, he was commended in a letter from Lord Mohun:

My honoured friend
    We are extremely obliged to you for your care and trouble. I protest your last supply of £200 was soe seasonable that without it we had starved. We shall be extremely beholdinge to you for some of the money out of Silly [Scilly], about £500 will doe excellently well. For merchandizes in your hands, you shall doe us a great curtesy to gett us halfe, but pray ready money and as soone as you can.[2]

Hopton, Basset says, called the two hundred pounds the 'best money hee ever received in his life. It seemed to me he was in very great need of it when it came.'[3] Indeed he was, with Ruthin after him: and two days before Braddock. On 7 March Colonel William Godolphin acknowledged £200 from his 'cousin' Basset; the receipt is countersigned by Hopton, who seems to have been acting as a kind of adjutant.[4] Further receipts were signed by Hopton on 14 March, 16 April, and 10 May 1643.[5] The total sum of monies

---

[1] Harl. MS. 6804: 55.
[2] Letter dated 29 January 1642/3 at Warley House, Basset MS.
[3] Basset MSS. 50 (13), 55 (17) (double pagination).
[4] Basset MS. 57 (20).   [5] Ibid.

dispersed by Basset for the King in the period 21 October 1642 to 10 May 1643, disposed to Sir Ralph Hopton, was £1,328 9s. 8d.[1]

In so poor a county as Cornwall the need for ready money was acute. Thus, loans were frequent expedients in lieu of outright levies. On 23 January Hopton certified that £300, for which a bond had been given, had been taken for the King's service,[2] although, in many such cases, the security was no guarantee of repayment.[3] A more reliable source was the sale of 'merchandise', which Slanning's patrol of the southern coast was quick to commandeer. Parliamentary merchant ships venturing out of Plymouth did so at their peril. A Mr. Robert Trelawny of that city came through the first three months of 1643 with little profit. In January his ship, the *Richmond*, was raided by Royalist privateers: it yielded 681 oz. of plate and '1 gold hatband of 99 links and of 3 oz. weight'. Of more immediate use was 150 bushels of wheat, which Francis Basset was happy to receive at St. Michael's Mount. So as not to kill the goose that was laying golden eggs, the vessel itself was allowed to proceed. In March it was boarded again, along with another of Robert Trelawny's ships, the *Little Richmond*, and a third ship called the *Tiger*, also of Plymouth. The loot, purveyed to Falmouth, yielded three and a half barrels of powder, eight muskets, six swords, seven skeins of match, and 1,032 barrels of salt from the *Richmond;* from the *Little Richmond*, 147 bushels of French wheat and thirteen sides and one hogshead of pork; from the *Tiger*, twenty-two chests of sugar.[4]

There is some question as to whether the Royalists had enough ships, apart from privateers, for ordinary transport. At Hopton's command early in 1643 two were dispatched to Scilly, one from Padstow and one from St. Ives. The expedition, financed by Basset,[5] was probably for grain. The Venetian diplomatic correspondence, for what it is worth, illustrates the Royalists' dependence on fortuitous supply. On 9 January Hopton, at Falmouth, seized three ships with wine from Málaga, claiming the King's right to use them for the transport of munitions.[6] On 20 February grain ships on their way to Parliamentary forces in Ireland, intercepted by a 'fortunate wind' and driven into Falmouth, were seized by the governor: 'They

[1] Basset MS. 50 (13).
[2] MSS. of the Rt. Hon. Earl Spencer at Spencer House, St. James's, fol. 'C' (H.M.C., App. to 2d Rept., 23).
[3] See Ch. v, n. 9. [4] *C.S.P.D.*, 1641–43, 449 (43).
[5] Basset MS. 60 (25). This item, undated, is listed by Basset's widow.
[6] *C.S.P.V.* 1642–43, 226.

proved of no little service to the army of Sir [Ralph] Obton [*sic*], who has shut up the earl of Stanford [Stamford] with the Parliamentary forces in Plymouth, and who remains master of the county of Cornwall.'[1] On 13 March the Venetian secretary, Gerolamo Agostini, reported to the Doge and Senate that the negotiations before Plymouth had been a boon to the Royalists: Hopton, 'now viscount' (which he was not), had gained time for a merchantman to arrive with munitions from Bordeaux.[2]

Where fortune was unfavourable and persuasion ineffectual, coercion, or the threat thereof, might sometimes be employed, though the implementation and extent of such force is hard to gauge. At Chard in June 1643 one John Harvey, as he himself alleged over two years later to the Committee on Compounding, was ordered, with others, to make a rate for the King, being threatened, upon refusal, with imprisonment and having his head and heels tied together. Under pressure from Hertford and Hopton, Harvey apparently succumbed, though later asserting his loyalty to Parliament and denying that he had ever borne arms against the Parliamentary forces.[3]

Sequestration continued. On 10 July 1643 a commission from Oxford directed Edmond Windham, Esq., high sheriff of Somerset, John, Lord Poulett, Sir John Stawell, and seven others, or any three of them, to inquire by oath or witnesses what persons in the past year had been in rebellion or aiding those in rebellion and if they had 'any Lande Tenamente or other hereditamente, or any goode ready Money Plate Cattell or Chattells reall or personall or any debte owing unto them by any person or persons within this County'. These magnates were authorized to 'dispose of such Lande Tenamente and hereditamente', etc. as 'his Majesty from tyme to tyme under his Signe Manuall shall direct and not otherwise'.[4]

The financing of the Cornish army at best was a piecemeal and uncertain affair, overdependent on the exertions of one man, and with few regular augmentations from official sources. Small wonder, then, that pay was often in arrears; that billeting was generally based on free quarter; that diet was seldom more than an adequate-to-scanty allowance of hard biscuit, cheese, and beer. Conditions were unlikely to improve as the troops marched farther away from the Tamar.

---

[1] *C.S.P.V.* 1642–43, 243.   [2] Ibid. 252–3, 257.
[3] *Cal. C.C.* 995 (reported 27 Nov. 1645).
[4] Black, *Docquets* . . . , 55–56.

3. Intelligence

'Meale . . . [and] intelligence', as Colonel Slingsby observed, were the 'two necessary things for an Army'.[1] Sir John Berkeley, as commissary-general, was served by a staff quartermaster[2] and regimental quarter-masters. They appear to have had no counterparts in the sphere of relaying and co-ordinating information: there is no record of a scoutmaster. Hopton was hospitable to clergymen, and messages often were conveyed by trustworthy men of the cloth,[3] such as Dr. William Cox, prebendary of Exeter, who, after Stratton, had brought the Cornish the news of Hertford's and Maurice's advance from Oxford. Local men known to the commanders might be employed in several capacities: thus, one Hugh Fry, of Billerica Parish, Witham Friary, Somerset, allegedly acted as commissary of provisions and intelligencer for the King's forces, acting under Hopton's warrants.[4] Perhaps such *ad hoc* solutions served the turn when the Cornish army was still an isolated unit, but after the Oxford regiments joined them correspondence was hampered by a lack of *rapport* among the members of the civilian staffs. Even setting the Cornish aside as virtual outlanders, there was a lack of understanding between Hertford's and Maurice's regiments. It was alleged that their chaplains and secretaries seldom gave true intelligence, but 'rather as their affections lead them, supposing that if such things were done, they must be done by such and such Persons'.[5] The incompatibility of the two principal commanders provided some basis for this assertion: the King himself, after the battle of Bristol, 'discerned plainly that the prince and the marquis would never agree together'.[6] It must be allowed, however, that a more convincing explanation lies with the aberrations of a civilian staff, even more ignorant of military strategy and manoeuvres than their masters.

In contrast to this muddledness, it is intriguing to consider David

---

[1] Hopton, 97.

[2] A 'Mr. Cory', according to Parliamentary intelligence: see App. II.

[3] Bailey, 308, 319, 451; *Wilts. Arch. & Nat. Hist.* xxxiv. 166–7.

[4] *Cal. C.A.M.*, 980–1 (reported 6 Aug. 1649). Hopton may have assumed scout-master's duties as marshal of the field. See Henry Hexham, *Principles of the Art Military* (Delft, 1642), C1–C2. Of Hugh Fry nothing is known beyond the surmise that he was probably a yeoman. In the S.R.O. is an abstract of title to Bellerica Farm in Witham Friary parish which recites back to 1677 and a diary-cum-account book of Edward Curl, the Parliamentary agent in the county, for part of 1649–50. Unfortunately the diary stops just short of August when references to Fry might have been found.

[5] Atkyns, 29.   [6] Clarendon, vii. 155.

Lloyd's assertion that Hopton set up a press to print orders, declarations, messages, and 'other Books to instruct and undeceive the people'.[1] The assumption is doubtful: Hopton was on the march too much.[2] Still, the Earl of Newcastle had a press; Arthur, Lord Capel, Hopton's nephew by marriage, had one at Shrewsbury. Peripatetic presses were sometimes used. Besides the royal press at Oxford, the King may have appointed his printers when his forces took over a particular locality.[3] So the possibility exists that Hopton had access to printing presses even if he had none of his own.

4. Discipline and Command

Enhancing morale through prayer and propaganda was a necessity both at the early stage when the Cornish were relatively untrained and later when their liaison with the Oxford regiments exacerbated regional differences among the Royalists. As Richard Atkyns put it, most of the Cornish foot 'could not well brook our Horse (especially, when we were drawn up upon Corn) but they would many times let fly at us'. Doubtless, he admired them, yet he could not forbear to qualify his admiration: 'These were the very best Foot that ever I saw, for Marching & Fighting; but so Mutinous withal, that nothing but an alarm could keep them from falling foul upon their officers.'[4] Plainly cavalier honour and ethics required a strong dose of religion for stability. The conflict between piety and hearty hedonism is amusingly described in an anecdote of Captain Atkyns. In the middle of June 1643, as the Royalists moved up towards Bath from the south, he went to his quarters at Glastonbury where the house had been totally plundered: 'neither Bread nor Bear in it; but only part of a Cheddar Cheese, which looking blew, I found my Foot-boy giving it to my Greyhounds'. The lad was reproved, but protested there was nothing else to give them. For this cheese, Atkyns says, he was later arrested in London and fined £100. This was hard for a man like himself whose piety was so exemplary that he had turned down an invitation from Maurice to share a buck with the other officers. Atkyns preferred, instead, that his troop be given the sacrament. Major Thomas Sheldon, who was to die from that same explosion of powder-kegs that so seriously burned Hopton, could not

---

[1] Lloyd, 343.

[2] Dr. Ian Roy, of King's College, University of London, who has done a study of the Oxford army, holds this view.

[3] Seyer, ii. 419.   [4] Atkyns, 24.

understand: 'Hang't, hang't Bully, said he merrily thou may'st receive the Sacrament at any time but thou cann'st not Eat Venison at any time.'[1] Thus devotion and discipline were mitigated by occasional, perhaps necessary, distractions.

Order, if not harmony, was the responsibility of the provost marshal, often a civilian,[2] who, besides the discipline of the camp, was charged with such diverse duties as the selection of an ammunition park, the retention of prisoners,[3] and sanitary arrangements. In addition, temporary marshals might be appointed from the local populace: Richard Callow, of Warminster, Wiltshire (near Hertford's seat), was accused by the Parliamentarians after the war of having served Hopton in this capacity, keeping the Black Swan in Devizes, the house of Robert Edney, as a prison for those adhering to Parliament.[4] This was probably just after the battle of Roundway Down.

In determining the components of success, it is not out of place to consider the motto ascribed to Hopton by Lloyd: 'Pay well, command well, and Hang well.'[5] Administration, leadership, discipline: by maintaining, despite lapses, a consistently high degree of efficiency in these spheres, the Cornish overcame initial set-backs and the attrition of long periods of inaction, numerical odds against them, financial arrears, and the limitations of a lingering '*posse* mentality'. Their morale was greater, perhaps, on their native soil; but they fought as well in Somerset as in Cornwall. Their prowess was unimpaired by the deaths of their principal commanders: Slanning's regiment under Thomas Bassett; Bevill Grenvile's under his son, Sir John Grenvile, continued to do good service. If truth lies less in the word than in the performance, the King's letter of thanks to the Cornish must surely be accepted as no more than a fair and just statement of their deserts:

Charles R.

We are so highly sensible of the extraordinary Merit of Our County of

---

[1] Ibid. 28–29.

[2] In the Cornish army, this post was filled by a 'Mr. Crue', according to Parliamentary intelligence: see App. II.

[3] Major O. F. G. Hogg, 'Forerunners of the Army Council', *J.S. Army H.R.* xi. 109.

[4] *Cal. C.A.M.* 943 (reported 18 and 25 Aug. 1648).

[5] Lloyd, 343. The last admonition may be taken to mean 'punish judiciously'. Though the threat of hanging was a wholesome check to mutiny and rapine, capital punishment was little used in the western army until that advent of Irish troops at the end of 1643. In a civil war more than in others, indiscriminate hanging would have proved the bane of recruiting.

Cornwall of their Zeal for the Defence of Our Person and the just Rights of Our Crown, (in a time when We could contribute so little to Our own Defence, or to their Assistance, in a time when not only no Reward appeared, but great and probable Dangers threatened Obedience and Loyalty) of their great and eminent Courage and Patience in their indefatigable Prosecution of their great Work against so potent an Enemy, backt with so strong, rich and populous Cities, and so Plentifully furnisht with Men, Arms, Money, Ammunition and Provisions of all kinds, and of the wonderful Success with which it hath pleased Almighty God (though with the loss of some eminent Persons, who shall never be forgotten by Us) to reward their Loyalty and Patience, by many strange Victories over their and Our Enemies, in despite of all human probability, and all imaginable disadvantages: That as We cannot be forgetful of so great Deserts so We cannot but Desire to publish to the World, and perpetuate to all Time the Memory of these Their Merits, and of Our Acceptance of the same. And to that and We do hereby Render Our Royal Thanks to that Our County, in the most publick and lasting manner we can devise, commanding Copies hereof to be printed and Published, and one of them to be read in every Church and Chapel therin, and to be kept for ever as a Record in the same; That as long as the History of these Times and this Nation shall continue, the Memory of how much that County hath merited from Us and Our Crown may be derived with it to Posterity. Given at our Camp at Sudeley Castle, the Tenth of September, 1643.[1]

However their exploits may be regarded, it can hardly be denied that the animating impulse of the Cornish was supplied by their native commanders. The high calibre of their officers was the *sine qua non* of their success. At the same time the role of Sir Ralph Hopton in recruiting, drilling, and deploying these regiments on the battlefield was of paramount importance. The army had survived three set-backs (at Exeter, Plympton, and Sourton) to achieve four substantial victories (at Braddock, Launceston, Stratton, and Lansdown) and contribute materially to two more (Roundway and Bristol). It had saved the west for the King. In so doing Hopton and the Cornish army became a legend. Perhaps there is no more telling proof of how Hopton was regarded by the Parliamentarians as the Royalist paladin of the west than those newsletters of the winter of 1642–3 in which his death was reported so many times that it must have become a joke even among the roundheads themselves. The motto of the Parliamentary newsmakers seemed to be:

---

[1] Rushworth, v. 360; Basset MS. 14; George Granville, Lord Lansdown, *A Letter to the Author of* Reflexions Historical and Political . . . Etc. (London, 1732), *passim*. Another copy is on display in Stratton Church, and there are others throughout Cornwall.

'When in doubt, kill Hopton.' On 5 December 1642 he was reported to be 'either dead or dangerously sick'.[1] On 9 February 1643, it was bruited that he had been created 'Baron Glastonbury', but had been slain with 600 men before Plymouth.[2] A report of 20 February related that Sir Nicholas Slanning had sent one of the master gunners in Plymouth a letter offering him £100 if he would charge his guns with powder and paper and give false fire. The mayor of Plymouth discovered this, imprisoned the gunner, and returned the letter in the gunner's name, agreeing to the proposal. On this premise, Hopton set upon the outworks; but the Plymouth men charged their pieces with small shot and slew 800 men, 'amongst whom Sir Ralph Hopton was one'.[3] This wild rumour was succeeded by another on 6 May from Exeter, relating his death on Sourton Down.[4]

A few disclaimers appeared. On 15 May a letter from 'J.T.' (Sir Jonathan Trelawney) of Plymouth put the Londoners right: Hopton still lived; at least, warrants were still being issued under his name.[5] Later the Cavalier poet John Cleveland was moved to comment:

I wonder for how many lives Lord Hoptons soul tooke the Lease of his Body. First, Stamford slew him: then Waller outkilled that halfe a Barre: and yet it is thought the sullen corps would scarce bleed were both these Man-slayers never so near it.[6]

But rumours discredited by history may become the stuff of legend; and it is easy to imagine the peasants of the west country, and even the London burghers, responding to the resilience and recuperative power of the Cornish army—so often outnumbered, so often in retreat—as to a phenomenon preternatural, if not supernatural. In the lines of a Royalist poet, Sir John Denham, penned after Sourton Down (25 April 1643), this sentiment found rousing voice:

'A Western Wonder'

Do you not know a fortnight ago
How they bragged of a Western Wonder?
When a hundred and ten slew five thousand men
With the help of lightning and thunder.

---

[1] N. & Q., 7th ser., xi (17 Jan. 1891), 46.
[2] Cal. of the MS. of the Duke of Portland, i (H.M.C., 13th Rept., Pt. I, 95).
[3] Good Newes from Plymouth, being a true relation of the death of Sir Ralph Hopton, in Catalogue of the Thomason Tracts (London and Oxford, 1908), i. 235.
[4] N. & Q., 7th ser., xi (17 Jan. 1891), 46.
[5] Ibid.   [6] N. & Q., 9th ser., ii (10 Dec. 1898), 465.

There Hopton was slain, again and again
Or else my author did lie;
With a new thanksgiving for the dead who are living
To God and his servant Chudleigh.

And now on which side was the miracle tryd,
I hope we at last are even;
For Sir Ralph and his knaves are risen from the graves
To cudgel the clowns of Devon.[1]

[1] E. H. Young, 286–7.

IX

LORD HOPTON, MARSHALL OF THE FIELD:

Bristol to Arundel

(July 1643–January 1644)

'IN war the supreme commander must often consider politics as a branch of military science: the achievement of a political synthesis among his followers may be the main reason for his victory.'[1] In the seventeenth century Cromwell had this knack, as to some extent did William of Orange and Henry of Navarre; it was a talent denied, however, to Charles the First. Ambitious personalities in his court and army, forming rival juntas, divided his councils and hampered the progress of his arms.[2]

This deficiency was particularly evident when confusion arose from the conflicting claims of two grandees or magnates to exercise local authority in the King's name. After the battle of Bristol field operations were suspended ten or twelve days while the principal commanders wrangled over the question of who was to become governor of the city. Hertford had already appointed Hopton to this post; and the marquis's right was hard to question as he was both commanding general of the western army and lord lieutenant of Bristol. Prince Rupert, however, had obtained a patent for the same office, the King being unaware at the time of Hertford's prior disposition. The ensuing contretemps threatened to embarrass the King's affairs: 'the greatest of the Court being ready to take partes in it'. Charles finally came to Bristol to settle the matter in person, having beforehand sent Sir Ralph a conciliatory letter:

Charles R.

Trusty and well belov'd wee greete you well, wee rather intended to have testifyed unto you the acknowledgement of your great services unto us, by some reall testimony of our favours, then to have told it you this way in writing, but wee cannot at this time be silent, because haveing heard that the Marquess of Hertford haveing intended to make you Governour of our

[1] Hugh Thomas, *The Spanish Civil War*, 610.
[2] Ian Roy, 'The Royalist Council of War, 1642–6', *Bulletin of the Institute of Historical Research*, No. 35.

recovered Cittye of Bristoll, and wee haveing thought fitt to confer the same upon our Nephew Prince Rupert, Wee have thought it necessarie to assure you, that in this wee have bin so far from intending you thereby any disrespect, as we never heard, nor imagined that you should have bin named to that command, knowing how necessarie your continuall presence is to our Westerne Army, assuring you that wee can thinke noe man fitter for that command than yourselfe (it being by farre too little a recompence for your great deservings) and therefore haveing dealt thus freely with you, and haveing expressed our estimation of you (which wee shall better expressed in our actions than wee have done in words) wee are most confident that you will not onely rest satisfyed in this particular, but also make knowen to all your friends the true vallue wee sett upon you, and hinder any misinterpirtations, that malitious people may sett upon this accion of ours, for certainely wee too much esteeme our Nephew P. Rubert, to make him a means of putting any disrespect upon any Gentleman especially upon one wee so much esteeme as you, and wee are confident that his particular estimation of you is such, that he will rather seeke ways to oblige you then to give you any distast. And so we bid you hartely farewell. Given at our Court at Oxford the 29th day of July 1643.

Hopton, 'abhorring verie much that His Majesties affaires should be disturbed by any concernement of his, disposed all his endeavours to the composing the business betweene the two great Lords, and for himselfe wholy submitted to his Majestie's pleasure'.[1] It may be that his capitulation to Rupert was due to the tenderness he reserved for the children of the Queen of Bohemia;[2] but the chances are that the King's preference was itself sufficient.

With no inclination, then, to push himself, he was content to be commissioned as Rupert's lieutenant-governor and remain at Bristol with six very small and 'ragged' regiments, totalling no more than 1,200 men, mostly Cornish, in addition to 200 of Maurice's horse. The King and Rupert marched to the siege of Gloucester; Prince Maurice took what was left of the western army into Dorset. A letter from Sir Anthony Ashley Cooper, the future Earl of Shaftesbury, to the mayor and corporation of Dorchester, urging their submission,[3] was complied with next day; the surrender of Weymouth, the best port town of the county, followed at once.

Devonshire also was ready to capitulate. In the north, Barnstaple and Bideford had remained Parliamentary, though their garrisons

---

[1] Hopton, 58–59.   [2] Sealy, 104.
[3] Tanner MSS., LXII, 217: Anthony 'Astley' Cooper, 'Geo.' Naper, and John Hele, dated at Sherborne, 3 August 1643.

were unable to relieve Exeter because the Royalists under Colonel John Digby blocked them at Torrington.[1] The Devon towns fell in quick succession: Barnstaple on 28 August, Bideford on 31 August, Exeter on 4 September;[2] Dartmouth held out until 6 October.[3] Four western counties—Cornwall, Devon (except Plymouth), Somerset, and the strategic parts of Dorset, excluding the ports of Poole and Lyme Regis—were now secured for the King.

Hopton, one year after proclaiming the commission of array at Shepton, and with conspicuous successes behind him, had reverted to a familiar role. His correspondence with Rupert reveals the scope and weight of his responsibility, with Bristol an entrepôt, arsenal, and training ground for the whole west.

Within a week after the siege of Gloucester was joined on 10 August he sent the prince a full account of his problems. Though declaring his full intent to comply with the King's warrant for thirty barrels of powder, he begged Rupert to remember that

I had but 31 barrells left me here, and by all the industry I cann yet use, I have not gott me 30 barrells more, and truly Sir I feare there is not att this time in any of his Majesty's servants hands, west of the camp att Gloucester, nor in all of them, 100 barells of powder more, and I canot by any industry I have used gett the mill wrights or saltpeter-makers from Oxford that were promised me.

Another great lack was money. A fortnight after the local contribution of £1,500 a week had begun, less than £300 had been received, insufficient for half a week's pay. He had borrowed heavily to pay the sergeants, corporals, drummers, and common soldiers; but even if the whole contribution came in it would not be enough. One reason for the arrears was that

the cuntry hath other great burdens upon it, I have here enclosed sent your highnes, Coll: Carys warrant which he sends to the same part of Sumersettshire where our contribution should rise, even close to the gates of this cyty and demands no less the[n] 804£ a weeke, I humbly beeseech your highnes to consider of it and to remove him, else I and my garrison here must necessaryly starve or disolve. . . .

With two commanders canvassing the same district, it is hardly surprising that Hopton found it difficult to maintain his forts and increase his stores. As for ordnance: 'we have here in effect none at all', since 'those we have were taken of severall shipps wherof now

[1] Alexander and Hooper, 86–87.   [2] Clarendon, vii. 197–8.
[3] Burne and Young, 119.

the most are in his Majesty's service and Sir John Pennington demands theyr gunns agayne'. Order had been taken for the casting of more cannon at the King's works in Shropshire: thirty pieces in all. Small arms, too, were in short supply. Sir Ralph had fetched 400 spare weapons from Bath, and the workmen of Bristol had promised to send in 200 muskets and thirty brace of pistols a week.[1]

The system of distribution was haphazard, to say the least; the problem of equitable allotment to scattered forces was aggravated by questions of accountability and precedence. Hopton on 15 August had informed the prince about the arrival of a frigate from Dunkirk with arms procured by the Queen. The supply of muskets, pistols, hand grenades, and round-shot was most welcome. But delay was occasioned by the ship captain's desire to go to Oxford and tell the Queen in person. Meanwhile, the news was bruited in Bristol;[2] the assumption is that the growing levies were becoming impatient for weapons. Hopton concluded his long letter with a plea to the prince to help him secure muskets from this store, assuring him that it would soon be made up again from the workmen's contributions. He also asked for 100 pairs of pistols for his regiment of horse, then in Devon, urging its deserts as one of the 'old regiments'. The Prince must have received this letter by 16 August; he went to Oxford to make inquiries, but with scant success. Henriette Marie was jealous of her husband's nephew; the King left the siege to pacify her.[3] Operations were held up for several days. By 20 August they were moving again: Hopton received a warrant from Gloucester for 100 pairs of pistols.[4] His own request for pistols to equip Maurice's regiment was finally answered by a royal order of 1 September for 192 pairs.[5]

[1] B.M., Add. MS. 18, 980: 93 (115–16), undated. Though the pagination follows 18,980:92 (114), dated 6 Sept. 1643, it is clear from the context that this letter must have been written shortly after 15 August. In the first line Hopton reports the death 'this day' of Lt.-Col. Nathaniel Moyle. Although Clarendon, vii. 133, says that Moyle died 'within few days' after the battle of Bristol, it is conceivable that he lingered a week or two longer. Hopton reports that the Somerset contribution had begun two weeks before: it was still pending 28 July—see a letter from the King to Rupert in Eliot Warburton, *Memoirs of Prince Rupert and the Cavaliers* (London, 1849), ii, 268, n. 1. The Prince was still within the environs of Bristol on 9 August—ibid. 280; the siege of Gloucester began on 10 August; on 15 August Hopton wrote to Rupert concerning the arrival of the Queen's frigate with arms from Dunkirk—see note 2, below.

[2] Warburton, ii. 278, n. 1.

[3] Ibid. 278, 282–3; Clarendon, vii. 177.

[4] Ref. from Shire Hall, Gloucester: D-115/11—a warrant to Lord Hopton as governor of Bristol for 100 pairs of pistols, to be delivered to Sir John Mennes, 20 Aug. 1643.   [1] Harl. 4712, f. 233.

Despite shortages and set-backs, recruiting went so well that Hopton towards the end of August was able to send 500 musketeers to Gloucester under the command of two of his own officers: Captain Neale Mackworth (who, in May, 1639, had served as his cornet at Newcastle)[1] and Captain Thomas Randall. The men, he reported later, came in 'freely' to the new government, confident of 'reasonable' means of subsistence.[2]

His employment had its more agreeable side. While the siege languished, he wrote on 16 August to Sir Francis Ottley, governor of Shrewsbury, on behalf of Captain Thomas Gay, from whom 'three Butt of Spanish Wine' had been 'violently taken' by the round-heads during the Parliamentary occupation of Bristol. He requested Ottley to assist Captain Gay's agent in recovering the wine from the hands of Richard Betton, vinter, of Shrewsbury and any other of Gay's goods which might be found within the governor's jurisdiction.[3] No doubt this disposition to do favours enhanced the esteem in which he was held. The day following his dispatch for the wine-butts, the common council of Bristol concurred that 'It is thought meet and soe agreed that there shalbe a present conferred and bestowed uppon the lord Hopton the present Governor vizt. a But of sack two hogshead[es] of claret one of white and a c[wt.] of sugarr'. It cost the city £22.[4] This gratuity was more than a token: on 14 September the council went further: 'The house think[es] fitt that the Lord Hoptons Freedom of this incorporation be tendered to him under the Cittyes seals for gratulatory token of the Cities affection toward him'.[5]

The declaration of affection to 'Lord' Hopton substantiates the truth that Sir Ralph's services had been rewarded with a peerage. The honour must have been conferred immediately after the battle of Bristol and partly as compensation for his graceful yielding to Rupert in the matter of the governorship. It was confirmed by letters patent on 4 September 1643:

A Patent of Creation graunted to Sir Ralph Hopton Knight of the Bath of the honor of Baron Hopton of Stratton in the County of Cornwall entayling

[1] (Add.) S.P. 16: 538: 91.
[2] Hopton, 60.
[3] William Phillips, ed., 'The Ottley Papers Relating to the Civil War', *Transactions of the Shropshire Archaeological Society*, 1875, 2d series, vii, Pt. ii, clxxxiii.
[4] Bristol: The Council House: MS. of the Proceedings of the Common Council 1642–9, 35 (17 Aug. 1643).
[5] Ibid. 36.

the same upon the heires males of his body forever and for want of such Issue the same entayled upon Sir Arthur Hopton Knight [Sir Ralph's uncle] and the heires males of his body.[1]

The title presaged greater duties, but for a time administration continued routinely. On 1 September Hopton wrote to Rupert requesting explicit directions for repairing the works of the Windmill Hill fort and begging him to 'remember this poore garrison for arms'.[2] Three days later he sent the prince a 'hansom body of men': five foot regiments of 2,000 men plus Prince Maurice's regiment of horse, 500 strong, including officers. He sent after them eight barrels of powder and 1,500 lb. of match, promising to send next day by wain 22 barrels of powder, 2,400 lb. of match,[3] and 2,000 lb. of musket balls. This left only two foot regiments in Bristol: Rupert's and Hopton's;[4] the former had 'full 300 whole men', but only 93 were armed.[5] To guard the wains with the second supply of munitions, Hopton could spare only a lieutenant and a few horse.[6] Yet all his apprehensions and exertions seemed wasted: that same day (5 September 1643) the siege of Gloucester was raised. Next day Colonel Richard March, having been informed of this by Hopton, composed an immediate reply to a letter from Henry, Lord Percy, general of the ordnance, declaring his readiness to dispatch as directed the serviceable armour from the Dunkirk store, as soon as he knew where to send it.[7]

Within a few weeks after the fall of Exeter on 4 September some

[1] Black, *Docquets* . . . , p, 71: breviate of Sir Ralph Hopton's patent for his barony. This is the only authority for Hopton's creation and for thirty-five others out of the total of forty-five which took place between 28 June 1643 and 1 September 1646. It is edited from the original Crown office docquet book. There are no enrolled patents, privy seals, or signed bills relating to peerages between these dates. The Long Parliament passed an Act 4 Feb. 1651/2 making void all titles of honour conferred by the King after 4 Jan. 1641/2—see *Complete Peerage*, ii. 454.
  A copy of Hopton's patent, in Latin, may be found in B.M., Add. MS. 15,856, f. 43b: 3 pp. quarto. There is a printed copy in the collection *Monastic Remains of Witham, Bruton, and Stavordale, Com. Somerset*, by Sir Richard Colt Hoare, Bart. (Frome, 1824), 33. Notice of the creation is also given in the Ashmole MSS. (Bodleian), 832: 186.
[2] B.M., Add. MS. 18,980: 90 (112).
[3] 2,500 lb., according to Add. MS. 18,980: 92 (114), dated 6 Sept. 1643, below.
[4] Hopton, 60.
[5] B.M., Add. MS. 18,980: 91 (113), dated 4 Sept. 1643. This letter never reached the Prince. Hopton reports in ibid. 92 (114), dated 6 Sept. 1643, below, that the messenger was forced, 'for his owne security to cast it away'.
[6] B.M., Add. MS. 18,980: 92 (114), dated 6 Sept. 1643.
[7] Rawlinson 395, f. 140, dated 6 Sept. 1643.

of the Cornish who had gone with Maurice, including Lord Mohun,[1] left his service, professing to apprehend a threat from the Parliamentarians' western outpost at Plymouth. Of six troops of horse and four of dragoons which returned to Bristol, four troops of horse and two of dragoons were from Hopton's own regiment, all 'very weake and wholly disarmed'. Two fresh troops were 'something stronger' but without arms. How to pay them was a problem as yet unsolved. The ubiquitous Colonel Cary, by the King's order, was entitled to a share of the contribution, though Hopton viewed with scepticism his optimistic promises to bring in hundreds of horse, doubting he could find half that number. The *de facto* governor of Bristol complained to his superior that business was so great and went on so slowly that he needed a deputy. He suggested Sir Francis Hawley, he who had held the left flank at Marshall's Elm the previous year and been wounded at Chagford in February, a man 'who being likewise this cuntry man, his alliance will assist me in raysing the contribution, and many assistances which cannot be so well affected by any that were not this cuntry man'.[2]

These administrative burdens partly explain why Lord Hopton missed the first battle of Newbury, which took place on 20 September. Hardly any troops were left in Bristol; the greater part were still Cornish.[3] It is uncertain whether these veterans were regarded only as a garrison force or as a potential reserve. Just before the King engaged with Essex, he sent orders to Hopton to draw out what troops could be spared and bring them himself to Newbury, over sixty miles distant. The messages did not reach their destination until after the battle had begun. Hopton drew out between seven and eight hundred foot and four or five hundred horse, leaving only 1,200 foot to hold Bristol in his absence. By 1 p.m. he was on the march. Quartering at Marshfield that night he reached Marlborough next day and learned the result of Newbury fight:[4] after heavy losses on both sides, the King, on the information that powder was failing, had given

---

[1] Black, *Docquets* . . . , 78: commission of Oyer and Terminer for Cornwall directed to Lord Mohun, Justice of Assize 'for the tyme being' and others, dated 4 Oct. 1643.

[2] B.M., Add. MS. 18,980: 96 (119), dated 17 Sept. 1643. Hawley didn't get this post immediately: it was given to Lt.-Col. Walter Slingsby (Hopton, 62), though on 30 Oct. Hopton refers to Hawley as 'my Lieut. Governour'—S.R.O., Phelips MS., 75. The distinction between a 'lieutenant governor' and a 'deputy governor' is unclear.

[3] *J.S. Army H.R.* xviii. 31.

[4] Hopton, 61.

orders to retire toward Oxford. Essex had kept his army intact and managed a retreat through Reading, though harassed again and again by Rupert's horse. He reached London safely. Thus a great chance to destroy the enemy's main field army had been lost.

A hinge had turned, a door had closed. It was conceivable, however, that it could be opened again. The Parliamentary party's Solemn League and Covenant with the Scots on 25 September was a portent, though as yet a dim one. Despite delays in the north and in the west, the King's fortunes were running at high tide. He retained the loyalty even of those who might have had reason to oppose him on religious grounds. Dr. Samuel Ward, master of Sidney Sussex College, Cambridge, archdeacon of Taunton, and prebendary of Wells, was a leading puritan and Calvinist. But he refused the Covenant in 1643. When he died in September of that year, his last words by report were: 'God bless the King and My Lord Hopton!'[1]

In this season of prosperity and equipoise, the problem for the Royalists was how to overcome the inertia, distractions, and lack of design that had limited their best efforts in the past: how to correct deficiencies in organization and command: how to devise a strategy for victory. The outline of a plan can be discerned: an advance on London from three sectors at once—north, centre, and west. In the absence of specific documentation the concept of such a plan must rest on inherent military probability; the evidence is restricted largely to individual surmise, mainly in terms of 'what might have been'.

As early as March 1643 Parliamentary intelligence had hinted at the possibility of a 'trident' attack, asserting that Charles was planning to join his Oxford army with the Earl of Newcastle's army from the north and Hopton's from the west.[2] While there is no evidence that the Royalists tried to implement such a sweeping strategy, it is clear that the King considered at least a two-prong approach. Between the fall of Bristol and the siege of Gloucester he sent an express to Newcastle, then before Hull, advising him that if he found the siege too difficult he should block up the port to protect the country and march toward London through the associated counties of Norfolk, Suffolk, Cambridgeshire, and Essex. The King at the same time would march toward the capital through the valley of the Thames.

---

[1] John E. Bailey, *Life of Thomas Fuller* (citing Pope's *Life of Bishop Ward*, Ch. iii), 105.

[2] Luke, *Journal*, 35 (Thurs. 16 Mar. 1642/3).

Newcastle's answer is a strong testament to the strategic limitations of a war fought by civilians. He reported that his best officers refused to march unless Hull were first taken.[1]

This 'fatal vanity of leaving no enemy's standard flying in their rear'[2] was a basic flaw of Royalist strategy. While the northern prong of the 'trident' was wedged at Hull, the middle was stuck at Gloucester and the western, clumsily wielded by Maurice, jammed by the profitless siege of Lyme Regis. For a month or two after Bristol, the pursuit of greater objectives was held up by attempts at a piecemeal reduction of the districts already overrun. Though the wisdom of the united front at this time could be debated, there were those who, at least in retrospect like Richard Atkyns, could see favourable conditions wasted and chances thrown away: 'If the armies before Lyme or Gloucester had come in, or the Field Army gone up to London to join with Newcastle, then successful in the North . . .'.[3] The 'if's', of course, tended to overlook or conceal the liabilities of a trident: the greater losses incidental to the offensive, the greater employment of soldiers necessitated by acting on exterior lines,[4] the problem of combining rapid movement with the effective co-ordination of widely separated forces.

These questions, however, might have been more easily answered if a more basic problem had been solved: the most effective employment of the best troops. That the fragmented Cornish infantry should be watching Plymouth, besieging Dartmouth, or guarding Bristol instead of coming to push of pike with Essex in Berkshire appears preposterous in the age of general staffs, but was no anomaly in a day when successful command still turned on personal followings and martial vigour on proximity to native soil. An advance on London, then, might be best supported by recruitment from the region of the capital, especially in the south-eastern counties of Sussex, Surrey, and Kent, which, if not exactly a 'soft underbelly'[5] from the Parliamentary standpoint, were much less cohesive than the counties north of the Thames. As early as 3 July 1643 a commission to raise a regiment of 500 horse had been issued to Sir Nicholas Crisp of London and a like commission to Sir Edward Dering, M.P., of

---

[1] Clarendon, vii. 177.
[2] Warburton, ii. 273.
[3] Atkyns, 44.
[4] Winston S. Churchill, *The World Crisis*, 1911–1914 (London, 1923), 62.
[5] Except in the topographical sense. Apart from the chalk cliffs, the soil of this region tends to be soft and sticky.

Kent.[1] By the middle of September the Commons was informed of six Royalist regiments of horse threatening Southampton. In addition to Crisp's and Dering's there was one led by Colonel Sir Edward Ford of Sussex; and from farther west others led by the Earl of Crawford, by Colonel Sir Humphrey Bennet of Hampshire, and by Sir George Vaughan, sheriff of Wiltshire. The informant, Colonel Herbert Morley, begged Speaker Lenthall for a new force. Otherwise, the southern counties would be lost and London itself imperilled.[2]

Charles's withdrawal to Oxford after failing to press his advantage at Newbury was brought off, no doubt, with this larger aim in view. Hopton, now nearly recovered from his wounds, was summoned to meet on 29 September with a committee of the Lords at Oriel College.[3] Here, by order of the King, he was given command of new regiments and told to clear Dorset, Wiltshire, and Hampshire of the last Parliamentary strongholds before marching as far as he could toward London.

Now at last it would seem he had been given a mission worthy of his devotion and skill. But it was the sad flaw of Charles that, while missing or ignoring what was under his nose, he too often devised grand schemes without taking proper measures for realizing them. Unlike Montaigne's man of experience, he could not always keep his celestial thoughts in accord with his terrestrial actions. Hopton, who, aspiring to less, was more adept at fitting means to ends, was forced to begin his work with only parts of an army, all horse cadres. These included, on paper, the six regiments of the Earl of Crawford (250), Sheriff Vaughan of Wiltshire (60), Crisp (100), Dering (120), Ford (260), and Bennet (no figures) just mentioned. Hopton had, besides, 250 horse and dragoons of his own; at his disposal were 100 of Hertford's and 150 of Sir Edward Stawell, son of Sir John Stawell of Somerset. Other cavalry and dragoon regiments were supplied by Sir James Hamilton of Worcester (50), Sir Horatio Cary, a veteran of the German wars (100), a Colonel Spencer[4] (60), and a Colonel Covert[5] (80). There is no evidence,

---

[1] Black, *Docquets* . . . , 54.

[2] Nalson MS. III: 31 (60), dated at Farnham, 16 Sept. 1643.

[3] Dr. Roy, 'The Royalist Army . . .' (typescript), p. 76 thinks this committee was a 'junto' of courtiers presided over by Francis, Baron Cottington, the Lord Treasurer, which sat regularly at Oriel.

[4] An Edward Spencer received a commission to raise horse in July 1643— Black, *Docquets* . . . , 61.

[5] John or Thomas—a son of Sir Walter Covert of King.

however, that Dering and Crisp's regiments were ever joined to the new army. All told, the number could not have been much more than 1,400 men.[1]

As for foot, Hopton was left to draw what he could out of Bristol. From his own regiment there, he was able to spare 500, which must have included some Cornish. Maurice's regiment could provide 250; Hertford's, under Colonel Bernard Astley, and the Welsh troops of Colonel Conyer Griffin, or Griffith, could draw 400. Sir Allen Apsley might supply 300, Colonel Washington 200, and Sir James Hamilton 450. There were some 300 others from cadres of regiments in Dorset and Somerset, bringing the total to about 2,000.[2] Such, on paper, were the dispositions of the new western infantry.

In organizing and supplying these troops, however, Hopton was left to his own ingenuity. He was dependent on his own stores for ordnance and munitions. Though £6,000 was promised him within fourteen days, he received only £1,500, which forced him to pledge his share of the Bristol contribution for twenty weeks to obtain £3,000.[3] True, he was allowed muskets out of the stores at Weymouth, though no more than 2,000.[4] Fifty pounds were paid to Andrew Grove, a Dane, 'for making of fireworks under Lord Hopton'.[5] Otherwise, it would appear that disinterested ardour was meanly served.

On his way back to Bristol,[6] Hopton was met near Tetbury by a messenger from Major George Maxwell, governor of Berkeley castle, a Royalist outpost half-way between Bristol and Gloucester. From the latter city, grown bolder since the collapse of the siege, Colonel Edward Massey had advanced on Berkeley, seizing the church and forcing Maxwell into the castle. Hopton at once sent orders to Colonel Walter Slingsby, his deputy governor at Bristol, to dispatch Major Spurr with 200 mounted musketeers to meet him

---

[1] Harl. 6804, f. 224, item 171. The rough draft has been edited by Dr. Roy.
[2] Ibid., item 137.   [3] Hopton, 61.
[4] Rawlinson MS. 395, f. 47: warrant from the King to Henry, Lord Percy, general of the ordnance (countersigned by Secretary Edward Nicholas), dated at Oxford 1 Oct. 1643. Hopton is here called 'Feild Marshall of Our Western Army'.
[5] S.P. 16/498/15: warrant of the King under the Privy Seal to the Treasurer and Under-Treasurer of the Exchequer, dated at Oxford, 5 Oct. 1643 (see also S.P. 16/498/8, p. 4, 11 Sept. 1643).
[6] H.M.C., App. 4th Rept., 296: MSS. of the Rt. Hon. the Earl de la Warr (Baron Buckhurst) at Knole Park, Co. of Kent. The Earl of Bath to his wife, dated 1 Oct. 1643, reports he saw Lord Hopton take leave of the King and Queen after the afternoon sermon.

at Sodbury, a dozen miles south of Berkeley and a like distance north-east of Bristol. The rendezvous was effected promptly; but the enemy, getting wind of it, retreated before the relief force arrived.[1]

After inspecting the fortifications, Hopton continued on to Bristol, to take the dispositions of his new troops. The lists, by design or error of the officers, were faulty; he discovered that the total number of foot fell far short of the 2,000 he had expected, being closer to 1,500. The horse were closer to his expectations. Besides his own cavalry and dragoons, there were Hertford's and Sir Edward Stawell's regiments. Sir George Vaughan's were still in Wiltshire. Others were forming in Somerset and Dorset. Most, however, were small, and Hopton's estimate that they might come to 1,600[2] would seem optimistic.

The cadres had to be filled. On 10 October 1643 the King, by his own hand, granted new powers to his 'Man in the West': a commission directed to Hopton as 'Feild Marshall of the westerne Army', giving him authority 'to presse raise and levye' as many foot and horse within the counties of Devon, Dorset, Somerset, Wiltshire, and Hampshire as 'in his judgment and experience [he] shall thinke fitt as well for supply of fitting Garrisons in the said Countyes as for securing of the same and suppressing the present Rebellion'.[3] Cornwall, significantly, was exempt from impressment, doubtless the privilege of previous valour, bestowed after a realistic appraisal of its '*posse* mentality': the Cornish army, of course, was still a going concern, though its components were scattered. The commission was extended on 27 October to include Sussex, Surrey, and Kent, giving Hopton the title 'Field Marshal General'.[4]

---

[1] B.M., Add. MS. 18,980: 98 (122), dated at Sodbury, 3 Oct. 1643; Hopton, 62; Nalson III: 42 (82), Col. (Sir) Edward Massie (Massey) to the Earl of Essex, dated at Gloucester, 6 Oct. 1643.

[2] Hopton, 62.   [3] Black, *Docquets* . . . , 85.

[4] H.M.C., 15th Rept., App. Pt. II, pp. 94, 99: MSS. of John Eliot Hodgkin, Esq. Rough drafts of a commission to raise horse, foot, and dragoons and to command the 'Trayned Bands volontiers or others' of the same.

'Lord *Hopton*, Field Marshal General of the West and Southern Countries'—Sir Edward Walker, *Historical Discourses Upon Several Occasions* (London, 1705), 7.

Black's *Docquets* reveal that several 'field-marshal' commissions were issued from Oxford in 1643/4. Hopton's appears to have been the first. The title can be equated roughly with 'colonel-general' as denoting a regional command, embracing several counties, with the duties of recruiting, organizing, and training new troops as well as leading them in the field. Such a commission was directed on 19 December 1643 to John, Lord Byron, appointing him field marshal of forces in Worcester, Salop, Chester, and six Welsh counties—Black, 113–14.

'Strugling through all exigentes as well as he coud',[1] the tireless governor, in addition to his military duties, sat on the commission of Oyer and Terminer for Somerset and Bristol,[2] at the same time directing most of his energy towards solving the eternal problem of money. To find quarters for his command, since barracks were unheard of, meant foisting it on the country. The inequity of 'free quarter', however, had been mitigated by some attempt at system. Maurice's regiment was sent to Wells to be settled in convenient houses according to their quality at these rates: common soldiers at 2s. 6d. per person per week; ensigns and other inferior officers at 3s. 6d.; superior officers at 6s. Allowance was to be made out of the weekly contribution of the county.[3] Naturally there were grumblers. Henry Davey of Bridgwater complained: 'we are squeezed like wax in our weekly payments, still mounting'. He himself paid 15s. 6d. a week besides billeting 'five Troops' at free quarter.[4]

There was no alternative, however; not only was the success of the new eastward advance at stake, but Gloucester still posed a threat. The morning of 25 October Hopton received word from Colonel Thomas Veel at Berkeley Castle that Massey had descended again and that the surrounding country had come in to the rebels. Hopton sent some horse and cannon and a warrant for a fortnight's provisions, but protested in a letter to Rupert that the castle guard was as yet unpaid. Meanwhile, some of his own foot and almost all of his horse had already advanced toward Winchester, 'in great want'. It would be vastly more convenient, as he had declared before, if he and his treasurer, Captain George Walrond, had full control of the moneys assigned to them. As it was, he stood less in fear of defeat from Massey or Waller than from Mr. Edward Kirton,[5] who

[1] Hopton, 63. [2] Black, *Docquets* . . . , 81, 88.
[3] Acts of the Corporation of Wells, 249: letter to the corporation from Hopton, dated at Bristol, 8 Oct. 1643, signed 'your very loving friend'.
[4] Bristol City Library, pamphlet-letter, dated 27 Oct. 1643, p. 2.
[5] B.M., Add. MS. 18,980: 105 (131). Edward Kirton, Esq., of Castle Cary, Som. In the 1630's and early 1640's he is described as an 'officer to the Lord Marquesse Hertford'. M.P. for Milborne Port in the Long Parliament, he was disabled in Aug. 1642, after which he came to Oxford as a 'servant of the King's'.—*Som. Assize Orders*, Thomas G. Barnes, ed. (Frome, 1959), item 184, n. 4; Keeler, 242, n. 55; Clarendon, xiii. 96.

The official rank of field marshal was introduced into the British army from Germany by George II, who, on 12 Jan. 1736, bestowed it upon George, first Earl of Orkney, fifth son of the Duke of Hamilton. Two days later John, second Duke of Argyll, was granted the same honour. Both had served with distinction in Marlborough's campaigns.—*J.S. Army H.R.* xxxviii. 84.

must have been one of the King's servants responsible for collecting the subsidies.

A few figures will show Hopton's dilemma. From Oxford he had received £1,500; the Bristol contribution, at an estimate, brought him £600 a month. The cost of a musket and bandoleer was 24s.: to arm 2,000 infantry therefore would have cost £2,400, or £1,800 for the 1,500 infantry he had actually raised, if we may assume, for the sake of illustration, that they were all musketeers. A carbine cost more than a musket—32s.—but here was less of a rub, since dragoons themselves were lacking. A pair of pistols, with holsters and spanners, cost 56s., perhaps because of the leather, though it might be inferred that the cavalry, in many cases, would supply their own. Match was 40s. the hundredweight and powder £15 15s. the hundredweight.[1] It can be seen, then, that the main expenses lay with the foot. In comparison, the maintenance of two or three thousand Cornish pikemen had been a drop in the bucket.

To gather the reins of control more tightly into his own hands, Hopton on 30 October addressed a letter to the lords and gentlemen of Somerset, authorizing three or more of them to meet for the following purposes:

To examine weekly contributions: by whom received, to whom paid, and by what orders.

To inquire into the county's forces: how they were regulated and ordered, and how garrisons were fortified to assist levies of horse and foot. They were to provide arms and munitions; to prevent marauding, and to apprehend straggling soldiers, 'especially those that come from Ireland', for the speedy conveying of them to their colonels.

To give Hopton a particular account of the 'true Estate of the

[1] MS. Clarendon XXII: 1729 (sheet 137): articles of covenant and agreement made and concluded between Henry, Lord Percy; Henry, Lord Jermyn; Sir John Culpeper, Master of the Rolls; and John Ashburnham, Esq., with John Van Haesdonck, who agrees 'at his owne Adventure' to deliver at the haven or castle of Weymouth into the hands of the governor of the town or castle:

4,000 muskets and bandoleers	at 24s.	£4,800
1,200 pr. pistols, w/holsters & spanners	at 56s.	£3,360
600 carbines, w/belts	at 32s.	£960
20 tuns of match	at 40s. Cwt.	£800
400 barrels of powder	at £15. 15s. Cwt.	£2,300
	TOTAL	£12,220

To be paid for at time of delivery.

Van Haesdonck is permitted to sell to anyone not in open war or rebellion against the King. His losses will be borne by Percy, et al., on behalf of the King.

County' by maintaining constant intelligence with Sir Francis Hawley, lieutenant-governor of Bristol.

Five hundred pounds a week were to be added to the weekly contribution. Arrears were to be made up. But he assured them that allowance would be made for billeting and quartering. 'Plunderers' were to be court-martialled, the gentlemen of the county sitting as a tribunal. Hopton noted that most of them were colonels, adding that he never knew the King's business to proceed better than with the advice and assent of the 'gentlemen of worth' in the county. (This is the key to his own importance as 'King's Man in the West'.) The weekly contributions had been assigned to him for collection and disposal through Captain George Walrond, treasurer of the army and garrison.

He sent them copies of an order of the council of war at Oxford and one of his own authorizing Walrond to pay the garrisons so that they would know the numbers of horse and foot to be retained for the defence of the county. He commanded them to note the horse and foot remaining over and above those mentioned in the orders and to send them to Bristol with their officers; if they were colonels' companies not to oblige the colonels to come without commands fit for them. Those needed against the rebels of Gloucester would stay in Bristol; the rest would go to the army.[1]

It is a pity that Hopton did not have a lieutenant as able as Sir Francis Basset to take charge of finances and day-to-day business, leaving him free for command. As the army formed, it was clear that to co-ordinate the movements of this motley array would be no light task. The background and experience of its components were various in the extreme. In the south-east new cavalry were being raised by the provincial gentry and office-holders, neither grandees nor veterans of foreign wars, whose strength was their local influence and standing in the country running from Hampshire to Kent.[2] In the same region Sir Nicholas Crisp was commissioned to raise a

---

[1] S.R.O., Phelips MS. 75. In a P.S. Hopton says he has heard bad reports of 'Young Mr. Bisse of the Lodge' keeping company with 'riotous lewd fellows', trespassing on his neighbour's park and deer stealing. Since he respects this young man's forbears, he does not wish to proceed rigorously, but desires they send for Bisse and see he is 'better ordered' hereafter.

[2] Roy, 'The Royalist Army . . .', 122–3 (typescript). This force Dr. Roy calls the 'Sheriffs Army' since some of the colonels held this office: e.g., Sir Edward Ford of Sussex. One Robert James was nominated by Sir William Boteler, high sheriff of Kent, to serve as muster master in Kent, Surrey, and Sussex—Harl. 6852 f. 218: dispatch from the King to Hopton via Walker.

regiment of 1,500 foot.[1] The new levies, however, would be useless without stiffening from more seasoned units.

The dearth of experienced infantry made very welcome the arrival by the end of October of two Irish regiments commanded by Sir Charles Vavasour and Sir John Poulett: between four and five hundred foot, 'bold, hardy men, and excellently well officer'd, but the common-men verie mutenous and shrewly infected with the rebellious humour of England'.[2] It is conjectured that his next move was to forestall an outbreak from the ranks. He resolved to use them immediately in his design to surprise Wardour castle, north of Salisbury on the Shaftesbury road and commanded for Parliament by Edmund Ludlow. Fetching four iron guns for this purpose from Weymouth, pretending they were for use at Bristol, he had the Irish quartered about Bath, secretly advising their officers to lead them on another twenty or twenty-five miles in the direction of Warminster and Hindon, under the pretence of finding them more suitable quarters. This would put them in an excellent strategic position for falling upon Wardour, and from there upon Lyme Regis and Poole, the clearing of which would allow him to advance without fear of an enemy at his back.

Confident as he was that this plan would succeed, it was thwarted by a command from the King to move up and support Sir William Ogle, who had just taken the castle at Winchester. Resolved, then, to try the next best, he sent Vavasour's regiment with the four guns to join at Hindon with Captain Henry Bowyer and Lieutenant Francis Bowyer, brothers, who had been commanding two troops of dragoons as security against a possible sortie from Wardour. Hopton himself met with the chief gentlemen of Dorset at Blandford to compose their differences and inspect their forces, dividing among them the whole contribution of the county, £1,000 a week. He intended to leave Colonel Bernard Astley as major-general of the county, commanding Hertford's weak regiment of foot, along with a weaker unit under Colonel Conyer Griffin, to maintain a blockade against Lyme and Poole. Astley, however, fell sick; and to complicate matters further, Sir Anthony Ashley Cooper went secretly to Oxford and obtained orders forbidding the division of the contribution. 'And the rest of the Gentlemen, though intending very well to His Majesties service, yet proveing unsuccesful in their proceedings, the King's affaires impair'd apace in that County.'[3]

---

[1] Black, *Docquets* . . . , 99 (dated 4 Nov. 1643).   [2] Hopton, 62–63.   [3] Ibid. 63–64.

Sending before him Colonel Allen Apsley with 600 foot and Major Philip Day with dragoons, Hopton brought the rest of his force together at Amesbury, eight miles north of Salisbury. The horse, ordnance, and munitions arrived safe, but the only foot which showed up were 300 of his own regiment from Bristol. Notwithstanding, he resolved to advance with what he had and pressed on another fourteen miles to Andover. Here he was met by the Earl of Crawford and Colonel Charles Gerard, who informed him that Sir William Waller had come that night to Alresford, seven or eight miles east of Winchester. With him were five thousand foot and between two and three thousand horse, with a good train of artillery. In this exigency, 'there being little hope but the reputation that he had there, rather than in his strength',[1] Hopton gave orders to march an hour or two before dawn, with secret instructions to the artillery to send only two guns with him, the rest, with the foot, to turn back toward Amesbury, while Hopton himself with the horse went on to Winchester. This strategem served its purpose: Waller, thinking his enemy's force bigger than it was, retired to Basing House, eighteen miles north-east of Winchester, Hopton reaching the latter city on Monday 6 November.

His reputation had gone on ahead of him. That same day the Venetian secretary in London reported 'Viscount Obton' to be marching through Sussex toward Kent: 'If he succeeds it will be the veritable rod to draw the water of penitence from this hard stone of scandal.'[2] Such dispatches, though inaccurate, might give the impression of a Royalist effort to invade London through the 'back door'. The idea is valid as a reasonable hypothesis of inherent military probability, but there are no first-hand sources to prove that it was a subject of profound or prolonged study by the Royalist council of war.

At Winchester Hopton spent ten or twelve days consolidating and equipping his forces. From Donnington castle he received two additional pieces of ordnance,[3] from Oxford a load of arms and munitions.[4] Desiring to augment the few foot which had come on

---

[1] Ibid. 65.   [2] *C.S.P.V.* 1643–47, 36–37.

[3] Rawlinson, 395: f. 141, dated at 'Denington' 12 Nov. 1643. Casimirus Sturt, the Governor, informs Lord Percy he will obey his warrant, received that day, to supply Hopton, but that he needs two pieces more, being continually threatened by enemy scouts 'and having such ill neighbours as the factious town of Newbury'.

[4] 15 Nov. 1643: 'for carriage of a loade of Armes and Aññunicōn for Co: Gerard from Oxon to Hungerford & soe after ye Lord Hoptons Army being 35 myles at 6*d*. p myle

. . . . oo/o7/o6'

from Amesbury, he remembered the Irish troops near Wardour. Certain that only money would move them, he went back himself towards Hindon with £300 for that purpose. At Fonthill he met Sir Charles Vavasour and Lord Arundell of Wardour, who brought the unsurprising news that the Irish regiment at Hindon was in a high state of mutiny. Hopton at once arranged a rendezvous with Sir George Vaughan's horse and the Bowyer brothers' dragoons. Next morning they fell on the town, seized the principal mutineers and ordered the rest of the regiment to move out. 'And upon that terror, and the execution of two or three of the principale offendours he drew the Regiment quietly to Winchester.'[1] A new regiment of 300 foot, raised in Dorset on Hopton's commission by Colonel George Barnes, was left to maintain the Wardour blockade.

Returning to Winchester Hopton was cheered to meet on the way the Prince of Wales' regiment—200 horsemen commanded by Sir Thomas Byron.[2] The Irish infantry were increased by Sir John Poulett's regiment from Bristol, Hopton making Poulett major-general of his foot, which now numbered about 2,000. They were needed for instant service, the Marquis of Winchester, hard pressed by Waller at Basing House, having sent out an urgent request for relief. After sending reassurances and communicating with Oxford Hopton marched north to rendezvous at Kingsclere, nine miles north-west of Basingstoke, with Sir Jacob Astley, who had drawn '900 excellent foote' out of Reading. The horse regiments of Lord Percy and of Colonel John Belasyse, the latter under command of a Major Bovill, were also added to the array. This 'very hansome little army' now had nearly 3,000 foot and dragoons, some 2,000 horse, and a good train of artillery.

These movements were anticipated by Waller. Learning from his scouts that Hopton has passed within six miles of Basing and that Astley was drawing out of Reading, he decided to retreat, especially since the City regiments were threatening mutiny.[3] From 13 to 15

---

[1] Hopton, 65.   [2] J.S. Army H.R. xxiii, no. 95, p. 109.
[3] Cal. Portland MSS., H.M.C., 13th Rept., Pt. I, 155: Waller to Lenthall, dated at Farnham, 16 Nov. 1643; Hopton, 66.

The same Cartt lying still 3 dayes at 2s. 6d. p diem ye summe of
   . . . . 00/07/06'
—(March 1644) 'An account of Moneys disbursed for his Majesty's service by Captaine Henry Stevens Waggon-Master-Generall of his Majesty's Army', *The Papers of Captain Henry Stevens, Waggon-Master-General to King Charles I* (transcribed and edited by Margaret Toynbee, printed for the Oxfordshire Record Society 1961, issued for the year 1962), 23.

November he withdrew his forces some fifteen miles into Surrey, establishing his headquarters at Farnham. On the 14th a detachment of Hopton's men drove in the Roundhead pickets at Basingstoke and relieved the Marquis of Winchester at Basing House.

For the next two weeks the parties skirmished, Waller from Farnham, Hopton from Odiham, eight miles west of Farnham and a like distance east of Basingstoke. On 16 November Parliamentary horse and sixteen of every foot company were sent to beat up Hopton's headquarters, but the Royalists had pulled back temporarily toward Alresford, Hopton summoning all Hampshiremen between sixteen and sixty to appear for the King at Winchester in arms. On the 19th the Royalists reappeared upon a hill two miles from Farnham. The Parliamentarians drew out of town into the park and mounted their ordnance. About 3 p.m., after several hours of exchanges between the horse, the Parliamentary scouts rode out and killed several Royalists. At night a strong party of Parliament-men were sent against the foe, who fled, but held off pursuit by lining the hedges. Next day the action was repeated, the Royalists marching toward Farnham, its defenders charging to drive them back, taking eight prisoners. The Parliamentarians were reinforced by a Kentish regiment from Guildford and five companies of Sir Arthur Hazelrig's regiment of foot. Entrenchments were begun at Farnham; warrants were issued to summon all men of fighting age.[1]

There is little doubt that Hopton had shaken his enemy's confidence. Local report had it that 'Sir William Waller is quite routed' and predicted that 'the Lord Hopton will easily subdue Kent'.[2] 'The Lord was like to hopp betweene London and Waller which if hee had, hee made no question but to have routed his army.'[3] One calculation was that the Royalists would try for Surrey via Guildford, ten miles east of Farnham.[4] Parliamentary intelligence, however, was groping in the dark: the scouts were careful to qualify everything:

Henry Cunington returned this day and sayth that he came from Oxford and saith that the King and Queene are there and that there are very few forces there and (that they say that) Prince Robert is with a party neare Northampton and that the Lord Hopton is marched from Basing House

[1] T.T., E. 76 (24), *Mercurius Civicus* for Mon. 20 Nov. 1643; T.T., E. 78, *A True Relation of the whole Proceedings of Sir William Waller his Army; from the 20 day Nov. to the 9 of Decemb.* (internal dating uncertain); G. N. Godwin, *The Civil War in Hampshire* (Southampton and London, 1904), 124.

[2] Luke, *Journal*, 196 (Wed. 22 Nov. 1643).

[3] Ibid. 200 (Mon. 27 Nov. 1643).   [4] T.T., E. 78, above.

(and as they say) towards Kent and that there went out of Oxford one Saturday last 6 loade of amunition out at the south gate (and as they say it is gone) to Basing House.[1]

As Waller explained succinctly to Speaker Lenthall, his army's want of money and want of clothes had produced want of obedience and want of health.[2] His adversary, however, was scarcely in better plight. As usual, Royalist pay was in arrears, the Wiltshire contribution being set at £1,200 weekly[3] in an attempt to make it good. The men and horses were 'completely wearied out' and many officers absent. Hopton was driving them hard, commanding eight men and mounts out of every troop to report for duties at his own headquarters.[4] When Sir John Berkeley joined him at Odiham with additional horse and 1,000 foot, the field marshal general decided to try a general advance towards Farnham. His approach with an advance-guard of 300 horse and 1,000 musketeers was challenged in a 'warm skirmish for neere 2 howers'. Waller drew out his foot into the park under the tower of the castle, keeping his horse close by him, as there were only ten troops, the rest being quartered in out-villages. As the whole Royalist body pressed forward toward the park, they were met by musket-fire that drove them back to the heath, from which Waller's culverins shortly forced them to retreat, without great loss. Waller, in his report to Lenthall, lamented that his dragoons had not been supplemented by the extra horse for greater execution. He urged reinforcements or the enemy would overcome him. In a curious, broken phrase, he concluded: 'My oulde freind is so [vio]lant an enemy.'[5]

What followed, in Hopton's opinion, was the turning-point of his career. By a new stroke of strategy he decided to forward his designs by trying a different route into the territory south of the Thames. The pass at Midhurst, twenty-six miles east of Winchester and sixteen south of Farnham, was the vital launching point. Hopton sent orders to Lord Crawford, Astley, and Berkeley to dispatch dragoons to Midhurst for the taking of Cowdrey House next morning. Unfortunately he was anticipated: the enemy put men into Cowdrey House that night,

[1] Luke, *Journal*, 195 (Mon. 20 Nov. 1643).
[2] Nalson MSS., III: 93 (179).
[3] Black, *Docquets* . . . , 101 (dated 22 Nov. 1643).
[4] Rawlinson 395, f. 193: Lt.-Col. Holtby to Lord Percy, dated at 'Murrell, five mile from Farnham', 24 Nov. 1643.
[5] Hopton, 67–68; Nalson, III: 105 (203), dated at Farnham 28 Nov. 1643.

which fayler proved to be the beginning of the Lo: Hopton's misfortunes, for till thattime, it had pleased God to blesse him from the beginning of the warr with reasonable good successe, without any considerable disaster. But, by this fayler, he was prevented in the most important part of his designe, which was, by fortifying the passe at Midhurst, to have had that winter a fayer entrance through Sussex into Kent.[1]

It is tempting to consider the scheme of a thrust through the 'underbelly' of Sussex and Kent to cut the umbilical cord of the Thames and prevent supplies from flowing into the ravenous maw of London. This plan allegedly had been considered, as early as the previous June, as a possible joint operation for one army commanded by Hopton and Hertford.[2] The chance, however, it was becoming clear, had been lost. At the end of November the posts at Basing and Odiham were withdrawn. Early in December a council of war decided that the army should separate into four brigades and go into winter quarters. Despite the protest of a younger officer who thought such a division might be dangerous, Hopton retired to Winchester. Vavasour took his Irish seven or eight miles east to Alresford. The Earl of Crawford and Colonel Richard Bowles proceeded to Alton, ten miles north-east of Alresford and a like distance south-west of Farnham. Colonel Joseph Bampfield (who had marched with Hertford and Maurice to the west the summer before) went to Petersfield, ten miles south of Alton and the same distance west of Midhurst.[3] The whole front formed a triangle based on Winchester.

As a final ploy Hopton, after consultation with Berkeley, decided to bypass Midhurst and seize Arundel Castle, twenty miles south-east of Petersfield on the Sussex coast, a favourable position from which to launch a spring offensive. The move was successful: Sir Edward Ford, high sheriff of Sussex, was made governor of the castle; Colonel Bampfield was given command of the district.[4] But Arundel never became a strategic springboard: it remained an outpost—the farthest advance of the western Royalists. It was evident that their initiative was beginning to fail. At Winchester ominous signs appeared: the licence of the soldiery showed the danger of shared authority between Hopton and the civilian governor, Ogle. As John Trussell, City Clerk, complained, when officers

---

[1] Hopton, 68.

[2] Ibid., n. 2, citing *King's Pamphlet*, E. 105, No. 8.

[3] Col. Joseph Bampfield, *Colonel Joseph Bamfeild's Apologie* (The Hague?, 1685), 7–8. The younger officer was probably Bampfield himself.

[4] Hopton, 69.

'drincke, dice, and drabb', small wonder private soldiers do the same, or fall to plundering.[1] The one remedy was to put them to work building 'sconces': defensive works.

Indeed the King, however much he might appreciate his efforts, had little reason to be pleased with the accomplishments of his man from the west. To be sure, Hopton's strategy was hampered by the terrain. The region he was trying to cross was flat, open country composed of soft marl; the roads at this time were quagmires[2]—an exhausted cavalry would be swallowed up. As Hopton, reflecting the spirit of the Cavaliers at the end of 1643, explained to Rupert:

> The truth is, the duty of the service here were unsupportable, were it not in this cause, where there is so great a necessity either of prevailing through all difficulties, or of suffering them to prevail, which cannot be thought of in good English.[3]

This was one way of saying that he had been given inadequate means to accomplish an impossible task.

Upon receiving intelligence that Waller had recruited a fresh force from London and suspecting Alton to be his object, Hopton sent word to Crawford to send out scouts and, if they confirmed his suspicions, to withdraw at once and retire to Winchester. Waller however, marching all night with 5,000 horse and foot, including the Westminster regiment, eluded the scouts by keeping to the woods; and arrived before Alton at 9 a.m. on 13 December, coming within half a mile of the place without being detected. Crawford, in the town with 500 horse, drew out 300 of them toward Winchester; met by the enemy horse he retreated to the town and then, hotly pursued a good part of the way, fled south to Hopton. Meanwhile the foot, all musketeers, drew into their works near the church, deploying themselves in a half-moon in double trenches. After two hours, and a desperate attempt to hold off the inevitable with a smoke screen, the Royalists surrendered, yielding 900 prisoners, 200 horse, 1,000 arms, and, according to the Parliamentary newsletter, 'divers Irish men and women'.[4] A few days later Hopton wrote to Waller

---

[1] Winchester City Archives: Account of John Trussell, Clerk of Winchester (a Royalist), f. 99. These annals of Dec. 1643 et seq. are composed in rhyming couplets.

[2] S.P. 16/498/76: Mr. Brunelle, a friar, signing himself 'J.M.', to the reverend Capuchin Father Robert de Ventelet at Paris, dated (London?) 23 Dec. 1643; C.S.P.V. 1643–47, 51.

[3] B.M., Add. MS. 18,980: 134 (160), dated at Alresford 12 Dec. 1643.

[4] T.T., E. 78, above.

lamenting the loss of 'many a Hundred brave Men'[1] and declaring
Alton to be the 'first evident ill success I have had'.[2]

Rumours of a Royalist try at Kent still persisted,[3] but Sir Anthony
Ashley Cooper's appraisal to Sir Edward Hyde came closer to the
truth: the King's forces were too weak and ill-paid[4] to do more
than hold their own. The fall of Alton was a threat to Arundel.
Hopton assured Bampfield that, if Arundel were besieged, he would
march to his relief. He sent the King a dispatch requesting eight or
nine hundred foot from Oxford: the reply was 'a verie gratious
message from his Majestie full of goodnes, and favour to him; But
the desired supply came not'. With Waller appearing before Arundel
on 19 December, Hopton tried for infantry again: 'Instead thereof
the Lord Wilmot was sent unto him with a thousand of the King's
horse, which, although it was a gallant body, yet it was not proper
for that service.'[5] Bampfield, meantime, was making one mistake after
another. Instead of keeping only the troops he needed to defend the
castle and letting the others go to swell Hopton's relief, he took them
all into the castle with him. He also had been improvident in stocking
it with bread and malt, losing most of his supply with the town. He
was unfortunate, too, in having an ox fall into the best well, making it
unfit for drinking; the one well remaining was insufficient for so many.[6]

In short, 'someone had blundered', not only the unlucky ox. On
Sunday 31 December 1643 it was reported that the Royalists were
reduced to 'a small quant[it]y of wheate, beife and salt, and noe hay
or provander being constrayned to instead thereof to give them ivye
leaves which grew against the castle wall'.[7] The famished garrison
had overestimated the odds for survival, assuring Hopton that they
had enough wheat for two weeks, making him think that he could
spare the time to gather his foot.[8] On 4 January 1644 Waller's
battery assaulted Arundel. The Royalists parleyed, asking leave to
march out with arms, mounts, and baggage.[9] Sir William, however,

---

[1] *C.J.* iii. 345.

[2] William Curtis, *A Short History and Description of the Town of Alton* (Winchester and London, 1896), 49.

[3] S.P. 16/498/85: from one Harrison to an English gentleman named John Bradley at 'College de Turnay' (Paris?), dated at London? 28 Dec. 1643.

[4] *Cal. Clar. S.P.* (Ogle, Bliss, Macray, and Routledge, eds.), 4 vols. (Oxford: Clarendon Press, 1869 ff.), i. 245, No. 1734.

[5] Hopton, 72, 73.   [6] Ibid. 73.   [7] Luke, *Journal*, 227.

[8] Hopton, 73–74.

[9] T.T., E. 81 (12), *An Exact and True Relation of the taking of Arundel Castle* ... etc.

made sterner demands: besides the castle, he wanted delivery of all
colonels of horse and foot, all horses, arms, munitions, and military
provisions. He guaranteed that all commanders, officers, and gentlemen
would have fair quarter and civil usage; all soldiers would have quarter
for their lives. He demanded the person of Sir Edward Bishop for
security.[1]

The garrison was in no condition to dicker. Between 9 and 10 a.m.
on 6 January it surrendered. Only 200 of the original garrison of
900 marched out: some had been killed, a few had escaped, many
were dead of the 'bloody flux, and spotted fever'.[2] For the Parliament
troops the siege of Arundel had been only a little less grim: 'The
weather was cold, the nights long, and the season of the yeare
troubled us, who lay in the Field extreamly with high winds and
extraordinary showres of rain. . . .'[3]

Again it was the 'bitter season of the year'.

---

[1] *T.T.*, E. 81 (21), *Certain Propositions made by Sir William Waller at the Surrender
of Arundell Castle* . . . (London, 11 Jan. 1644), *passim*.
[2] Bampfield, 10.   [3] *T.T.*, E. 81 (12), above.

X

ARUNDEL TO ALDBOURNE:
Defeat at Cheriton

(January–May 1644)

As the rain turned to snow, Hopton lay at Winchester, immobile —no more, though, than his enemy at Arundel. His power was on the wane. The Prince of Wales's regiment of horse and Lord Wilmot's had drawn off, leaving him not more than 1,100 horse and 1,100 foot. At parting Wilmot 'very nobly' expressed his regrets: 'being commanded', he had no choice. Hopton, thanking him for his kindness and favour, urged him to let the King know the Winchester garrison's needs.[1]

Oxford's neglect, or interference, roused him shortly to protest. When Rupert, through Sir Lewis Dyve, demanded the sum of £50 12s. from certain hundreds in Wiltshire, Hopton's receiver in that county, a Mr. Paddon, retorted upon Dyve's messenger with 'some expressions' highly displeasing to the Prince. While apologizing for his man, Hopton pointed out that the Wiltshire moneys had been his most dependable source of income—in contrast, at any rate, with the scanty contributions from Somerset, Dorset, and Hampshire, whose remissness, he said, had been the 'first cause of my being in any danger of being out powered by the rebell in these parts'. Now that the old horse regiments had left him, and with a numerically superior enemy in front, he could ill afford to have all means of supply cut off behind him. With restrained bitterness he mentioned his agent's news that Colonel Charles Gerard's regiment was being sent to quarter in Wiltshire, 'which first hazarded these parts by the officers and afterwards the souldiers deserting the service'. His devotion to the royal interest, however, was unimpaired: 'Sir, I thank god I cann confidently say, I have not att all considered my self whither low or high prosperous or unprosperous, but the just interests of the King and this poore bleeding Kingdome.'[2]

---

[1] Hopton, 76.
[2] B.M., Add. MS. 18,981: 151 (7): Letter to Rupert, dated at Winchester 12 Jan. 1643/4.

155

There is no reason to believe the King ever doubted the truth of this vehement avowal. Nonetheless, the estimate of Hopton's capabilities had changed after his failure to challenge Waller decisively at Farnham and later to relieve Arundel. He had come to be regarded as 'a man of great honour, integrity, and piety, of great courage and industry, and an excellent officer in an army for any command but the supreme, to which he was not equal'.[1] The justice of this view will be considered in the conclusion to this treatise. If Hopton were out of favour, as the Venetian secretary Agostini alleged,[2] the letters from Charles were still full of 'comfort', though the orders were to withdraw to Marlborough, a pull-back of over thirty miles.

But now came 'a great season of frost and snow', increasing daily and continuing for nearly a month. During that time the ways to Winchester from Arundel were impassable. Hopton seized the chance to assert a measure of independence from the royal command, assuring the King that

for the present the weather had releived him, so as he lay in noe danger, for the Enemy could not attempt him, that it might be hoped, that the wether might last till his recrewts, for which he had already dispatcht his orders, might be ready to come to him, that if there were any counsaillable meanes to preserve that County [Hants.], so useful and so well affected to His Majestie it would very much import to his Majestie's service, that, if, by his quitting of these quarters, the Enemy should drawe downe to Winchester and possesse himselfe of that place, all the plaine of Wiltshire would lay open to him; He therefore humbly ofer'd it to his Majestie's consideration, whither His Majestie would be pleased to trust him with the time of his retreate; Which His Majestie most graciously did.[3]

The recruits continued to come in, to the number of 2,000 foot and 2,000 horse. Parliamentary intelligence still bruited the intent of the Royalists 'to march into Kent upon their old designe'.[4]

The command structure, however, was undergoing a significant change. Hertford's commission as lieutenant-general was given to Prince Maurice, with authority for the western counties and for Kent, Surrey, and Sussex.[5] The civilian grandee yielded to the rough young veteran. To Hampshire was sent the septuagenarian Patrick Ruthven, Earl of Forth, who had captained a regiment of Scots in Sweden in 1612 and had been knighted by Gustavus

[1] Clarendon, vii. 401, n. 3 (3).
[2] *C.S.P.V.* 1643–47, 51 (dated 18 Dec. 1643) and 74 (dated 19 Feb. 1643/4).
[3] Hopton, 77.   [4] Luke, *Journal*, 261 (dated 6 Mar. 1643/4).
[5] Black, *Docquets* . . . , 140 (dated 1 Feb. 1643/4).

Adolphus.[1] Hopton met him on 14 March at Newbury.[2] In the old soldier's train were 1,200 foot, 800 horse, and four cannons; even more gratifying was the earl's affability, which hardly allowed for the exigencies of his new command. His role with the King had somewhat resembled that of a modern chief of staff, and at first he may have seen himself principally as Hopton's senior adviser. Lord Hopton, however, was quite ready to give way before rank and a military record which, for sheer duration, was almost beyond rival. Under his deferential pressure, Forth was persuaded to take charge.[3] Officially the two commanders had 'full power', in conjunction with Wilmot[4] and Sir Jacob Astley,[5] to frustrate Waller's movements. But from February to May 1644 the divisions in the Royalist high command were such as badly to hamper the effective co-ordination of individual efforts. The supreme commanders—Charles at Oxford, Rupert at Shrewsbury, Maurice in the south and west—were too distant to touch the autonomy of regional chiefs; and within these area commands the lack of distinction between line and staff was detrimental to efficiency. Forth, the recent 'chief of staff', gouty and largely confined to his coach, was now commanding general; Hopton, a *de facto* commander-in-chief for the greater part of a year, had relegated himself to a staff position, accountable for most of the work, but without the spur and sanction of ultimate responsibility.

Waller's dilemma was different. He still commanded the forces of the Southern Association, but amendments to the ordinance for that Association, as he saw it, threatened to limit his actual power. His original commission from Lord Essex, nominal commander-in-chief of all the Parliamentary armies, had given him virtually a free hand, subject only to orders from the Houses or from Essex himself. The new amendments subordinated him to the superior officers of Essex, stripped from him the right of commanding the garrisons within the Association, and disabled him from creating his own general field officers. Vehemently protesting against these three measures, he did not dissent from the last change—that the Association forces might be diverted and divided at Essex's pleasure—because he, Waller, was confident that the Earl would never command any out of his own circle.[6]

[1] *D.N.B.* xvii. 511.   [2] Dugdale, 63.   [3] Hopton, 77–78.
[4] Sir Edward Walker, *Historical Discourses upon several occasions.* . . . (London, 1705), 8.   [5] Roy, *The Royalist Council* . . . , 162.
[6] Tanner MSS., LXII, 619: letter from Waller to Lenthall, dated 10 Mar. 1643/4 at Wickham.   [6] Ibid. 627, dated 13 Mar. 1643/4.

Waller's argument for flexibility points up a contrast between the Parliamentary and Royalist positions. The former party needed to delegate more authority to individual field commanders; the latter, on the other hand, needed greater co-ordination at the top. Waller's relationship to Essex, however, was not unlike Hopton's to Forth. Each was an instance of a regional field commander being too dependent on higher headquarters, a junior officer hamstrung by a lethargic superior.

Hopton was still obsessed with the idea of subduing the 'back country'. Towards the end of winter he had sent Sir Francis Doddington to besiege Wardour Castle, still holding out under Sir Edmund Ludlow. Ludlow's plea for moderate terms found little favour with his hard-grained antagonist: on 18 March the castle surrendered. The Parliamentary commander, in Doddington's custody, was conveyed to Winchester. On the way Sir Francis showed him a letter from Hopton desiring Ludlow's conversion to the Royalist party, using such arguments as the justice of their cause, the probability of their success, and the 'inconsiderableness' of Parliamentary strength in those parts. In Lord Ralph's quarters the prisoner was closely examined. How, Hopton asked, could he, a gentleman, be content to bear arms against his King? Ludlow replied that he was justified by the laws both of God and Man. Hopton replied, 'Well, I understand you are so fixed in your principles, that I am like to do little good upon you by my perswasions; but shall desire the archbishop of Armagh [James Ussher] to take the pains to speak with you, when you come to Oxford; and if he cannot work on you, I know not who can'.[1] The archbishop, it goes without saying, had no better luck: Ludlow ended his Civil War career as a regicide.

With Poole and Plymouth the only remaining Parliamentary bastions behind him, Hopton took heed, as spring advanced, that his enemy was preparing to do likewise. On 26 March 1644 word came that Waller, adding to his array 1,800 horse and dragoons under command of Sir William Balfour, had marched out of Sussex and come as far as West Meon, ten miles south-east of Winchester.

Forth and Hopton conferred; the earl, seized with gout, ordered

[1] *The Memoirs of Edmund Ludlow*, C. H. Firth, ed., 2 vols. (Oxford: Clarendon Press, 1894), i. 70, 81, 84. In a letter to the Speaker dated 3 Jan. 1652 (Tanner MSS., LIII, 192) Ludlow explains how Lord Arundell of Wardour (Henry, third Baron) procured a power from Hopton to give him his life if Doddington demanded it.—Ibid. 455–6.

Lord Ralph to draw out the whole force; the army marched at 3 p.m. to spend the night in the fields.

> My foes reunite, my frends refuse to staye
> And my auxilaries are drawne awaye.
> Those regiments that heer were quartered and
> Were under the Marshall generalls Commaund,
> Honord Lord Hopton, are drawne fourth to face
> Wallers great body which comes on apace.[1]

Forth, with difficulty controlling his pain, came up before dawn. The enemy, in the meantime, had encamped at Warneford in the direction of Alresford. Marching thither, the Royalists found the foe *in battalio* on a hill, which, judging from Stratton and Lansdown, would appear to have been the favoured Parliamentary position. After failing to lure them to more level ground, the Royalists switched from tactics to strategy. Hopton, knowing the lay of the land well, suspected that Waller would send Balfour to seize Alresford. Possession of this town would secure him a position within easy striking distance of Winchester, less than eight miles; at the same time, if forced to retreat, he would be close to the London road.

It was urgent, therefore, that the King's men get to Alresford first; and speed was the more necessary as the enemy already stood closer to the goal. Hopton sent off in the lead his own regiments of horse and dragoons, followed at half a mile by Sir Edward Stawell's brigade. As they approached Alresford, they could see on their right hand less than a mile away Balfour's men marching level with them in the next lane. Hopton, riding with Stawell behind his own troops, called to them to make haste, giving orders that, once they had entered the town, the dragoons should dismount and erect barricades, while the cavalry should concentrate themselves in the market place to back them up.

The forlorn hope reached Alresford in time; Stawell's hundred horse came after them; Forth followed more slowly, taking up quarters in the town. The enemy, checked, retired less than three miles south to the village of Cheriton. The main Royalist army bivouacked just north of Tichbourne Down, half-way between Alresford and Cheriton, facing toward the foe.

---

[1] Winchester City Archives: Account of John Trussell, f. 99. For this citation and many of the following I am grateful to Mr. Richard Sawyer, surveyor, of Winchester, who has devoted twenty years of study to the battle of Cheriton.

Tichbourne Down is the narrow, western end of a ridge which widens to the east. This ridge looks south on an open vale, rising above it to a height of about one hundred feet. The valley is nearly a mile across. A lower ridge flanks it on its south side. The two ridges curve in a horseshoe, forming one mass of high ground at Cheriton Wood. The antagonists, reconnoitring and skirmishing on 28 March, found the site ideal for a battle: the northern and southern slopes, with the wood at their eastern extremities as a bridge or

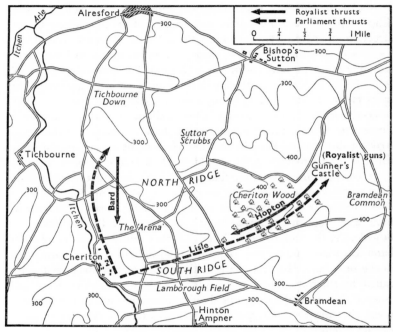

Map 5. Battle of Cheriton
29 March 1644

saddle between them, formed a kind of grandstand enclosing on three sides the field of combat.

The Royalist scouts, threading the lanes and dense woods on the south ridge, found their enemy just beyond it encamped in Lamborough field, surrounded by a ditch and thick hedges, their ordnance planted on a further hill behind them. Surveying their advantage, Forth and Hopton that night sent a party of 1,000 musketeers and

500 horse under Colonel George Lisle to hold the south ridge. The main army deployed behind the north ridge, Hopton, at their head, sleeping in his coach, while Forth and the other general officers retired to lodgings in town.

Thus the scene was set for the last round of the contest which since the previous autumn had run on so sporadically, with few and temporary gains for either side. Lisle's forlorn hope lay so close that the sentinels could hear one another talk. Hear, but not see: at some time between the dark and the dawn, which was obscured by thick mists, Waller sent four files of musketeers from the London brigade of foot, led by a Captain Thompson, to take Cheriton Wood,[1] which they accomplished before the sun appeared to disclose them. This manoeuvre was an opening wedge for supplementary tactics: working from cover the Parliament-men either could turn the Royalist flank and sweep the north ridge; or, by close, concealed fire prevent the main body from advancing in a straight line across the open 'arena'. Lisle, deceived by the sound of their wagons, told Hopton, who told Forth, that he thought the roundheads were withdrawing. They had, in fact, the preceding afternoon, considered a retreat;[2] but the successful seizure of the woods drove such thoughts from their minds. Thompson's forlorn hope was augmented by 1,000 musketeers.

The Royalists, however, that misty morning of 29 March 1644, had some basis for optimism. True, their array of 6,000 fell several thousand short of the enemy's and included ill-assorted and incompatible units: Irish and French troops; a small contingent of Cornish;[3] recent levies of ill-trained and badly armed Hampshire foot. Still, there were strong grounds for confidence in their commanders. With Forth had come other experienced senior officers, including Lord John Stuart, brother to the Duke of Lennox and Richmond and a distant cousin of the King; and a French veteran, M. de Pluvie, commanding the Queen's regiment of horse. Lord John Stuart served as lieutenant-general of the horse; John Paulet, Marquis of Winchester, as major-general of the foot. Under Stuart were two major-generals of horse: on the left wing (towards Cheriton Wood), Sir Edward Stawell; on the right, Sir John Smith, whom Hopton

---

[1] B.M., *T.T.*, E. 40.1 and E. 40.9: 'Winchester Taken together with a fuller relation of the Great Victory at Al[re]sford', by 'A.A.' (London, 1644). An eyewitness report. Copy in Winchester City Library.

[2] Burne, 185–6.

[3] At an estimate, no bigger than a brigade of two regiments, 1,000 to 1,500 men.

called a 'jewel'. At breakfast Smith bade his men 'feed heartily, for they should have Princely sport anon'.[1]

The 'sport' began at 8 a.m. when Hopton on reconnaissance visited the south ridge. Though the sun had been up two hours, the mists were just beginning to clear. As they broke up Lord Ralph could see that the wood to his left bristled with men and cannon. The Royalists in that quarter were almost, though not quite, out-flanked.

Lisle's advance-guard withdrew to the north ridge. Hopton, after a hurried conference with Forth, drew up a body of horse and musketeers; by 9 a.m. he was ready to drive the enemy from their post of vantage:

And placing the foote and horse that the E. of Brainford[2] [Forth] brought with him on the right whing, himselfe with his owne foote and horse drew to the left, which was over against that woody ground that the Enemy had newly possest, and where they understood themselves (as indeede they were) upon a great advantage under the covert of the wood, and having lin'd the hedges next to us with store of muskettiers. This the Lord Hopton observing tooke his advantage likewise of the ground he was on, and drew all his horse and foote in order on the side of the hill that was from the Enemy, and being there within muskett shott, and yet secured commanded [Lieutenant] Coll. Appleyeard (now Sir Mathew Appleyeard) to draw out of the foote a com-manded pa[r]ty of 1000 muskettiers, which he did, and devided them into 4 divisions, and in that order (as he was commanded) advanced towards the Enemy; But the bodyes of our men no sooner appear'd on the topp of the Hill, but the Enemy shewed how well they were prepared for us, and gave fier very thicke and sharpe, which our men very gallantly received and return'd; But the Lord Hopton foreseeing that our party could not long hold out upon so great disadvantage, and observing an opportunity to cast men into the wood upon the flanke of the Enemy, he drew of Lieutenant Coll: Edward Hopton[3] with one division of the commanded muskettiers, and commanded them to run with all possible speede into the wood upon the Enemyes flancke, where there was likewise a crosse-hedge to cover them, which they had noe sooner done, and given one volley from thence but the Enemy fell in disorder; and began to runne, and Coll. Appleyeard with his party pursued them, and had

---

[1] B.M., *T.T.*, E. 53.10: Edward Walsingham, *Britannicus Virtutis Imago* (London, June 1644). A somewhat flowery, but vivid and moving account. Smith's remark is given in the reference as a direct quotation.

[2] Ruthven was not created Earl of Brentford until May 1644.—Clarendon, viii. 28.

[3] Of Hereford. He served with Sir Allen Apsley's regiment of foot, the 'Red-coats'. So far as I can ascertain he and Ralph, Lord Hopton were unrelated: at least there is no apparent connexion for eight generations before the latter's birth.

the execution of a part of them through the wood, and tooke a horse and Colours and some prisoners, but none of theire cannon, for they being light gunns were drawen off.[1]

The Royalists took the wood as the Parliamentarians moved up on the south ridge. Now began the climax of this fluctuating battle. Hopton sent to Forth telling him of his success and that, if he were so pleased, he would with 1,000 horse and 1,000 musketeers sweep down the enemy left flank and drive them from the ridge. The earl, however, opted for immobility: holding, as he thought, the advantage of ground, he was convinced that the enemy either would have to charge a formidable position, which, at best, they could hope to take only with great loss, or else retire from the field. While this almost mathematical weighing of facts and probable outcomes is an attribute of one kind of successful generalship, it often allows too little for possibilities and alternatives beyond the facts; it cannot always cope with the unexpected. In the light of what was soon to happen, however, there is no reason to suppose that Hopton's more aggressive tactics would have proved more successful. Around noon a junior officer on the Royalist right wing, later named as Sir Henry Bard,[2] had an impulse which entered into his commander's plan and destroyed its shape.

Hopton settled his guards on the left wing and walked back to confer with the lord general, well satisfied with his 'solid advice'. Approaching the middle of the north ridge he saw that the right wing had advanced too far and was fiercely engaged with the enemy. As he came up Forth, greatly troubled, told him that certain officers had charged without orders. He sent Hopton as his adjutant to order 1,000 horse forward to charge the enemy in the common below. Hopton chose Stawell's brigade, which charged bravely for half an hour, only to be scattered and driven back. Sir Edward himself was wounded five times in fighting his way to the enemy cannon, where he was taken prisoner. As the hours passed the Royalist attack was stepped up. Regiment after regiment went down into the arena, to be met and repulsed by the Kentish horse. The toll of officers was high. Lord John Stuart and Sir John Smith were both mortally wounded. Hopton, holding together 300 horse at the entrance to the common, was supported mainly by the Queen's regiment under the doughty French commander M. de Pluvie. Hopton's horse was

---

[1] Hopton, 81–82.   [2] Hopton, 101: Col. Slingsby's account.

hit in the shoulder by musket-shot; Pluvie had his leg torn off to the ankle by a cannon ball, and soon after died.

But already the decisive moment had gone. By descending into the arena the Royalists had gradually exposed their right wing. About 2 p.m. three or four hundred Parliamentary musketeers marched around the mangled cavalry, advancing towards the west end of the north ridge. For three hours they poured their volleys on the hedges. By the time the attack was well launched the main body of the Royalists, saving nine of their eleven cannon, had begun a slow retreat. A rearguard of horse and dragoons gave the foot time to reach a low ridge that is today half a mile south of Alresford railway station. Here they deployed for the last time, shouting as their cavalry came up, 'Face them, face them, once more face them!'[1] Face them they did; the attackers held off; respite was granted for the next move.

It was close to evening; the field cries—the Royalist 'God and the Cause!' and the Parliamentary 'Jesus Blesse us!'[2]—had subsided. Hopton, knowing the country well and the weakness of the Winchester garrison, advised Forth to make for Basing House. Always a master of orderly retreat, he suggested that the ordnance move off in the direction of Winchester as a bluff, but after marching a mile make a right turn and move north. The foot, with a hundred horse as a rearguard, should avoid the high road and march through the lanes and woods. At the same time the horse could escape over the downs. All was carried out according to plan. One contingent made for Winchester Castle with the train of wounded. When the artillery had left, Forth sent off the horse, placing 1,000 musketeers in the town to cover his own getaway, 'remayning himselfe with his page last upon the ground'. The enemy horse followed after him in hot, though futile, pursuit. Hopton took charge of the foot, withdrawing the musketeers at the very last, and reaching Basing House about 1 a.m. without hazard. After a day's rest, with the prospect of soon meeting the King, he set out again toward Reading.[3] Meanwhile, the Lady Hopton, who had been with her lord at Winchester, escaped from thence with her plate and jewels in two coaches, each drawn by six horses. Intercepted by Balfour, she was treated by him

---

[1] *T.T.*, E. 40.1 and E. 40.9: Eyewitness report of 'E.A.', above.

[2] B.M., *T.T.* E. 40.12: letter from Captain John Jones, dated at Alresford 29 Mar. 1644 (London, 1644). The earliest report of the battle, with list of commanders slain and taken prisoner.

[3] Hopton, 83–84. At this point Hopton's personal narrative, *Bellum Civile*, ends.

and by Waller with all courtesy and given an escort to Oxford.[1] It was a chivalrous war.

Apart from the deaths of some notable leaders, the number of Royalist casualties at Cheriton, thanks to the cohesion of their withdrawal and the spirit of their last rally, had not been large. In the aftermath the main sufferers appear to have been the civil populace and the wounded left behind. John Trussell, poet-clerk of Winchester, after the city surrendered to Waller, complained that poor market people were being robbed of their carts and horses and forced to redeem them in money. As a result fewer provisions were being brought in, and prices were going up. As for the invalid soldiers:

> The wounded dressing want, surgeons wherewithall
> Playsters to make; the sick and weake doe call
> for Comfort, but nor food nor physicks found
> to fill the stomacks or clense the wound. . . .[2]

The army itself, through good management and Parliamentary slackness, had been preserved: Waller, like Charles at First Newbury, had failed to follow up his initial advantage.

Nevertheless, Cheriton[3] was a strategic as well as a field victory for Parliament. The attempt to invade Sussex and Kent had failed; and this failure, as the sequel proved, was irrevocable. Rupert's triumph at Newark on 21 March was a fillip to Royalist hopes, but the tide was slowly starting to turn. What the stars revealed may be of little concern to an historian, but it is interesting to note that on 30 March 1644 an amateur astrologer, William Lily, was conning his practice book for a figure on the 'success betweene Sir W. Waller and [Lord] Hopton beeing then supposed to be in fight'.[4]

Four scouts were paid £10 each for bringing news of the 'routing' of Hopton's forces to Westminster.[5] The Lords and Commons ordered a public thanksgiving for Waller's victory. Next day, 2 April, Sir Arthur Hazelrig gave a full relation of the battle in which he himself had been a pivot: the commander who had swung his own cavalry around Sir Henry Bard's after that rash young officer's

---

[1] Rushworth, vi. 655.
[2] Account of John Trussell, f. 99, above.
[3] This fight is variously called the battle of Cheriton, the battle of Alresford, and the battle of Bramdean Heath.
[4] Bodleian Library: Ashmole MSS. 184: 1. This astrological practice book covers the period 30 March 1644 to 4 June 1645.
[5] *Cal. C.A.M.* 1492: warrants for payment of money, 2 April 1644.

impetuous charge, cutting him off from the main Royalist body.[1]
Tuesday 9 April was the day of thanksgiving 'for the great victory
obtained by the forces under Sir Wm. Waller and Sir Wm. Balfour
over the army of Sir Ralph Hopton', with a collection taken up for
the sick and maimed soldiers who 'will be ready again to venture
their lives for the defence of all our lives, liberties and religion'.[2]

The paradox of Cheriton is that, though the bulk of the Royalist
army was Hopton's, he himself served in a subordinate and junior
capacity during the battle, often detached from any position where
he could have general oversight of the field. Though many of the
senior commanders were able men, Forth, the commander-in-chief,
courageous and experienced as he was, had advanced so far in years
as to lack the requisite quickness and resilience required in a military
tactician. He was also, according to Clarendon, both deaf and
bibulous,[3] although there are no grounds for assuming that he drank
deep before the fight. On the day of the battle he was advised and
cautioned in the following dispatch from Oxford:

You will henceforth receive an order from his Majesty to the commanders
for all the forces with your Excellency to obey Lord Hopton's orders in your
absence, his Majesty being much troubled that your indisposition will not
permit you to be abroad with the army.[4]

The council of war apparently realized that Forth's gout and deafness
might incapacitate him. At the same time it had faith in Hopton's
competence. Clarendon's estimate that the latter had 'a good understanding, a clear courage, an industry not to be tried, and a generosity
that was not to be exhausted (a virtue that none of the rest had)' is
unequivocal. Even though qualified by the observation that he took
too long to make up his mind, 'which rendered him rather fit for the
second than for the supreme command in an army',[5] this stricture
applies specifically to debates in council. Although he was content
to accept Forth's plan for holding their position, Hopton was resolute
enough in wanting to sweep the south ridge from Cheriton Wood

---

[1] *C.J.* iii. 444 (1 & 2 April 1644). Hazelrig's colleague Denzil Holles, however,
later accused him of cowardice at Cheriton, asserting that Hazelrig bellowed, 'Ah,
woe is me, all is lost! we are all undone!'; so that a Scots officer wished him to leave
the field and not stand 'gudding' (crying) to dishearten the troops.—'Memorial of
Denzil, Lord Holles . . . in Normandy, 1648', printed in Baron Masere's *Select
Tracts relating to the Civil Wars in England in the Reign of Charles I* (London, 1815),
i. 206.

[2] S.P. 16/501/64.   [3] Clarendon, viii. 29.
[4] S.P. 16/501/53.   [5] Clarendon, viii. 31.

before the earl held him back. In the field on his own he was seldom lacking in decision and initiative. If he had a flaw, it lay in an exaggerated respect for nominal superiors. Even his limitations, though, might be construed as excesses of virtue. His failure to move decisively had stemmed in part from a consciousness that the new infantry were under strength and too undisciplined for the task. His Parliamentary opponents were convinced that he could not make up his foot 'most part of this summer'.[1] How he must have yearned for the equivalent of five stout regiments of Cornish pikes and musketeers!

The chance and challenge of independent command was now at an end. At Cheriton his force had been integrated with the main field army and so was to continue till the war's end. When the King's army mustered on 10 April 1644 at Aldbourne Chase in Berkshire, Hopton appeared as colonel of the first regiment in Sir Edward Stawell's brigade of horse. He brought also a regiment of foot, the Blue Coats, with five colours.[2] Twelve days later he was ordered, as field marshal general, to draw the local pressed men out of Winchester Castle and replace them with men from remoter parts.[3] On 29 April he met the King and Rupert at Wallingford; the prince promised to settle £500 on the garrison at Bristol.[4] To that city on 26 May he was sent, as 'Field Marshal General of the West' with 200 horse for convoy, to strengthen the fortifications and 'to give life' to a new western association. He was back where he had started. Charles at Oxford waited for Essex to show his hand. The winter campaign had come to naught. That spring Royalist strategy looked to the defensive. Now the western counties had to be saved from all-out invasion.[5]

---

[1] *T.T.*, E. 40.13: Sir Wm. Balfour's letter of 30 March (London, 1644).

[2] Harl. MS. 986 ('The Diary of Richard Symonds'), pp. 83–90; Peter Young, 'King Charles I's Army of 1643–1645', *J.S. Army H.R.* xviii (pp. 27–37), 33.

[3] Harl. 6802, f. 122.

[4] Dugdale, 65–66; B.M., Add. MS. 18,981: 277 (167), dated at Oxford, 6 May 1644.

[5] Walker, 16; Dugdale, 68; Bayley, 192; Seyer, 426–7.

XI

THE LAST COMMAND:
Debacle at Torrington and return to Truro

(May 1644–March 1646)

AFTER the Aldbourne muster Hopton's star begins slowly to
fade. From the late spring of 1644 to the end of the first
Civil War two years later the record is too sparse for more
than a highly impressionistic account of his fortunes, which, along
with those of the Royalist cause itself, were generally in decline. In
the north the incursion of the Scots threatened to arrest the progress
of the Marquis of Newcastle: on 2 July 1644 his army was shattered
at Marston Moor in Yorkshire and the counties beyond Trent were
lost to the King. Oxford, Wales, and the west were preserved for the
time by the enemy's failure to take concerted action. The performance
of Cromwell's cavalry at Marston, however, presaged a new impetus,
which the following year was to become predominant.

Waller's taking of Winchester had opened up the whole plain of
Wiltshire to enemy encroachment. Early that summer Hopton's
former prisoner Edmund Ludlow, having been exchanged after
several months of detention at Oxford, towards the end of June
assumed new office as Parliamentary sheriff of Wiltshire. With him
were members of the Somerset committee, including the Popham
brothers, Alexander and Edward, and William Strode. From Devizes
they kept close watch on Royalist activity in the neighbouring county.
Ludlow marched as far as Hopton's seat at Witham, seizing one
hundred of Lord Ralph's cattle to pay his soldiers. The Royalist
guard was given liberty to go home in return for giving up its arms,
and an outpost was established at Woodhouse near Hornesham in
Wiltshire, towards Frome—the property of Henry, third Baron
Arundell of Wardour. Between 6 and 7 July the main body of
Ludlow's force advanced from Devizes to Warminster, close to the
county line. Meantime, Hopton had sent his adjutant Sir Francis
Doddington from Bristol to quarter about Woodhouse with troops
of horse and dragoons, following himself with 1,000 horse upon
receiving word of an increase in Parliamentary strength. On 8 July

the scouts of both parties met and fought. Hopton charged and scattered the roundheads, but, being tired from his night march, could not pursue them. Doddington, though, chased them sixteen miles to Salisbury and another six beyond, slaying about 100 and taking as many more prisoners, along with 100 pairs of pistols and about 40 muskets. Less than 40 out of the original 300 escaped to Southampton.

Doddington then turned again to Woodhouse. His plan to reduce it was not realized until the King came to Somerset a week later. Charles marched from Lansdown to Bath on Monday 15 July, being met by Hopton and Sir Thomas Bridges, the governor and sheriff of Somerset. They continued to Mells, the house of Sir John Horner, a leading Parliament-man. In this march two soldiers were hanged for plundering. Though Hopton must have approved such sternness as no more than just in view of the provocation, two days later he displayed again the moderation and magnanimity which had won the trust and praise of James Chudleigh. Doddington, with a party of foot and two cannon given him by the King, who had reached Wells, approached Woodhouse on 17 July, made a breach, and took it by assault, killing twenty and taking eighty prisoners. Using them as rebels, he sentenced a dozen or so, most of them clothiers, to be hanged. After these executions had been carried out, he 'could hardly be induced to spare the rest': they were saved by Hopton's timely intervention, ordering such butcheries to cease.[1]

His name still carried weight: rumours of his activity and impending presence kept Parliament on the defensive in all directions. From Henley in Oxfordshire on 16 July Major-General Richard Browne, in an apprehensive postscript, passed on to the Committee of Both Kingdoms the false news that Hopton, then allegedly quartered at Almonsbury in Gloucestershire, was planning to visit Basing or Reading: 'I would we were more able to resist him.' At the same time Colonel Edward Massey complained that his own moves towards the garrison at Windsor were frustrated because 'the Lord Hopton's forces have long lain most upon that passage'. Next day the Committee informed Sir William Waller of a Parliamentary attempt to take Wareham in Dorset, prevented 'by a body of 800 horse of Sir Ralph Hopton's',[2] whose active sphere at that time comprehended no more

---

[1] *D.N.B.* (1908), xii. 256; Ludlow, i. 92, 95–98, 459–60; Richards Symonds, *Diary of the Marches of the Royal Army During the Great Civil War*, C. E. Long, ed. (Camden Society, No. 74: 1859), 31–32; Waller, 39–40.

[2] *C.S.P.D.* 1644, 353–4, 354, 358.

than the distance between Bristol and the King's itinerary through Somerset. It would appear that, in the minds of the Parliament-men, almost any Royalist move in the west was likely to be instigated by Hopton, or at least a Hoptonian.

The King acknowledged the merit of his man. Upon the occasion of Hopton's ordering a number of ships to assemble at Falmouth— likely to ensure the safe embarkation of Queen Henriette Marie on 14 July for France—Charles expressed his gratitude for 'your remarkable affection and care in all that hath concerned us in these times of distraction'.[1] Such fidelity may have been the more appreciated since the royal progress seemed in no wise to prosper. True, when Charles asked the corporation of Wells for £500, the people, unable to provide so large a sum, at least showed their good will by sending £100 and 200 pairs of shoes.[2] When he attempted musters, however, the results were disappointing. To Kingsmore on 23 July the country people had been summoned to meet as a *posse*. Yet 'when they came to the point whether they would goe in person to serve his Majestie, few stood to it'.[3] Three days later the trained bands of Devon were summoned to meet at Exeter, but only a small number showed up.[4]

In the meantime, Essex, moving west from Weymouth with more than his usual speed, cut across the King's line of march and advanced by way of Tiverton to Tavistock, prompted by a desire to get between the Royalist army and the western ports. Encouraged by the renewed allegiance of Barnstaple, by his party's reduction of Taunton Castle, and by the importunities of Lord Robartes of Lanhydrock, he allowed the prospect of profitable mines and shipping to overcome his better judgement, and on 26 July, knowing nothing of the land and people he was invading, fumbled his way into Cornwall.

Once more the Royalist danger—and hope—lay beyond Tamar. From thence—motivated by bribes and native bile, by flattery and fidelity—marched 1,500 Cornish to join the King. Secretary at War Sir Edward Walker shrewdly appraised the reason for their loyalty: it was not due to 'a greater Measure of Judgment, or to more Humanity than others have, but unto that Obedience to their Superiours which the rest have cast off'.[5] Essex pressed on to Bodmin and Lostwithiel, sending a detachment south to take the little port of

---

[1] Coate, 137; Basset MS. 35, dated 20 July 1644.
[2] Corporation of Wells: Convocation Books, VII, f. 259 (18 Jul. 1644). Includes copy of a letter from Hopton urging support for the King.
[3] Symonds, 36.   [4] Ibid. 39.   [5] Walker, 50.

Fowey. It was as though time had come round: on 2 August Hopton arrived with Charles and Maurice at his old rendezvous, Launceston. Advancing to Liskeard and on to Braddock Down the main army waited while Sir Richard Grenvile—an excellent soldier, though lacking the exalted spirit and moral fibre of his brother Bevill— moved in upon Bodmin from the west. On 9 August a letter signed by seventy-eight of the King's chief officers was sent to Essex with overtures of peace,[1] virtually the last chance to end the war by means other than a field victory. The earl, on the grounds that Parliament have given him no power, refused to treat. Hopton, no 'bitter-ender', as his signature showed, moved out with 1,000 horse and 2,000 foot to meet Grenvile,[2] who on 11 August captured Bodmin. Essex, covered from the north-west, north, and east by four Royalist armies, was trapped in the narrow seven-mile-long river defile between Lostwithiel and Fowey, his escape blocked on either side by cliffs 400 feet high, his only outlet the sea.

This was the crest of the Royalist wave. Their line of battle lowered on the hills above Lostwithiel, its potential impact strengthened by changes in command and staff. Lord Wilmot, on the suspicion that he was intriguing with Essex to promote an easy peace, was removed as general of the horse and replaced by Lord Goring. On 14 August Hopton succeeded Lord Percy as general of the ordnance.[3] The noose tightened as 2,000 horse and 1,000 foot moved westward behind the enemy to 'stopp their landing of provisions by sea, and to hinder their foraging westward by land'. The King's supply line was unbroken. From Pendennis came 100 barrels of powder; and, the Parliament-men's cannonade doing little damage, the Royalists were able to use the expended lead.[4] By 27 August Essex reported that he had been forced to yield Lostwithiel.[5]

---

[1] Ibid. 59–61. [2] Ibid. 62; Symonds, 53.

[3] Symonds, 54; Stevens, 65; Walker, 65. The official commission, dated 20 Aug. 1644, appoints Hopton 'Generall of the Ordinance and Artillery of his Majestie's Army now under the command of the Earle of [Forth, and] Branford [Brentford] Lieutenant general of the same. . . .'—Black, *Docquets . . .*, 238. On 2 Dec. 1644 Hopton was invested as general of the ordnance and artillery of the King's armies throughout England and Wales under Prince Charles as first captain general and Prince Rupert as lieutenant general.—Black, *Docquets*, 240–1. Rough drafts may be found among the MSS. of John Eliot Hodgkin, Esq.—see H.M.C., 15th Rept., App., Pt. II, 95, 106. These commissions were confirmed by a warrant to Hopton from the Prince of Wales on 26 May 1645—*Cal. Clar. S.P.* i. 266, No. 1887. It is likely that this office was largely honorific. Dr. Ian Roy has found no more than half a dozen of Hopton's signatures among the Ordnance MSS.

[4] Symonds, 58. [5] *C.S.P.D.* 1644, 456.

N

He had not, however, yielded his army. His only chance of salvation lay in a breakthrough: the horse over land to Saltash; the foot, by boat from Fowey to Plymouth. Success depended partly on the weather: though the mornings and evenings of late had been very misty, the nights were starlit.[1] At last the chance came. The night of 30–31 August was dark and foggy enough to reassure the most prudent commander, of whom Essex surely was one. Even so, the Royalists have been warned: they had only to block the narrow passage between the main army and Maurice's troops to effect the capture or annihilation of the enemy horse. That this did not happen was due largely to the unresponsiveness of the new general of horse. George, Lord Goring, whose conduct then and subsequently reminds one of a likeable small boy, refused to take the intelligence seriously, continuing his jovial dissipations until it was too late.[2] Thus Sir William Balfour's cavalry managed to break through the bottleneck, with scarcely any trouble or loss.

The Parliamentary foot fared less well. Leaving them in the lurch Essex with some superior officers on 1 September escaped by boat to Plymouth. Deserted, and hemmed in by the sea on three sides, Major-General Philip Skippon sent propositions for a treaty. The King was clement, demanding only the heavy weapons. After yielding 6,000 muskets and pikes, with some forty cannon and a mortar, retaining only small arms, swords and one carriage to a regiment,[2] the surrendered troops were allowed to march away, defeated less by the Royalists than by the stubborn soil of Cornwall.

That same day the new general of the ordnance, writing to the mayor and burgesses of Wells from the army 'within a myle and half of Fowey', was advising them to choose as their new recorder the brother of Sir Francis: Mr. Christopher Doddington, 'whose integrity and abilityes to serve you and the publique are well knowne'. Besides this, Doddington's friends and connexions would conduce to the good of the town. In addition, by this choice they would 'shew your good respecte to one who desireth but to continue your assured loveinge freind'.[3] Fearing this letter might miscarry, he wrote again on 5 September from Okehampton.[4] Later Prince Rupert from Bristol wrote to Wells recommending Mr. John Bourne for the recorder's post.[5] Hopton's nominee, however, carried the day,

---

[1] Symonds, 57.   [2] Ibid. 66; Clarendon, viii. 118.
[3] Acts of the Corporation of Wells, 266.   [4] Ibid., dorse.
[5] Ibid. 267, dorse.

receiving nine votes, including those of the mayor and mayor-elect, while Rupert's candidate received only four and a third contender, Mr. Bull, but three.[1]

For Lord Hopton it was business, and politics, as usual.

———

So it continued for several seasons more. The campaign of 1644, a year of equipoise, ended on 27 October with the second battle of Newbury, in which the Royalists, outnumbered two to one, managed to extricate themselves from a Parliamentary trap by hard fighting and taking advantage of the enemy's badly-timed offensive. Hopton's record is an almost total blank. In addition to his nominal post as general of the ordnance, he also commanded a reserve of horse,[2] but did nothing, or had no opportunity, to win distinction.

In the opposite ranks his able adversary Waller, circling the King's camp by night, had again shown his skill as a shifter of ground. Among his own familiars, however, tokens of former prowess were few. The Cornish troops, reduced under Maurice to three thin brigades, had plenty of stomach, but no head. Echoes of more glorious battles throbbed like drums afar off.

Command, of course, is more than a single leader: it is leadership dispersed and controlled: the delegation of authority as a trust. For the supreme commander the only real sanction is the confidence of his lieutenants and subordinates, all the stronger if based on the affectionate respect or enthusiastic loyalty which moves men to accept a superior's judgement even while they may be repressing or deferring contrary opinions of their own. In the seventeenth century, royalty, along with religion, was the common source for which a common sacrifice might be made. While Hopton spent a humdrum Christmas at Bath, fresh plans were brewing at Oxford. On 26 January 1645 Charles, Prince of Wales was commissioned as captain-general, under the King, of an associated army of Somerset, Devon, Cornwall, Dorset, Bristol, and Exeter,[3] with his headquarters at Bristol and Hopton as his lieutenant-general. The Prince was only in his fifteenth year: one of the grounds for sending him to the west was to 'unboy' him.[4] In February Hopton was sent to Bristol to provide a house for his young master.[5] On 1 March, along with his nephew Lord Capel, he was sworn of the Privy Council;[6] on 17

[1] Ibid. 268, dorse.
[2] Young and Adair, 158, 163.
[3] Black, *Docquets* . . . , 252.
[4] Clarendon, ix. 7.
[5] Ibid. viii. 254.
[6] Dugdale, 77.

March the commission of admiralty was renewed for inserting their names.[1] On 5 March Hopton escorted the Prince towards his new headquarters, in the company of Capel, Sir John Culpeper, Master of the Rolls; Sir Edward Hyde, Chancellor of the Exchequer; the Earl of Berkshire, the Archbishop of Armagh, and the Bishop of Salisbury.[2] It was by far the ablest group of colleagues Hopton had ever worked with: indeed, Sir Edward Walker hinted afterwards that the King, by making his old councillors a council to his son and sending them all away from Oxford, may have been depriving himself of some able advisers.[3]

For the Royalists the outlook could hardly have been gloomier. Scarborough on the Yorkshire coast had fallen, as had Shrewsbury, an important recruiting district and nodal point between Oxford and Wales. In the west the Roundheads' occupancy of Taunton impeded communications and supply. When the Prince came to Bristol provisions were so scarce that he had to borrow from Hopton to buy bread. Elsewhere, Sir Lewis Dyve, colonel-general of Dorset, was finally forced to yield Dorchester, and the whole county except for Sherborne and Portland Bill fell into Parliamentary hands. Sir John Berkeley, colonel-general of Devon and Cornwall, was urged to help Dyve,[4] but, isolated behind the Parliament strong-holds of Lyme Regis, Taunton, and Plymouth, was himself dependent on uncertain help from west of Tamar, where Sir Richard Grenvile's stringent discipline served mainly to hold the line of the river and encroach upon Plymouth.

Through March and the first part of April Hopton was concerned with little more than the minutiae of the council. The memoranda of this body, extant for a period of only four or five weeks, reveal that he attended every session.[5] The business was largely routine. A volunteer regiment was to be established consisting of inferior gentlemen and the lords' servants, these to buy and keep their own arms and to be trained twice a week.[6] Prince Rupert had determined to set up a post between Bristol and Worcester.[7] The sheriff wanted boats to trade with Gloucester: it was agreed that one general warrant should be signed by Lord Hopton.[8] Sir John Seymour was committed

---

[1] Black, *Docquets* . . . , 269.   [2] Dugdale, 78.   [3] Walker, 125.

[4] *God appearing for the Parliament* . . . , etc. (London: 10 Mar. 1645): Sir Lewis Dyve to the Earl of Bristol, dated at Dorchester, 26 Feb. 1645.

[5] Staffordshire Record Office: Clarendon Memorandum Book (Salt MS. 2007), no pagination. The only detailed primary source for 1645.

[6] Ibid., 28 Mar. 1645.   [7] Ibid., 6 Apr. 1645.   [8] Ibid., 18 Apr. 1645.

for refusing to lend the King £300.[1] Expenses were a problem. It was ordered that a list be made of all the Prince's servants and the proportions allotted to them, while the lords' table, for the present, should be 'put down'.[2] A letter from the King exhorted them to take pains for victualling the castle: to effect this the mayor and aldermen of Bristol, attending the council, were admonished to pay the city's arrears of £400, either in money or on credit for beer, fish, salt, and butter.[3] The mayor was ordered to make an outlying house called 'Knoll' into a 'Pest-House', and remove thence people with the plague, for which purpose Hopton delivered to the mayor a warrant to dispose of the house.[4] Hopton also acted as provost marshal, executing the Prince's order to commit Colonel David Hyde and a Colonel Briggs, accused of robbery, to safe custody.[5] In addition, he carried out the committal of Edmond Smyth, constable of Ashton, who, allegedly incited by Sir Ferdinando Gorges, J.P., had led a resistance in his parish against the contribution.[6] Burdened as he was with trivial duties, Hopton was not exempt from greater ones, being commissioned under the Great Seal as one of a council to govern the city and university of Oxford, together with the counties of Oxford, Berkshire, and Buckingham, in the absence of the King.[7]

Nominally the Prince's deputy, Hopton functioned as a 'chief of staff' for the council and as civilian governor of Bristol, having little to do with the army itself. His credit with both King and Prince was undermined by Lord Goring, ambitious for an independent command in the west,[8] a fine soldier when his interest was satisfied, but jealous of serving under a superior. With Lord Digby, Secretary of State, he formed an alliance of court and camp which worked to diminish the influence of Hopton and Rupert. Hopton's lack of dependable court connexions partly explains the decline of his authority. With the former Secretary, Falkland—his mentor in the Long Parliament

---

[1] Ibid., 22 Mar. 1644/5.   [2] Ibid., 27 Mar. 1645.
[3] Ibid., 3 Apr. 1645.   [4] Ibid., 14 Apr. 1645.
[5] Ibid., 22 Mar. 1644/5.   [6] Ibid., 28 Mar. 1645.
[7] P.R.O., Deputy Keeper's Reports, IV, App. II, p. 188, citing Pell's Patent Book, No. 11, pp. 25–28 (dated 8 May 1645).
[8] Clarendon, ix. 20. Goring's earlier career is illustrative. In Dutch service in 1637, he was shot near the ankle-bone and lamed for life. After serving in the Scots wars, he took part in the army plot of March 1641, urging the army to seize the Tower. When his plan was rejected by his fellow officers, he told the Parliamentary leaders. Continuing to play both sides, he served Parliament as commandant at Portsmouth while taking money from the Queen. On 2 August 1642 he declared for the King.—D.N.B. viii. 245–6.

who had been killed the previous year at the first battle of Newbury—his relations had been cordial and intimate. Now it was clear that the wind had changed. The defence of a remote county like Devonshire, for example, depended to some extent not only on the good pleasure of an outlander, Sir Richard Grenvile, but on the influence which could be brought upon him through the good offices of a powerful peer like the Earl of Bristol—who happened to be Lord Digby's father.[1]

The problem of self-willed, independent commanders was brought to a head at the end of April by the difficulty of co-ordinating an attack on Taunton. Goring, more interested in pursuing Waller through Wiltshire, finally sent his foot and cannon thither. Meanwhile, Grenvile, approaching Taunton from the west, was shot in the thigh while viewing Wellington House, five miles distant. Since Grenvile's men refused to serve under Sir Joseph Wagstaff, Goring's subordinate, Hopton was approached to take command. Wisely he refused to take on such a disjointed crowd, preferring to wait until Goring, then skylarking at Bath, had been removed. In the interim the troops submitted to Sir John Berkeley, and Wellington House was taken; but no one did his duty in Grenvile's absence.[2] Hopton, as field marshal, went down to assist Berkeley; the siege of Taunton, however, was a wasted effort, the castle remaining impregnable; so they limited themselves to burning as much of the town as they could reach, an operation suspended by news from Sherborne that Sir Thomas Fairfax had been reported at Piddlestown near Dorchester.[3] Goring held off Fairfax long enough to allow the besiegers to withdraw, but Taunton was relieved on 11 May.

Goring benefited from these events. The King by a letter to the Prince on 10 May ordered that he should be admitted to all deliberations of the council, with authority to pass on commissions.[4] Lord Digby, speaking for the King, informed the council through Sir John Culpeper that Goring was to have the entire western command in chief, with Sir Richard Grenvile as major-general of the foot and Hopton retaining his post as general of the ordnance, these dispositions to be ratified by Rupert. The Prince of Wales, for his safety, was to remain in garrison—his headquarters, since the plague was

---

[1] *God appearing for the Parliament* . . . , above.   [2] Clarendon, ix. 15.
[3] *C.S.P.D.* 1644–45, 478; Tanner MSS., LX, Pt. I, 150–1: Sir John Culpeper to Lord Goring, dated at Bristol Sun. 11 May 1645 '5 of the clock'; John L. Sanford, *Studies and Illustrations of the Great Rebellion* (London, 1858), 624.
[4] Clarendon, ix, 31.

raging in Bristol, had been changed, without confirmation from the King, to Barnstaple on the north Devon coast. Later these orders were slightly amended: Goring was summoned to Northampton, while Hopton, informed by the King's own hand, was to command the forces under the Prince.[1] Lord Ralph's reply, displaying again his own self-abnegation, hints at the factious jealousies that crippled his efforts:

I have received your Majesty's of May 19 from Chetwynd [Salop.] and the duplicate of the same date, both containing your commands to me to stay here and command the western forces next under his Highness the Prince of Wales; truly, Sire I doubt that very expression in my former commission cost me great displeasure from Prince Rupert, though without cause on my part, as I shall be able to make appear when I have the honor to attend your Majesty. Now, Sire, having suffered much by the uncertainty of my commands [an understatement!] and my desires to be easy and forward in all things to your Majesty's orders [and] having much hazarded your business under my charge, I think it my duty in all respects to desire from the Prince of Wales express commission for what I shall take in hand, and then there shall not fail my best endeavors, though I foresee difficulty enough and find myself not so able to go through with it as I have been. Your Majesty will be pleased to believe that I cannot willingly disserve you, but can most willingly lay down my life [for your cause].[2]

The Royalist sun was beginning to set. On 14 June near the village of Naseby, close to the borders of Northampton and Leicestershire, Parliament's New Model Army, led by Fairfax and Cromwell, proved the destruction of the King's Oxford army, the core of his command. With it went the last chance to take London. The war had a year to go, but the end was inevitable.

With this defeat Charles ceased to lead. The fantastic muddle of the Cavalier command is revealed in an ambiguous letter from Digby to Goring on 2 July. The King, Digby said, was leaving it to Goring and Rupert to do 'what you shall think best', issuing no directions himself. Presumably this applied to the garrison at Bristol, which it was now Rupert's duty to defend. Charles played with the plan of raising a new army in South Wales: this may have been the 'resolution' which Digby vaguely referred to as having been originally proposed by Goring and confirmed by the 'unanimous advice' of Rupert and the Prince of Wales' council, though apparently a final decision waited on the King's hearing from Rupert again. Digby also reassured Goring concerning Sir Richard Grenvile's new commission as field

[1] Ibid. 43-44.   [2] C.S.P.D. 1644-45, 511 (from Bath).

marshal of the associated armies in the west: it was titular only, though it might create problems in the eventuality of Goring taking over the united commands of Rupert and Hopton. The personal differences between Grenvile and Thomas, Lord Wentworth, serving in Goring's army before Taunton, were for Rupert to worry about, 'being improper for the King to interpose in'.[1]

From that time the new, matchless Parliamentary army moved westward with the irresistible force of a juggernaut. By early July Fairfax was in Somerset. Langport, thirteen miles east of Taunton, fell on 10 July; Bridgwater on the 23rd. Before the end of summer there were no royal garrisons left between London and Exeter;[2] Oxford and Bristol were nearly isolated. Yet in August the court received a 'cheerful letter' from Hopton: he had 6,000 Cornish foot well armed and was on the march to join with 3,000 more before Plymouth. He promised to 'make Fairfax as weary of the West as Essex was last year'.[3] His optimism, no doubt, was displayed for the sake of morale. While Goring showed no initiative whatever, Bristol fell into Fairfax's net: as explained in a letter to Speaker Lenthall, the Parliamentary army could not have marched from Sherborne into Cornwall with that city a hostile garrison at its back[4] (even though Hopton had done just that three years before). Censured by the King, Rupert had grounds for justifying his surrender on 11 September. He noted that though the garrison troops were supposed to number eight or nine hundred, only five or six hundred were effective. The auxiliaries and trained bands, due to pestilence, poverty, and other pressures, were down to 800. The mariners, having no employment in Bristol, had taken themselves off.[5] Cogent enough: thus, the line of the Severn was sealed off; and the three remaining circles of Royalist resistance—Oxford, Wales, and the west—girded for a last-ditch defence.

So scanty were their resources that the Prince of Wales wrote to

---

[1] H.M.C., 13th Rept. Pt. I, 232: *Calendar of the Portland MSS.*

[2] Joshua Sprigge, *Anglia Rediviva* (original London, 1647), Harry T. Moore, ed. (Gainesville, Fla., 1854), iii. 146.

[3] *Calendar of State Papers, Ireland*, 1645, 408: George, Lord Digby, to the Marquis of Ormond, dated at Cardiff 2 Aug. 1645.

[4] Bristol City Library: *A True Relation of the Storming of Bristoll And the taking the Town, Castle, Forts . . .* , etc.: letter from 'J. R.' (John Rushworth), dated 13 Sept. 1645.

[5] The name: *A Declaration of His Highnesse Prince Rupert with a narrative of the State and condition of the City and Garrison of Bristol, when His Highnesse Prince Rupert came thither* (1645).

Fairfax requesting a safe conduct for Hopton and Culpeper with twelve servants to attend the King and urge overtures for peace, all desiring to manifest to the world their earnest endeavour 'to stoppe the issue of Bloud,'[1] a plea which appears to have been either ignored or denied, as we find the King two weeks later dispatching strict directions to Culpeper for ensuring the Prince's safety by having him embark for France.[2] This the Prince's council resolved to defer, lest his going sink the spirits of the people and make a bad case more desperate yet. Besides, without royal intervention, it was plain that Grenvile and Goring would never agree. The latter's contempt for the Cornish was unendurable: before Taunton, clapping an Irish soldier on the back, he would declare he was worth ten 'Cornish cowards', in the hearing of these same Cornish, many of whom 'had reason to believe themselves not inferior to any who had served the King'.[3] Fortunately, though too late to do any good, Goring found himself physically depleted; on 20 November 1645 he left for France to recover his health. The council must have drawn a sigh of relief. There was still Grenvile, but Sir Richard at least was a strong disciplinarian who could control his troops, and he ruled Cornwall absolutely.

By the middle of October Fairfax had advanced into Devon, though no farther than Cullompton, thirteen miles north-east of the court at Exeter, where sickness among his troops made him pause. The plague appears to have continued through the autumn: in November Elizabeth, Lady Hopton, writing from Exeter to a Dr. Martin, thanked him for his services in alleviating her own illness:

Good Doctor, I doe willingly take of the time of my rest to give you harty thankes . . . acknowledging the Blessing of your care for me and blush still when I thinke how much I am a debtor to you for me and mine, I thanke god mine owne health is of late better . . . then it was, But my Betty [a grandchild by her first marriage] hath of late been very ill, but now I bless god mendes againe, But because the night is soefarr past upon me, I have appointed Ann Hill to write particularly how shee is and hath been, I have often wished for you but wee hath been soe obstructed as I can not hope it but shall . . . in very harty respects and thankful acknowledgments remaine. . . .

Your freind to serve you
Eliz. Hopton[4]

---

[1] S.P. 16/510/115, dated 'At our Court at Exeter', 15 Sept. 1645.
[2] Clarendon, ix. 96.   [3] Ibid. 100.
[4] Nalson MSS., XII, 165, dated 17 Nov. 1645.

On 27 November Hopton, at Truro, reported in a letter to his brother-in-law Sir Baynham Throckmorton that Fairfax had drawn back eastward. Again it was only a pause; the juggernaut was poised for the last lunge. Exeter was abandoned; the Prince took himself and his retinue to Launceston. By the middle of January 1646 his command was on the verge of collapse. Grenvile complained he had ordered Major-General Harris to guard one of the Tamar bridges; Harris had returned word he would receive orders from no one but General Sir John Digby; Digby, in turn, said he would receive orders from none but the Prince. A party of Lord Wentworth's horse approaching a troop of Grenvile's guard and neither accepting the commands of the other, they had fallen out, and two or three had been killed. 'It was absolutely necessary that his highness should constitute one superior officer, from whom those independent officers might receive orders.' At last! Grenvile recommended the Earl of Brentford or Lord Hopton to command in chief.[1]

The Prince chose Hopton to take charge (it was almost too late to take command) of 'a dissolute, undisciplined, wicked, beaten army'. Hopton accepted the order, telling his master it was the custom now for men to decline an unwanted task by saying it was against their honour. In the present case he knew his own was at stake. 'But since his highness thought it necessary to command him, he was ready to obey him with the loss of his honor.'[2]

Again in a time of necessity he was ready—let 'honor' die.

Some of the names and faces were reassuring: Walter Slingsby, Richard Arundell, Jonathan Trelawny, and Sir Christopher Wray, the latter a colonel at eighteen. The picture, however, was enough to make him despair. The Cornish trained bands had shrunk to about 150 and 'how full of necessities, complaints, and all kinds of distempers': Wentworth's horse: 'Amongst them were divers gallant men, but in general I cannot say they were exact upon duty.' As for the artillery: 'Of that I had none.'[3]

The total came to 4,190 men, not counting five or six hundred foot under Grenvile, who again had become contentious. Upon receiving written orders on 15 January from Prince Charles to be

---

[1] *Cal. Clar. S.P.* i. 298, No. 2090, dated at Worington, 16 Jan. 1645/6.
[2] Clarendon, ix. 133–6.
[3] Thomas Carte, *Original Letters* (London, 1739), 109–10: Hopton to the Prince of Wales.

lieutenant-general of foot under Hopton, he demurred strongly—
odd and erratic behaviour in view of his suggesting Hopton in the
first place, but Sir Richard was a man of strong and strange humours
and had always cherished his semi-independent command. Self-willed
and obdurate, he sulked in his tent four days until the Prince, losing
patience, had him arrested and committed to Launceston gaol.[1]
Goring's horse under Wentworth were more amenable: they agreed
to receive Hopton on condition that he would not supersede Goring,
should Goring return.[2] Their clinging to this remote chance is a
minor example of the unrealism which now pervaded Royalist
counsels and plans, though in this particular instance the motive may
have been simply to save face. One scheme was to raise in Brittany
and Guienne 4,000 foot and 1,000 horsemen for the reinforcing of
the western army, though the relator—Sir William Devenant,
writing on 17 January from Paris to Culpeper and Hyde—warned
that success depended on that of which human nature is least capable,
'Selfdenialls'.[3] The King, who had returned to Oxford, corres-
ponding with the Prince's council on 2 February, purposed to march
at the end of that month through Surrey and Kent to Rochester with
1,500 horse and 1,000 dragoons. He had directed the Queen to land
5,000 men out of France at Hastings. His concluding remarks,
however, testify to his uncertainty,[4] and the proposal went the way
of many another half-baked scheme. Charles was no longer even
shadow-boxing: the King was cornered.

Meanwhile, his Man in the West, for whom romantic enterprises
were inconceivable—sustained by that cool realism that rarely forsook
him, knowing he must lose most of what reputation he still had—
left the Prince at Launceston on 6 February and advanced into north
Devon, giving up Exeter as lost. Fairfax also abandoned his siege of
that city: with Dartmouth in his grip he could afford to wait. On
19 February Hopton was at Torrington; four days later Fairfax left

---

[1] Roger Granvile, *The King's General in the West* (London and New York,
1908), 162–3. Granvile regards Sir Richard Grenvile, his ancestor, as, more properly than Hopton, the King's principal commander in the west and his refusal to
serve as natural enough. This reluctance he traces back to August 1644 when the
King, Prince Maurice, Hopton, and Grenvile were laying the trap for Essex at
Lostwithiel, each with a virtually independent and equal command. After his
arrest, Grenvile accused Hopton of sending an officer to survey his goods, who
afterwards broke open all the trunks, boxes, and chests and plundered them.—
Ibid., above and v–vi. 155–7.
[2] *Cal. Clar. S.P.* i. 300, No. 2101, dated 21 Jan. 1646.
[3] Tanner MSS., LX, 371.   [4] *Cal. Clar. S.P.* i. 301, No. 2110.

Crediton with 10,000 men and reached Chulmleigh, thirteen miles south-east of Torrington.

The latter town presents some of the most attractive features of topography to be found in the west country:[1] most strikingly, on the south side, a long and very steep hill which descends windingly about a mile to the hamlet of Little Torrington and the river Torridge. To the north of the town is a large common: here Hopton posted his horse. To the east the country is more enclosed; on this side the Royalists reinforced the thick hedges with a line of barricades. Assuming a spirited defence, the position was almost impregnable.

On Sunday 15 February Fairfax sent out a few horse for reconnaissance. The following day Colonel Edward Massey's brigade was sent to block the Barnstaple road, while the rest of the army at 7 a.m. marched for Torrington. A series of skirmishes developed with the Royalist advance-guard under Major-General Webb at Stevenstone House, which turned into full-scale engagements. About 5 p.m. the King's men, though delaying the enemy's progress, were forced to give up their post. Falling back from hedge to hedge they maintained a slow retreat and resistance until after dark; around eight o'clock Hopton called them in, and the main body of foot was posted along the hedges four fields east of the town.

A pause of about four hours ensued. Then, near midnight, Fairfax, inspecting the watch, heard a sound like tattoo and suspected a retreat. To make sure he sent a party of dragoons to fire over the barricade. When almost upon it they were met by a hot blast and rattle of musketry. Hurriedly the Parliamentarians brought up more troops, and a general fight broke out along the whole line of the outer defences. The Royalists fought well at first, but were no match for the discipline of their enemies, who, seizing the turnpike, cleared a way for their horse to enter. At this critical juncture Hopton's horse charged and twice drove them back. Fresh Parliamentary horse galloped up; Lord Ralph's horse was shot and he himself wounded; but, finding another mount, he rode to the north common and returned with 500 of Wentworth's cavalry, making one charge more that failed from lack of foot to back it up.

It was the beginning of the last retreat: first the foot, then the horse, the Prince's Life Guards leaving last of all. Streaming back

---

[1] The author is indebted to the Rev. P. G. Harrison, Vicar of Great Torrington, Devon, for a conducted tour of the church, town, and battlefield in June 1964.

through the town they rode or ran down the plunging hill to the river and over the bridge and fords to the lanes that led westward. As they fled the din of battle was punctuated by the roar of an exploding powder magazine. They had left their munitions—eighty barrels—in Torrington church, which the Parliament-men later had converted into a guardhouse for prisoners. As scores of surrounding houses were blown up, prisoners, guards, and citizens perished in the blast. The estimates for numbers of Royalists killed range between one and three hundred.[1] The parish register tells only part of the grim story: the burial between 16 and 21 February of sixty-three soldiers, roundhead and cavalier alike.[2]

The disintegrating Royalist army, having taken four days to advance twenty-five miles to Torrington from Launceston, returned in one, the foot following hard by a few hours on the horse. These last, from the standpoint of subsistence, were in unfavourable country: the depredations and rapines allowed by Goring had diluted the ardour even of the loyal Cornish. If not prepared to go over to the enemy, they were in no mood to resist him. The day after the battle Edward Hyde was still reassuring the Queen: his letter from Pendennis to Paris described Hopton and Capel still at Torrington with 6,800 horse and foot (greatly exaggerated), Exeter resisting Fairfax, and Barnstaple well prepared: the west might yet be saved.[3] Next day the Prince ordered Hopton to make a stand about Stratton.[4] It was a futile flourish. By March the country people were greeting the New Model as a deliverer. John Rushworth passed on to Speaker Lenthall a rumour, later confirmed, that Lord Mohun, one of the five regimental commanders of the original Cornish army, was 'unwilling to obey Lord Hopton's commands, but rather stands upon his guard'.[5]

The Parliament wave rolled on. When it reached Bodmin the Prince, Hyde, and Culpeper left Pendennis for Scilly, the latter continued to Paris. Hopton and Capel drew into Truro. On 5 March

---

[1] Clarendon, ix. 139, 142–3; Carte, Alexander, and Hooper, 89–92, citing P.Q. Karkeek, 'Fairfax in the West', paper read before the Devonshire Assn., 1876, including Fairfax's personal account and a bibliography of pamphlets; E. H. Young, 293.

[2] Parish Register, Church of St. Michael and All Angels, Great Torrington, Devon.

[3] Cal. Clar. S.P. i. 303, No. 2121, dated 17 Feb. 1646.

[4] Ibid., No. 2124, dated 19 Feb. 1646.

[5] H.M.C., App. 6th Rept, 102: House of Lords Calendar, dated 1 March 1646, confirmed 2 March.

Fairfax sent them a letter offering to treat. He proposed that all soldiers should have liberty to go beyond the sea or to their homes: those who chose to stay at home would have liberty of their persons and immunity of their estates from pillage, yielding only horses and arms. Gentlemen would be allowed to retain horses for themselves and arms befitting a gentleman in time of peace. Officers who wanted to go beyond the sea for other service could take their arms with them and horses sufficient to fulfil their duties. Inferior horse-officers and troopers might receive twenty shillings by turning in their horses and arms. Passes would be granted to English gentlemen of considerable estates. Lastly, for himself, Hopton might be assured

of such mediation to the Parliament in your behalf, both for my self and others, as for one, whom (for personal worth and many vertues, but especially for your care of, and moderation toward the country) we honour and esteem above any other of your party, whose Errour (supposing you more swayed with Principles of Honour and conscience then others) we most pity, and whose happinesse (so far as consistent with the public welfare) we should delight in more then in your least suffering.[1]

On 8 March Hopton replied:

Sir,

I Received yours, bearing date the fift of this Moneth; wherein I must acknowledge much kindnesse from you, and a very Christian consideration of sparing blood: But one thing there is, I am confident you have too much honour to expect from me; which is, that to avoid any danger, or to enjoy any worldly advantage, I will renounce my Masters House, to whom I am both a sworne Subject, and a sworne Servant; That I must professe I am resolved to undergoe all Fortunes with him, and, if there shall be cause, to suffer anything, rather then in the least poynt to taint my honour in that particular; and I hope there is not a man of any consideration in this Army under my command, that is not so resolved: yet all honest and honourable wayes to procure the peace of this Kingdome, and the sparing of Christian blood, I take God to witnesse, I am, and still have been most desirous: And I heare from good hands, that our gracious Soveraigne is at present so farre advanced in a Treaty with the Parliament, as that he hath promised to passe four of the principall of their Bils proposed, whereof the entrusting of the Militia for seven years, in hands agreed between them, is one. I desire you to deal freely with me in that particular; for if that be so, it will spare the labour of further Treaty, being for my part, ready to obey whatsoever his Majesty shall agree to. God hath indeed of late humbled us with many ill successes,

---

[1] *A Summons From His Excellency Sir Thomas Fairfax to Sir Ralph Hopton And his Forces now in Cornwall* (London, 11 Mar. 1645/6), 7; Sprigge, 205–6—see pp. 220–31 for articles of treaty.

which I acknowledge as a very certaine evidence of his just judgment against us for our personal crimes: yet give me leave to say, your present prosperity cannot be so certaine an evidence of his being altogether pleased with you. It is true we are reduced to a lower condition then we have been in, yet have we a gallant Body of Horse, that being preserved to a generall accord, may be for good use against our common Enemies; and being otherwise present, I may say it without vanity, want not resolution, at lest, to sell our selves at a deare rate against any oddes. Your Propositions, though they be not wholly consented to, yet if a generall accord, much more desirable, be not in a likely forwardnesse to prevent them, I shall be willing that eight Commanders of ours, with three Country Gentlemen, give a meeting as soon as you please, to any equall number of yours, at any indifferent place, to consult of this great businesse, and to conclude of some Propositions that may be reasonable and honourable for both Parts; wherein I hope God will so blesse our cleer intentions, as may produce a probable inducement to a generall Peace, according to the unfained desire of

Your Servant
Ralph Hopton[1]

Fairfax's reaction was sceptical. Declaring that there was no definite news of a treaty pending between King and Parliament, he asserted that the former was plotting to bring over Irish rebels and that Hopton's proposals were simply delaying tactics while waiting for supplies.[2] He did not, however, decline to treat and on 10 March entered Truro, while Hopton pulled back to St. Allen's, having the previous day sent his foot and munitions to Pendennis and St. Michael's Mount. A cessation was observed by both sides.

Hopton refused to treat in person, relegating that task to the horse commanders. The commissioners met for five days. During the talks the armies fraternized.[3] Desertions continued: the Parliamentary correspondent John Rushworth noted between thirty and forty Royalist lieutenant-colonels, sergeant-majors, and captains coming over during 11 March and others coming to visit, but not returning. In the evening a captain and forty esquires came in with their horses

---

[1] Sprigge, 209–10; Carte, 121–3—see pp. 109–26 for Hopton's account to the Prince of Wales, covering 15 Jan.–13 Apr. 1646.

[2] *Sir Thomas Fairfax His last Letter of the Treaty with Sir Ralph Hopton, . . . and other notable Observances, by way of answer to Sir Ralph Hopton.* A copy of Sir Ralph Hoptons Demands . . . , etc. By Parliamentary reckoning, Ralph Hopton is still a knight.

[3] *A late Letter from Sir Thomas Fairfax's Army now in Truro Relating the severall Passages in the Treaty and what is concluded,* 5. The letter is signed 'J.R.' (John Rushworth) and dated at Truro 11 March 1645/6, with a PS. dated 12 March. It was communicated to Parliament 16 March (*L.J.* viii. 211) and printed 17 March.

and arms. From Penryn came over one hundred common soldiers: forty more were going home.[1] A brisk trade went on in horse: the Royalist troopers selling their good mounts to the Parliament-men for bad ones, 'gayning twenty . . . or thirty shillings in exchange' then giving up the bad horses for twenty shillings in the formal surrender.[2] The disbanding of this strength, which began officially on 15 March, meant the end of the Royalist army as a field force. The officers were given passes on their promise never to bear arms against Parliament.[3] Hopton, for his own use, was allowed all his horses, provided they did not exceed forty, plus arms for himself and twelve men.[4] On 18 March his Life Guard was broken up.[5] All this time he had been forced to endure a more personal tragedy: for his wife had died,[6] the staunch companion of twenty-three years.

So Cornwall was reduced, the King's last bastion in the west: in the words of the puritan chronicler Joshua Sprigge

a Country having convenient Ports and Harbours both for France and Ireland, whose naturall situation was very strong and apt for defence, being all very mountanous, and enwrapt with the Sea on all sides, except toward Devonshire, and there bounded by the River Tamar, which in a right line, runs almost from Sea to Sea. From which advantages, it hath been in ancient times, one of the last places of retreat in the Kingdome, and hath ever made saving conditions for itself in those overflowing inundations both of Saxons and Normans. Since the beginning of our late Warres, it and its Forces have been more then once fatally disastrous to our former Armies, and had ever been from the beginning of the Warres in the possession of the Enemy, the people more generally disaffected to the Parliament then any other part of the Kingdome, from whence the King, as from a never failing Spring, was constantly supplied with a choyce and able Infantry.[7]

Thus, the man who in the autumn of 1642 had pleaded the King's cause so well at Truro sessions now, after more than three years of victories and vicissitudes, had been driven back to lay down his arms at Truro, all his efforts having come to a sorry issue and a dead end.

---

[1] *A late Letter from Sir Thomas Fairfax's Army* . . . , 2.
[2] Ibid. 4.
[3] *A more Full and Exact Relation . . . of the several Treaties between Sir Tho. Fairfax and Sir Ralph Hopton* . . . , etc. This is John Rushworth's third letter to Speaker William Lenthall, dated at Truro, 13 Mar. 1645/6.
[4] Sprigge, 225.   [5] Ibid. 217.
[6] *Cal. Clar. S.P.* i. 306, Hyde to Hopton, dated at Jersey, 16 Mar. 1646.
[7] Sprigge, 229–30.

XII

EPILOGUE:
The Years of Exile

(1646–1652)

HOPTON's last years, tinged with the sadness of defeat, are not pertinent to his military career. Nevertheless, a summary sketch to round off the general picture of his life will serve to fix his position in the frame of Royalist policy for the six years following the first Civil War.

Held in Cornwall for nearly a month by adverse winds, he and Capel arrived in Scilly on 11 April 1646 to join the Prince and Sir Edward Hyde. Next day an enemy fleet surrounded the island; luckily it was dispersed by a storm.[1] When this had subsided, the Prince's party embarked for the safer haven of Jersey; their ship *Le Noir Proudaigle*, cast anchor at the roadstead on Friday 17 April an hour before sunset. The following day Hopton went to survey Mont Orgueil to test its security for residence and defence. It is assumed that his report was unfavourable, since young Charles continued to live at Elizabeth Castle.[2] Their resources were meagre, dependent mainly on what the Prince, as Duke of Cornwall, could realize in the way of fines, rents, and pre-emptions of tin. His appeals for these dues in the form of specie or bills of exchange ignored the impoverished condition of the duchy;[3] but the only alternatives were piracy or help from France, and the latter recourse was extremely unpopular with the councillors except as a last resort.

The fear of French and Catholic influence, as personified by the Prince's mother, Queen Henriette Marie, then at Paris, was the main reason for their reluctance to let him pass out of their hands.

[1] *Cal. Clar. S.P.* i. 316, No. 2211, Hyde to Colonel Arundell, dated 15 May 1646.

[2] H.M.C., App. to 2d Rept. (London, 1870): '*Journal et Recueil des choses les plus remarquables en l'isle de Jersey, arrivées pendant les Guerres Civiles sous les regnes des Rois Charles Premier et Charles Second. Par Jean Chevalier, vingtenier de la ville de St. Helier*', 160 (copy). Most useful for corroborative details of the Royalists' residence in Jersey.

[3] Nalson MSS., I: 31 (63), the prince of Wales to his Receiver in Cornwall, dated at Castle Elizabeth in Jersey, 20 May 1646.

It could not be denied, however, in view of the King's surrendering Oxford, that his son's personal safety might be better supported at St. Germains. Towards the end of June, therefore, they acquiesced in his departure, though declining to accompany him and trusting that the Queen would make a favourable interpretation of their absence.[1] Prince Charles's last executive act as captain-general of the west, negotiated from the French court, was an attempt to relieve Pendennis Castle: the one remaining Royalist outpost in England. A nine-ton vessel commanded by Sir Thomas Hooper was dispatched from Jersey with a small supply of wheat and pork. It was apprehended, however, by Captain Francis Langdon.[2] Pendennis, holding out under the eighty-year-old Sir John Arundell of Trerice until it had only a day's victuals left, shortly after surrendered (17 August).

By the autumn of 1646 Jersey hung perilously between two threats: one emanating from Parliament, the other from Paris. Getting wind of a plan of Henriette Marie's adviser Lord Jermyn to hand the island over to the French, Hyde, Hopton, Capel, and Sir George Carteret, the governor, signed a pact on 19 October to defend their station against the foreigner, even resolving, if the design were attempted, to call in Parliament for help.[3] By December it was bruited in London that Hopton had set up two or three powder mills and several strongholds on great rocks, encompassed by the sea. Fishermen were not allowed to go to sea without a diligent search of their boats.[4] Rumour implied that a task force was building up to invade the mainland, though these measures were almost entirely defensive. At any rate, Hopton's name was still something to conjure with.

Jersey became a haven for exiled Royalists: 'Milord Hopeton et le chancellier [Hyde] étoient de grands amis, lesquels tinrent longtems table ouverte à ces pauvre fugitifs d'Angleterre, qui pour la plupart

---

[1] *Cal. Clar. S.P.* i. 323, No. 2248, Lords Capel and Hopton, with Sir Edward Hyde, to the Queen, dated at Jersey 25 June 1646.

[2] Nalson MSS., I, 66, the Prince of Wales to the governor and council of war at Pendennis, dated at St. Germains, Paris, 22 Aug. (N.S.) 1646; Tanner, LIX, 511, the Parliamentary committee in Cornwall to Speaker Lenthall, dated at Truro, 27 Aug. 1646.

[3] *Cal. Clar. S.P.* i. 338: articles of association entered into 19/29 Oct. 1646; H.M.C., App. to 2d Rept., 161–2; Wormald, 147.

[4] *Severall Prospositions Presented To the Members of the Honourable House of Commons, by Mr. Peters, Minister of the Gospell . . . with A Discovery of two great plots against the Parliament . . . The First, by the Queen . . . The Second by the Lord Hopton . . .*, etc. (London, 1 Dec. 1646).

n'avoient point d'argent.' The French chronicler, Jean Chevalier, gives a brief, complimentary picture of Hopton at this time: 'Milord étoit un homme fort grave, et d'une belle contenance, lequel se porta prudemment et sobrement pendant le tems qu'il resta à Jersey.'[1]

Having secured the island's defences, Hopton considered his own future. His estate had been disposed of; Parliament had decreed that he was not to be pardoned by the King except with the consent of both Houses.[2] Also he was fifty and perhaps weary. About the middle of February 1647 he prepared to quit Jersey. There was no reason to stay: the military administration was in the hands of Sir George Carteret, a thoroughly capable man. Many Royalists had retired to the continent: Capel had left in November for Holland. Lord Ralph decided to stay with his uncle Sir Arthur Hopton, sometime ambassador to Spain, at Rouen. By early March he was settled in that city. He had not, however, retired. Over the next five years—in peregrinations to The Hague, to Utrecht, to Bruges—he continued from time to time to play a part in the shifting pattern of English politics and their ramifications on the whole European scene.

Meanwhile, the King followed a melancholy road. In the spring of 1646 at Newark he surrendered voluntarily to the Scots, who the following year received £400,000 for turning him over to Parliamentary commissioners. Towards the end of 1647, after confinement at Holmby House in Northampton and later at Hampton Court, he fled to Carisbrooke Castle in the Isle of Wight, where he lived unmolested for most of 1648, the year of the Second Civil War. That conflict of a few months between the Independent Party's New Model Army and a Royalist-Presbyterian-Scottish coalition saw the triumph of Cromwell's Ironsides in the King's stoutest strongholds—Cornwall and the Welsh Marches; the execution, after the fall of Colchester, of two Royalist commanders; and the shattering of the Scots by the Puritan army at Preston. Cromwell's veterans seized power everywhere and, having expelled the King's men, began purging from their own ranks those elements antagonistic, or useless, to their design of establishing the reign of the Saints on earth. Colonel Thomas Pride's expulsion of the more moderate members of the

---

[1] H.M.C., App. to 2d Rept., above, 162.

[2] John Thurloe, State Papers, 7 vols. (London, 1742), i. 80. In the Parliamentary propositions for peace presented to the King at Hampton Court on 7 Sept. 1647 and in the negotiated treaty at Newport in the Isle of Wight 13 Oct. 1648, Hopton is listed among thirty-seven Royalists 'who shall expect no pardon'.—Walker, appendixes, 17, 57.

Commons on 6 December 1648 signified that the New Model had come into its own as the arbiter of a kingdom, which, with the execution of Charles the First on 30 January 1649, the continuing exile of his son, and the dismemberment of the Estates, became a trunk without a head.

During these years, along with the question of the militia, there loomed the overriding question of the Church settlement. On the Parliamentary side, Presbyterian grandees, Congregational soldiers, and sectarian agitators of all sorts were agreed only in opposition to the Episcopal Establishment. Among the Royalists sentiment ranged from the inflexibility of a conservative Anglican like Edward Nicholas to the more resilient and accommodating spirit of devout, but moderate, churchmen like Hopton, who, though they might be opposed to synods, had affinities of taste and temper with the puritans. This indeed became a subject of discussion, and some contention, between Hopton and Hyde. In the spring of 1647 the latter wrote considering the possibility of communion with the Huguenots and comparing the Church of England with other reformed churches. It was Hyde's opinion that any alteration in the 'old ways' of church and state would never bring peace. Those who were naive enough to think so would learn that such an alteration could never be made without 'a long continued vast change' and the 'trouble of any army': a veritable revolution that would permanently violate their security.[1] At the time Hyde was not unalterably opposed to communion with the Calvinists. A year later, however, taking up the question again, he opined that Hopton was too tolerant of the 'misreformed' churches. Bishops were the bulwark of Protestantism in England; lacking them the reformed churches, including the Kirk of Scotland, would be brought to ruin.[2] These exhortations perhaps influenced Hopton's negative reaction to the Royalist treaty with the Scots at Breda in 1650, though for him the Scottish-French alliance was a greater menace than Presbyterianism.

In the meantime he kept apprised of western developments: his correspondent Sir Edward Ford reported on the affairs of Wales, Devon, and Cornwall.[3] Somerset missed his presence: it was noted

---

[1] *Cal. Clar. S.P.* 379, No. 2529, Hyde to Hopton, dated at Jersey, 9 June 1647; Wormald, 185–6, 311.

[2] *Cal. Clar. S.P.* i. 420–1, No. 2770, dated at Paris, 20 Apr./2 May 1648. For a fine analysis of Hyde's views on the Church, see Wormald, 311, above. Hopton at the time was in Hampshire, it is presumed on secret business.

[3] *Cal. Clar. S.P.* i. 411, 419.

in the deed of election of the visitors to Sexey's hospital on 20 May 1648: 'Lord Hopton being absent and resident in some parts beyond seas.'[1] In the autumn of that year he took up his station with a few ships at Helvoort Sluys in Brabant. The Royalists had considered the possibility of landing troops from Ireland in the west of England and in Wales, though it might be hard enough even to maintain a beach-head. As Hopton explained to Rupert, then at The Hague:

I do adventure to continue the baker of this towne in his course of furnishing fresh bread to save your bisquett which will be the scarce comodite in Irland there is thrift in it, but I must pray your highnes now att the Hague to procure a certayne meanes of payment for it, else I must ly in pawne for it here is likewise a score due to the Carpenters who are 3 weekes in areere of thyr pay this night, and very earnest for it, it will come to neere 400 guilders.[2]

On 8 February 1649, little more than a week after Charles I's execution, he called upon the gentlemen of Cornwall to acknowledge and receive Charles II as their new King. He harboured few doubts as to their loyalty, 'having had pretty good experience of it formerly'.[3] His own reputation, of course, had helped to secure that loyalty in the past. Now, however, while it warranted that promotion of the King's cause in the west had been entrusted to 'a person certainly of great integrity',[4] it failed to raise the most Royalist of counties. The great invasion turned into a series of naval engagements. In April Hopton was reported as 'floting up and downe' the coast with twenty ships, 'insomuch that no ships can passe nor escape his fury'. He was said to command in chief that squadron and adjacent land forces; his colour was yellow with black bullets in the middle—probably the fifteen bezants of the arms of Cornwall[5]—and the motto in gold letters: 'For Charles the second.' On one occasion he set upon a fleet of merchants sailing toward Land's End. They exchanged broadsides, and the fight continued some hours until Hopton steered towards Scilly. He was chased six miles and three of his vessels were

---

[1] S.R.O., Deeds of Election and Surrender of Trust of Visitors of Sexey's Hospital 1648–1717 (SE. 41).
[2] B.M., Add. MS. 18,982: 472 (153), dated at Helvoort Sluys, 2 Jan. 1648/9.
[3] *A Declaration sent from the Right Honourable Ralph Lord Hopton To The Gentlemen and Inhabitants of Cornwall, . . . concerning his Ingagement for and in behalf of Prince Charles, who is now King Charles the Second . . .*, etc. (London, 19 Feb. 1948/9).
[4] H.M.C., Rept. on the MS. of F. W. Leyborne-Popham, Esq. of Littlecote, Co. Wilts. (Norwich, 1899), 10.
[5] Coate, 252.

sunk, as was a merchant ship with 100 sailors. The merchant fleet turned toward Land's End again; Hopton, 'being thirsty of revenge', gave chase, boarded them, and took the crews prisoner. Fear spread lest the 'Hoptonians' became masters of the British seas. A Bristol ship surrendered its cargo of cloth; after distributing this haul among his men, Hopton struck in at a creek near Pendennis for victualling. When the crew went ashore it was nearly captured by enemy forces, but these in turn were frustrated by the 'malignity' and vigilance of the Cornish before they could get between their prey and the water. A 'hot conflict' ensued; the Hoptonians retreated to their ships and cast off, escaping from pursuing Parliament ships with the loss of nineteen men.[1]

From this Hopton would appear to have been in the process of launching a naval career to match his military exploits. For the technicalities of sea war, however, he must have relied on professionals; his main concern was provisioning the fleet.[2] Such humdrum work was the more congenial because of friction in the higher levels of policy and command. At Calais in July 1648 Prince Charles met with members of the King's Council, dominated by his Queen-Mother's favourites, the Lords Jermyn and Culpeper. Of the anti-French faction the only prominent spokesmen were Hopton and Christopher, Lord Hatton, Hyde and Nicholas being then at Dieppe awaiting instructions. These Councillors were anxious to get the Prince out of France. Hopton therefore urged that letters be sent to Dieppe calling the whole Council into Holland. Perhaps his ploy was too obvious and too strongly put. Hatton more diplomatically suggested that the Prince stay at Calais until Hyde and Nicholas came to him. Charles agreed, but Culpeper thought it unfit that the Prince should wait on anyone. Hopton, taking it upon himself to know the opinions of the absent Councillors, declared they were all of a mind to follow the Prince to the Netherlands. This rash avowal, in defeating Hatton's argument, for a time strengthened the hand of Culpeper, who argued that such a voyage was unsuited to persons of their 'age and informities' and disinclination to the sea. As undeterred by these objections as he had been by those of opponents in the Long Parliament, Hopton

---

[1] *A Great Fight near Pendennis Castle in Cornwall Between The Lord Hopton, and the Parliament Forces, upon the landing of his men for the fetching in of provision* . . . (London, 2 April 1649). (From 'T. Jennings'.)

[2] *Cal. Clar. S.P.* 444, No. 2906, Hopton and Hyde to the Lords of the Council with the Prince at The Hague, dated at Helvoort Sluys 10 Nov. 1648; ibid. 446, No. 2919, Hopton to the same, dated at Brill, 19 Nov. 1648.

continued to press his point, though enduring harsh language from the royal secretary, Sir Robert Long. Even when it was resolved to spend a month at sea he continued to urge it; his perseverance finally won out, though in the long run with little advantage.[1] Privy Councillors absorbed in daily tasks were no match for experienced courtiers, whether at St. Germains or at The Hague. It is saying something for Hopton that, despite his bluntness, he never lost the personal respect of his colleagues, even though some of them, even without malice, continued to regard him as a lightweight in conciliar matters:

There was only one man in the council of whom nobody spoke ill, nor laid any thing to his charge; and that was the lord Hopton. But there was then such a combination, by the countenance of prince Rupert with all the other lords of the Court and the Attorney General [Sir Edward Herbert], upon former grudges, to undervalue him, that they had drawn the Prince himself to have a less esteem of him than his singular virtue and fidelity, and his unquestionable courage and industry, (all which his enemies could not deny he excelled in,) did deserve.[2]

In the spring of 1650 the Council was split into two main factions: those who favoured a treaty with the Scots Presbyterians as the short way to victory and, on the other hand, those who, like Hopton, Hyde, and Nicholas, were suspicious of such a treaty, fearing the old Scottish alliance with France.[3] Preferring to rely on assistance from the Dutch, the Danes, or the Germans, their main hope lay in the chance of a native uprising: their plan was to raise armies of resistance in those counties with a solid core of Royalist sympathy and strength, especially in the west and south-west.

Some details of this scheme leaked out a year later in the confession of a Shropshireman, Thomas Coke, before the Parliamentary Council of State.[4] Since he relied for the most part on memory his testimony must be received with caution, but it is sufficient to show that Hopton, however regarded by court and council, was still the darling of the

[1] Sir Edward Nicholas, State Papers, 3 vols., George F. Warner, ed. (Camden Society: 1886, 1892, 1897), i. 91–92: letter from Christopher, Lord Hatton to Edw. Nicholas, dated at Paris 29 Aug. 1648, signed 'Charles Parker'.
[2] Clarendon, xi. 84.
[3] David Underdown, *Royalist Conspiracy in England* (Yale University Press, 1960), 10–11.
[4] Nalson MSS., XVI, 72: Examinations and confessions of Thomas Coke of Drayton, Shropshire, made in Mar., Apr., and May 1651, reported from the Council of State 28 May. See refs. in *C.J.* vi. 579 and H.M.C., 13th Rept., Pt. I, 580–2: *Cal. Portland MSS.*

camp. A meeting was held at Salisbury to form a western association
for the 'Kings businesse'. Cornwall, still the country for infantry,
was to furnish 3,000 foot; the other five counties, 1,500 horse.
Jonathan Trelawny was to be major-general: there was 'some
contest' between Hopton and Sir Richard Grenvile about command.[1]
An army was also proposed for Kent, with Charles, Lord Gerard
commanding and Hopton as a candidate for lieutenant-general.

The King was more than interested. From Breda in the Netherlands, where he was treating with the Scots commissioners, he sent
Coke instructions. These were hidden under a loose board in the
room of one 'Mr. Hardie', a ground chamber in Coney Court, Gray's
Inn, Holborn. As the conspirators wanted the King to land a foreign
force to encourage them, Charles sent an equerry to Denmark for
men and supplies. The Danish King sent 300 men to Scotland as a
Life Guard; they retired to Jersey when the Scots would have none
of them. 'Duke Wolmar[Waldemar?]', allegedly 'base brother to the
King of Denmarke', came to Breda and offered 8,000 men out of
upper Germany if at least £50,000 were advanced and shipping
provided. Gerard, Nicholas, and Hopton were interested; the latter
went to Cologne to prosecute the design. But the proposal fell
through because the Scots commissioners were against it.[2]

To make matters worse for the 'country' Royalists, there were
divisions in their own ranks. Sir John Berkeley advocated treating
with the Scots: he could never conceive that a 'Cabal' consisting of
Nicholas, Hopton, and others would represent 'men of more tender
consciences than other men'. He argued that the opposing of 'an
imaginary power which the Queen has with the King is the strongest
link which unites these'.[3] In the latter estimate, Berkeley came close
to the truth, though suspicion of the Kirk was a tie equally strong.
From the viewpoint of Hopton's party English Parliamentary
Presbyterians were a different and generally more acceptable breed.

A meeting of the Privy Council was held on 6 April 1650 in the
castle at Breda.[4] After the first day's debate, Hopton and Nicholas
were 'set aside' because they opposed concessions made to the commissioners of the Scots Estates and Kirk.[5] Two months later, in

---

[1] S. R. Gardiner, ed., *Letters and Papers Illustrating the Relations Between
Charles the Second and Scotland in* 1650 (Edinburgh, 1894), 154–5, citing Tanner
MSS., LIV, f. 14.

[2] Nalson MSS., XVI, 72: 2d paper, p. 1; 4th paper, pp. 1–4.

[3] *Cal. Clar. S.P.* ii. 50, Berkeley to Hyde, dated at Paris 22 Mar. (N.S.) 1649/50.

[4] S.P. 18/9/25.   [5] Nicholas, i. viii.

answer to a query from Hyde,[1] Nicholas reported what Lord Jermyn had told Hopton at Beauvais: that 'those who obstructed the King's counsels ought to be removed from his counsels'.[2]

Early in May Hopton went to Utrecht, 'finding little business and less contentment at Breda', because he was not sufficiently trusted to be told the particulars of the treaty.[3] He continued to give advice by letter, still pleading for an invasion from the Channel Isles and from Ireland, to be co-ordinated with a western uprising. To create a climate of opinion for this enterprise he issued a declaration out of Plymouth, condemning the 'Serpentine Policy, simulated Piety, slie delusions', etc. of the 'Rebells' fomented by them in the name of '*Reformation, Liberty, Freedom*'. They had abolished religion, murdered the King, disinherited his heir, and established their own 'Princely Throne'. He hoped there were those who retained the hearts of 'true-bred English' that would rather bow to a king than to many tyrants—this 'Factious and broken crew of Mechanicks'. He desired them to join at the approach of his army; he would try to avoid 'Spoile, Forrage, Fyring of Houses, Plunder'.[4] However seriously this blast may have been received, the news that Hopton and Grenvile, 'the best heads and the stoutest hearts', were lurking somewhere off the coast brought three additional companies of foot to Exeter,[5] with the anticipation of more.

The King's policy, however, led him northward: on Sunday 12 June 1650 he took ship for Scotland. Hopton stayed behind,[6] compensated for his service by £500, which the French party doubted he deserved.[7] In the autumn, being reckoned among the 'honest counsellors',[8] he was summoned at the particular request of the Duke

---

[1] *Cal. Clar. S.P.* ii. 62, No. 326, Hyde to Nicholas (No. 15), dated at Madrid, 4 June 1650.

[2] Nicholas, i. 187, dated 17/27 June 1650.

[3] *Cal. Clar. S.P.* ii. 61 No. 322, 'J.T[rethewy]' to William Edgeman (Sir Edward Hyde's secretary), dated at Breda 1 June 1650; ibid. 62, No. 323, 'Ha. Na[sh]' to the same, dated at Antwerp 2 June 1650; S. R. Gardiner, ed., . . . *Relations Between Charles the Second and Scotland in 1650*, above, p. 90.

[4] *The Declaration of the Right Honorable Ralph Lord Hopton, Lieutenant Generall of all His Majesties Forces designed for the West of England . . .*, etc., from Plymouth, 20 May 1650.

[5] *A Message sent From The Lord Hopton, and Sir Richard Greenvill to the Prince, and a fight in the Isle of Guernsey . . .*, etc. (London, 7 June 1650), noted in a letter of 'T.S.', dated at Exeter 1 June 1650.

[6] Walker, 158; Nicholas, i. 186.

[7] Nicholas, i. 203, letter from Lord Hatton dated at Paris 19 Nov. (N.S.) 1650.

[8] Nalson, XII, 258 (No. 1), 'Doctor Stewart' to Nicholas, dated at the Louvre 12/22 Sept. 1650.

of York[1] to attend him at Brussels.[2] In December it was reported that he had gone into Germany;[3] in May 1651 a letter reached Nicholas from Wesel. Hopton, persuaded by Culpeper, who lived nearby, had been considering the possibility of compounding with Parliament for his estate, since other Royalists had done so, with the King's leave. Compromise was foreign to his nature, yet he had his own reasons for making inquiries of Edward Nicholas:

I am never a whitt the more perswaded to it; yet, if others have the Kings leave, I should be glad to have that testimony of his Majesties favorable care of me, that will cost him nothing. I desire you, if you think it fitt, to take the opportunity to move it forward as from yourself and to lay the fault on my modesty, as I protest it is, That I aske it not.[4]

In the following months he had time to consider the prospect further. After the battle of Worcester (3 September 1651), the defeated Royalists' last chance to contest Cromwell's rule, he wrote to Nicholas from Utrecht, using a numerical code:[5]

I perceave you had then the sad newes of our fatall overthrow att Wocester. And concerning what was considered betwen me and Lord Culpeper, truly it was nothing at all; but I writ cleerly my opinion in my last to me Lo. Ambassador, and it is that *in this sad conjuncture*, where little *hope is left of* suddaine *imployment* and where *the King cannot be* consulted *by us in the tyme of our danger, which is the end of this* moneth, *I will* endeavour *as warely* as I can *to save* some*thing of my estate and* wish *you and Sir Ed. Hide would doe soe too, and* to that end *send over one of your sonnes not* staying for *a pass, for* I suppose *neither of them* having bene *in armes* they *run noe danger*, and I wish yourself were here that wee might consult with more freedome then by letters. This advice *comes to me* severall *wayes from London, Paris and here* among *ourselves, and* indeed *the state of* the question *consists shortly in* this, *on one hand we shall in a* severe *way ruin ourselves, weaken the King and* profit *his enemy's, on the* other *in a more* doubtfull *way just the* contrary [coded words in original MS. italicized]. . . .[6]

---

[1] S.P. 18/11/24, one Nicholson *alias* 'Dean Stuart' to Nicholas, dated at Paris 21 Sept./1 Oct. 1650.

[2] Nicholas, i. 208, letter from Lord Hatton, dated at Paris 13/23 Sept. 1650.

[3] *Cal. Clar. S.P.* ii. 88, Hyde to Nicholas, dated at Madrid, 5 Dec. 1650.

[4] B.M., MS. Eg. 2534/75 (last part in code). See Nicholas, i. 241.

[5] For example: Hopton —520
               Hyde   —472
               and   — 49
               is   —503
               of   —186
               the   —474 (483)
—B.M., MS. Eg. 2534/108 and Nicholas, i. 268–9.

[6] Nicholas, above, dated 4 Oct. (N.S.), 1651.

After the Breda Treaty, Hopton's life resumed a more even course, brightened for a year by the prospect of a new marriage. The young woman was Lady Anne Douglas, daughter of Anne, Countess of Morton.[1] Sir Edward Hyde heartily approved the match and helped to promote it, lauding Hopton to Lady Morton as a man of 'honour and honesty'[2] and the most 'virtuous and pious man living'.[3] There seem to have been difficulties, however. Hyde hints at imputations made to the Queen against Hopton's character by 'mercenary informers';[4] rumours circulated that he had lost his head over another young lady at the French court—'but', Hyde tartly observed, as though in mitigation, 'that cursed place and company makes all people mad'.[5] In February 1651 Sir Edward wrote to Lady Morton again to tell her that 'things have not been well understood, but the mistakes may be at once found out and mended'.[6] Hyde continued to advise Lady Anne with respect to her engagement,[7] but though the marriage continued to be bruited there were no banns.

No longer directly involved in political and military engagements, Hopton continued to 'keep touch' as one of the circuit of Royalist correspondents.[8] In the summer of 1651 the veteran Colonel Slingsby approached him with a plan to surprise the castle at Poole,[9] which was still pending a year later. Toward the end of August 1652 he refused to be drawn into an intrigue against Cromwell: a scheme concocted by the Duke of Buckingham and other Royalists in conjunction with the Levellers to deflate the ascendancy of the New Model by

---

[1] The Countess was the daughter of Sir Edward Villiers (1585?–1626) and Barbara St. John; sister of William, second Viscount Grandison; and, in 1650 the widow of Robert Douglas, the eighth Earl of Morton. The House of Morton was ultra-Royalist; Countess Anne had been governess to the Princess Henrietta, with whom in 1647 she had escaped to France. Her father Sir Edward Villiers was half-brother to George Villiers, first Duke of Buckingham. Her brother William's daughter Barbara became the famous Duchess of Cleveland.—*D.N.B.* xx. 324; *Complete Peerage*, ix. 296. Another suitor to the young Lady Anne was James Livingston, Viscount Newburgh.

[2] *Cal. Clar. S.P.* ii. 49, No. 263, dated at Madrid 18 Mar. (N.S.) 1650.

[3] Ibid. 65, No. 338, dated at Madrid 21 June (N.S.) 1650.

[4] Ibid. 49, above.

[5] Ibid. 92, No. 471, Hyde to Nicholas (No. 21), dated at Madrid 29 Dec. 1650.

[6] Ibid. 96, No. 494, dated at Madrid 9 Feb. (N.S.) 1651.

[7] Ibid. 176, No. 981, Hyde to Lady Barbara Villiers, dated 18 Feb. (1653?).

[8] For example, he and Nicholas, through one George Wayte, were in contact with Major-General Edward Massey in Holland and a 'Mr. Spark'—possibly Edward Sparke, Charles II's chaplain—in Hamburg.—Nalson MSS., XVI, 128.

[9] Underdown, 68.

playing on its internal dissensions, with a by-plot to destroy Oliver himself.[1]

By this time, still pondering the chance of making an amicable composition for his estate,[2] he was living in semi-retirement at Bruges. Four years of war and wounds and six of exile had left their mark upon his vigorous constitution, as he approached the threshold of old age. With the waning of the year 1652 his strength ebbed; the autumn fogs and endemic dankness of the city brought on a chill; and in mid October Nicholas wrote sadly to Lord Hatton: 'Gallant and virtuous Lord Hopton died on Tuesday sennight [8 October, N.S.] at Bruges of an ague, in whom all honest and well affected men had a loss, but none so great as the King.'[3]

Edward Hyde at Paris, an often biased yet perceptive observer of men, in replying to this melancholy news, heightened his eulogy by first passing judgement on the current and still-young reign which he and Hopton had served with little reward and from which he himself was already beginning to feel estranged. After touching on the slackness of the Council, the 'softness' of the King, the corruption and licence of the French court, he briefly acknowledged his friend: 'as faultless a person as I ever knew man'.[4]

A year or two later Lord Hatton wrote to Nicholas requesting that his son be given the code number '520' that had been Hopton's.[5]

[1] *Cal. Clar. S.P.* 146, No. 800, 'R.F.' (R[ichard] Watson) to W(illiam) Edgeman.

[2] Nicholas, i. 311, Nicholas to Hyde, dated at The Hague 8/18 Jan. 1652.

[3] Nicholas, i. 284, to 'Mr. Smith' (Hatton), dated at The Hague 7/17 Oct. 1652.

[4] *Cal. Clar. S.P.* ii. 152, No. 839, Hyde to Nicholas, dated at the Palais Royal, Paris, 26 Oct. (N.S.) 1652.

[5] Nicholas, ii. 253, dated at Paris, 16 Apr. 1654 or 1655.

CONCLUSION:

The Civilian at War

HOPTON'S body was carried to Helvoort Sluys, where it remained unburied. In 1661 it was brought to Somerset and interred at Witham,[1] though there is no record of a grave[2]. Since Lord Ralph's uncle Sir Arthur Hopton had died in 1650, the barony of Stratton was conferred upon John, Lord Berkeley, Ralph Hopton's old Comrade in arms.[3]

As for Hopton's estate, in the absence of a will, an administration was granted in November 1662[4] to his four sisters. How they struggled to regain their brother's inheritance, and whom they married, are beyond the scope of this study. When the estate was restored by order of the Lords in 1672,[5] Witham Friary fell to the eldest sister Katherine, widow of Sir John Wyndham. Their son Hopton possessed Witham; upon his dying without issue the manor devolved on his brother, Sir William Wyndham, Bart., who died in 1683. Sir William's great-grandson, the second Earl of Egremont (d. 1763), sold his estate, including Witham, to an Alderman Beckford, whose son William Beckford, Esq., still living in 1824, sold it to a Dr. Trenchard and a Mr. Webb, surveyor. Later it was sold to the Duke of Somerset.[6] Time had come round: it should be remembered (see p. 2, n. 4) that Witham, before being seised to the first Sir Ralph Hopton, had been briefly possessed, prior to his attainder, by Edward Seymour, first Duke of Somerset and Earl of Hertford (the Protector), whose great-grandson William Seymour—first Marquis of Hertford and later second Duke of Somerset—was Hopton's lord general in the west. As of February 1964 Percy Hamilton Seymour, eighteenth Duke of Somerset—from his seat at Maiden Bradley,

---

[1] Edmund Lodge, *Portraits of Illustrious Personages of Great Britain* . . . (London, 1821–34), iii. 5.

[2] Witham Friary Parish Church, Somerset: inscription by portrait of Lord Hopton over font.

[3] Lloyd, 350.

[4] Archibald F. Bennet, Supervisor of Education, The Genealogical Society, Salt Lake City, Utah; Westminster: Somerset House, The Strand. The volume of administrations for 1662 is missing.   [5] *L.J.* xi. 53, 96.

[6] Sir Richard Colt Hoare, Bart., *Monastic Remains of Witham, Bruton, and Stavordale, Com. Somerset* (Frome, 1824), 25–26.

Warminster, Wiltshire—was still patron of the benefice of Witham Friary; but that part of his estate which included the manor of Witham had been sold to pay death duties.[1] The house at Evercreech still existed in 1824, though in a ruinous state. In an upper apartment a frieze with a wreath of hops alluded to the origin of the name.[2]

―――――――

Historical, as distinguished from literary, biography is less concerned with portraits than with careers and particularly with grafting the personal career of one man on to the main stem of institutions and events. In a work of this kind nuances of personality irrelevant to a more general picture must often be slighted. To assess an uncomplicated man of the early seventeenth century whose own account, though often colourful, is modest and impersonal can be done only within a larger frame of analysis.

There is some consensus that Hopton was the ablest of the Royalist generals,[3] at least after Rupert.[4] A judgement of this kind, which must rest on subtle and often invidious comparisons, can hardly be impartial and must be based to some extent on a predilection for the man himself, on esteem for his private virtues. Apart from his personal merit, there is the overriding consideration that he was fighting, after all, in a *civil* war; and his career throughout is as much that of a social and political leader as of a military commander. What won the west for the Royalists was not exclusively the tactical prowess of Field Marshal Hopton: it was also the character and status of Sir Ralph the country gentleman, local magnate, and deputy lieutenant of the militia.

His strength here lay in his assets as one of the wealthy gentry. In July 1644 he was one of four Royalist 'delinquents', from a total of eighty-seven, who were assessed at £3,000. Only four others were assessed at higher figures: three at £4,000 and one, Sir John Stawell, at £6,000.[5] This affluence is important in understanding, for example, Hopton's position as governor of Bristol. If necessary, he could afford to pay the expenses of recruiting and victualling out of his own pocket, as he did when drawing out the garrison in the autumn of

―――――――

[1] Letter to the author from His Grace, the Duke of Somerset, dated at Maiden Bradley, 17 Feb. 1964.
[2] Hoare, 27–28.
[3] John Richard Green, *History of the English People* (London, 1879), iii. 220.
[4] Young and Adair, 158.
[5] *Cal. C.A.M.* 436.

1643 and again when the Prince of Wales came to Bristol in the spring of 1645.

This burden was particularly his because few others of his command were sufficiently well endowed to share it; this was especially true in Devon and Cornwall. When in 1662 a sum of £60,000 was authorized for indigent Royalist officers, there were more claimants from Hopton's command than any other—113 in all.[1] Nor, it would seem, were all of the soldiers connexions or tenants of the gentry, rich or poor. In December 1649, twenty days after Pride's Purge, information was brought against John Turner of Cornhill, London, a servant of Thomas Lusher, citizen and linen-draper. Turner was accused of having been under arms with Hopton in Cornwall. His 'estate' consisted of two suits of clothes. Their worth being arbitrarily set at £15, he was fined £10 and discharged.[2] This poverty of resource, though an extreme example, explains the apparent ruthlessness with which monies were often levied in the counties.[3]

As one of the wealthier gentry, Hopton was expected to play an important part in politics. His activity, however, was confined largely to the period when he was a deputy lieutenant of Somerset and a member of the Long Parliament. Here he showed himself at first, in B. H. G. Wormald's phrase, a 'nonviolent parliamentarian', who supported reforms, but opposed 'root-and-branch' innovations. One is left with the impression that he thought little of politics except in the broadest, at times almost feudal, terms, as in his championing the right of the bishops to sit in the Lords and his unqualified, unfeigned deference for the House of Stuart. Unencumbered, in contrast to his colleague Edward Hyde, by legal refinements, his sense of the Constitution was traditional and practical; and he allowed his common sense to be guided by more astute and experienced parliamentary heads than his own. After fifteen years of training the militia, derelict lords lieutenant and unpaid muster masters notwithstanding, it was unthinkable for him to contest Culpeper's defence of the King's prerogative right to command it. On the Church—as a high Anglican, but no Laudian, with a tinge of personal puritanism and a tolerance for Calvinists who were unsupported by a foreign power—he could take the same stand as Falkland in supporting the reformation of episcopacy without the abolition of bishops. Brash in debate, he was considered discreet enough to lead the committee presenting the

[1] S.P. 29/68/19, sheet 65.   [2] *Cal. C.A.M.* 1176.
[3] *Cal. C.A.M.* 740, *Cal. C.C.* 977, 1046.

Grand Remonstrance. He was not active in the Oxford Parliament, though at the end of November 1643 he signed the letter of the Royalist peers to the Lords of the Privy Council of Scotland protesting against the Solemn League and Covenant.[1] As a privy councillor, he served as military adviser to the Prince of Wales; faithful in attendance, he was never foremost in directing affairs. Hyde's contention that he was indecisive is open to question. If Hopton's argument in the summer of 1648 that the Prince should leave France for the Netherlands is a clue, he could be blunt and tenacious, hanging on in debate as he did in battle. If his earlier reputation for possessing a hot temper is at all justified, it is likely that his usual aspect of gravity and benevolence, seldom shaken in the camp, may now and then have turned stormy at the council table.

The correlatives of war and politics, or war and society, though of secondary concern in a study of field operations, must be kept in mind when assessing Hopton's military record. The commanders in the Civil War cannot be judged by modern standards. Most were professionally unequipped, with few authorities to guide them, especially at the general command level.[2] Here, in the absence of field marshals and general staffs manipulating corps and divisions, it may be that the question of military 'genius' can be considered more easily in terms of personal charisma; yet Tolstoy's query cuts to the quick of it: 'Is a man a genius who can order bread to be brought up at the right time and say who is to go to the right and who to the left?'[3] At the same time, the Tolstoyan bias, by limiting a military commander to the roles of victualler and tactician, overlooks three-fourths of the attributes of generalship.

The necessary qualities of high command are thus summarized by Douglas S. Freeman in *Lee's Lieutenants:* 'administrative skill and diligence, strategical and logistical sense, military imagination, initiative, resourcefulness, boldness coupled with a grasp of practicality, ability to elicit the best of men, and the more personal qualities of character, endurance, courage, and nervous control'.[4] Most of

---

[1] Clarendon, vii. 287 (6).   [2] Burne and Young, xii–xiii.

[3] Leo Tolstoy, *War and Peace,* translated by Louise and Aylmer Maude (New York, 1642), 714.

[4] Douglas Southall Freeman, *Lee's Lieutenants,* 3 vols. (New York, 1949), i. xxvi. Lee's 'simplicity' and 'spirituality', Freeman thinks, were his essential qualities. They were among Hopton's assets, but, from the standpoint of command efficiency, could be regarded as liabilities as well. Twentieth-century parallels can only be suggested: the self-abnegating character of General George C. Marshall; the austerity of Field-Marshal Bernard Montgomery.

these attributes Hopton had. The recruitment of the Cornish army proved his administrative ability; his aptitude for solving problems of quartering and supply was such as to make this department an almost obsessive interest, distracting his attention from higher command problems. As a drillmaster and tactician he was both acute and tireless: the battle of Lansdown alone would establish him as a figure of exemplary steadfastness and the highest fortitude. His lapses must be acknowledged: there is no excusing the carelessness which provoked Chudleigh's surprise attack at Sourton Down. This incident points to a fundamental flaw: Hopton lacked strategic insight and military imagination. Much of the time he appears to have moved without a definite plan as to where he was going: wavering between Exeter and Plymouth, or between Oxford and Bristol, although it is true that his own movements had to be dictated to some extent by those of the enemy.

In this vacillation, to be sure, he was not alone. The first maxim of von Clausewitz, 'Pursue one great decisive aim with force and determination',[1] was rarely observed by the Royalist command. The 'design for Kent' is a prime instance of a great chance thrown away. The prolonged and fruitless siege of Gloucester in the late summer of 1643 and the failure to destroy Essex at the battle of Newbury shortly after, together with the King's supplementary instructions to clear the 'back country' first and the deficiencies in foot and funds: these obstructions and blunders, by delaying the execution of an autumn campaign and turning it into a winter stalemate, could have been surmounted only by a general of singular daring, willing to pull the beards of his superiors and make audacious demands—someone a little more like George Goring, then languishing in the Tower. A surmise as to the possible consequences if Hopton had shown more ambition, or even some of the brashness he had exhibited in the House of Commons—contradicting everything said 'without scruple' —must remain purely speculative.

He was neither a careerist nor a great military mind: but he was a great gentleman who could face and respect facts and who showed an extraordinary proficiency in the technical aspects of the military art. To repeat: in recruiting, administration, drill, and tactics he was as able as any amateur could be. He was, in short, a field commander of first-rate capacity. This is not precisely the same as being a great

---

[1] Karl von Clausewitz, *Principles of War*, translated and edited by Hans W. Gatzke (Harrisburg, Pa., 1942), 19.

general, but it is something more than being a good regimental officer or chief of staff. Throughout much of the war his position lay in a nebulous area of authority without the sanction of a command in chief. He never held the title of Lord General: this was bestowed on grandees like Hertford and Forth. His first commission was held jointly with three others. From Braddock Down to Lansdown he was first only in the field. It is hardly surprising that his leadership was more effective with cadres than with more integrated forces. Well aware that his professional military experience lay far in the past, he went out of his way to give precedence to Forth at Alresford. But as the earl's associate in that defeat, and as a result of his own failure to breach Waller's defence of Sussex and Surrey, he lost his chance for further preferment and from then on, until the last gloomy dinner at Truro with the taciturn Fairfax, could only follow as the King's star fell.

His caution was no lack of nerve but the necessary forbearance of a subordinate, one rarely admitted to inner councils and then seldom heard. His energy and initiative were stifled because he had to work in association with other commanders of equal or higher rank, and these did not always use him well: he was in fact 'perhaps as badly used a man as can be found amid the many who lost their all in the service of their King'.[1] Charles I as a generalissimo, though never deficient in bestowing honours and endearments, displayed a major weakness by the ineffective support he gave to his best commanders, especially those who, like Hopton, generally lacked a mediating courtier close to the royal ear. So, Hopton received horse when his need was for foot; so, when his request was for money, he was answered with assurances of the King's regard. His capacity for command was demonstrated only when he could act independently, as when leading the Cornish army and again when, stretching the King's instructions, he delayed his retreat from Winchester, pleading the snow. Otherwise, Clarendon's estimate of Hertford more properly applies to Hopton:

He often resigned an excellent understanding to those who had a very indifferent one, and followed the advice, and concluded upon the information of those who had narrower and more vulgar thoughts than suited with his honour, and were not worthy of such a trust.[2]

He was, indeed, too magnanimous in judging other men, willing to overlook not only their shortcomings but their more odious acts and

---

[1] Barrett, 284.   [2] Clarendon, vii. 156.

intrigues, partly because he could or would not stoop to their level, partly because he did not wish to waste time or weaken the King's cause with personal quarrels and recriminations.

His moral position is epitomized in S. R. Gardiner's characterization of an ideal commander:

> There is nothing which goes so far as the power of self-abnegation to make a commander of the first class. He must bear to be misrepresented and traduced, and be ready to work in harmony with or even in subordination to men whose behaviour is most distasteful to him. He must form no schemes, however glorious, which he does not believe himself capable of carrying into execution. He must be willing to relinquish the most assured success, if he sees that it will stand in the way of the ultimate interests of the cause for which he is fighting.[1]

To this extent, Hopton's reluctance to lead a force of weak foot towards Kent can be understood as a reflection on the inadequacies of Royalist recruiting and administration in general, if not on the command structure itself. If he were a loser, he could be blamed for personal oversights and deficiencies, but the blind alleys of a defective strategy were not his creation. The failure to concentrate power, to move swiftly, to follow up success—this responsibility lay elsewhere. Meanwhile, as he strove unremittingly to serve his sovereign Lord, Ralph Hopton might take what comfort he could from recalling his apogee with the Cornish army: for the better part of a year he had commanded the finest infantry that ever took up arms for the King.

[1] Gardiner, iv. 195.

THE COMMAND STRUCTURE OF THE CORNISH ARMY: MAY 1643

This is the most complete list of officers in the Cornish army, though, as a Parliamentary source, its accuracy is not unimpeachable. It is appended to a newsletter from 'J.T.' (Sir Jonathan Trelawney of Plymouth: a Parliamentarian, not to be confused with the Royalist 'Mr. Trelawny', below), dated at Plymouth 15 May 1643: *A True Relation of the proceedings of the Cornish Forces under the command of the Lord Mohune and Sir Ralph Hopton* (B.M., E. 102/17). Irregularities in spelling have been changed to standard usage; first names of general officers and regimental commanders have been added, where known.

GENERAL OFFICERS

Line

Warwick, Lord Mohun:
  Lord General
Sir R. Hopton:
  Lieutenant-General
Col. Wm. Ashburnham:
  Sgt.-Maj.-Gen.
(Sir John Berkeley included in
  commission)

Staff

Mr. Crue: Provost Marshal
Mr. Fuller[1]: Secretary
Mr. Weekley: Capt. of Carriages
Mr. Cory: Quarter-master

Foot Regiments

1. Sir Nicholas Slanning: Colonel
   Sir John Berkeley: Lieut.-Colonel
   Sgt.-Major Mannington
   Captains: Weeks, Cooke, Foster, Rich, Smallacombe, Rous, Piper,
     Poulson

2. Mr. Thomas Basset: Colonel
   Mr. Alexander: Lieut.-Colonel
   Mr. Button: Sgt.-Major
   Captains: Butler, Winter, Fisher, Rose, Frier, Reynolds, Ware

---

[1] Possibly Thomas Fuller, though he did not follow the war as Hopton's chaplain until later that year, after the battle of Bristol (July 1643).

3. Sir Bevill Grenvile: Colonel
   Sir Peter Courtney: Lieut.-Colonel
   M. Deroy: Sgt.-Major
   Captains: Piper, Estcot, Ford, Porter, Smith, Watts, Penvowne

4. Mr. John Trevanion (of Caerhayes): Colonel
   Mr. Edgecombe: Lieut.-Colonel
   Mr. Carey: Sgt.-Major
   Captains: Wise, Southcot, Hollyard, Bates, Stokes, Newton

5. Warwick, Lord Mohun: Colonel
   Sir Wm. Courtney: Lieut.-Colonel
   M. Parrey: Sgt.-Major
   Captains: Lambert, Glyn, Saul, Williams, Mannington, Cory

6. Mr. William Godolphin, Colonel
   Sir Thomas _____(?): Lieut.-Colonel
   Mr. Peters: Sgt.-Major
   Captains: Hill, Mountforke, Salter, Wotton, Furlow, Willis,
   Upton

7. Mr. Charles Trevanion (of Caerhayes): Colonel
   Mr. John Arundell of Trerice ('Jack for the King'): Lieut.-
   Colonel
   Mr. Trelawny: Sgt.-Major
   Captains: Grasse, Burlacy, Haswarfe, Boskoyne, Ballard, Frost
   Plus 1,400 horse.

THE HOPTONS OF SUFFOLK AND SOMERSET

1. Sir Arthur Hopton I, of Cockfield, Westwood, Suffolk
   m. Ann, d. of Sir David Owen, of Cowdrey, Sussex
2. Sir Owen, Lieutenant of the Tower
   m. Ann, d. and coh. of Sir Edward Itchingham
2. Sir Ralph I, Knight Marshal (d. 1572)
   m. Dorothy Pakenham
   Lease of Witham Friary, Som. (1538) and grant of same (1544, 1552), along with Ditcheat and other lands in Somerset and Berks. belonging to Glastonbury Abbey
3. Sir Arthur Hopton II, K.B. (son of Sir Owen)
   m. Rachael, d. of Edm. Hall of Gratford, Lincolnshire
4. Owen
   m. Dorothy, d. and h. of Sir Ralph I
4. Robert, of Witham, Som.
   m. Jane, d. and h. of Rowland Keymes of Vandry, Mon. and widow of Sir Henry Jones
4. Henry, *floruit* 1597
4. Sir Thomas, b. 1584. A gentleman pensioner of the court; acquired lands in his own right
4. Sir Arthur III, K.B. (1588–1650), sheriff of Somerest and ambassador to Spain through the Civil War
   Lands in Suffolk and Norfolk
4. Ann, m. Richard Cole

Children of Robert Hopton, Esq.

5. Sir Ralph II, K.B., Baron Hopton of Stratton (1596–1652)
   m. Elizabeth (1591–1646), d. of Sir Arthur Capel of Hadenham, Herts., and widow of Sir Justinian Lewen
5. William, b. 1598 and living in 1617; no record thereafter
5. Katherine, m. (Sir) John Wyndham
5. Rachel, m. (1) Thomas Morgan; (2) David Kemys of Kevenmably

5. Mary, m. (1) Sir Thomas Hartop; (2) Sir Henry Mackworth
5. Margaret, m. Sir Baynham Throckmorton, 2d Bart.

SOURCES: J. Collinson, *The History and Antiquities of Somerset*, ii. 234; Harl. Soc. xi, *Visitation of the County of Somerset in the year 1623*, F. T. Colby, ed. (London, 1876), 56–7; *Complete Peerage*, vi. 577, n. (c).

ROYALIST CONNEXIONS IN THE WEST

Based on Keeler's *Long Parliament*, the *Dictionary of National Biography*, *The Complete Peerage*, and various *Visitations* by the Heralds printed in the Harleian Soc. series. Courtesy, Prof. T. G. Barnes.

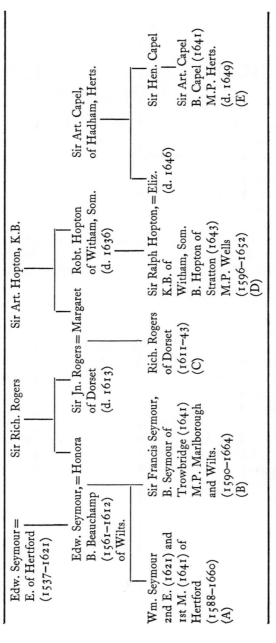

Edw. Seymour =
E. of Hertford
(1537–1621)

Sir Rich. Rogers

Sir Art. Hopton, K.B.

Sir Art. Capel,
of Hadham, Herts.

Edw. Seymour, = Honora
B. Beauchamp
(1561–1612)
of Wilts.

Sir Jn. Rogers = Margaret
of Dorset
(d. 1613)

Robt. Hopton
of Witham, Som.
(d. 1636)

Sir Hen. Capel
(d. 1646)

Wm. Seymour
2nd E. (1621) and
1st M. (1641) of
Hertford
(1588–1660)
(A)

Sir Francis Seymour,
B. Seymour of
Trowbridge (1641)
M.P. Marlborough
and Wilts.
(1590–1664)
(B)

Rich. Rogers
of Dorset
(1611–43)
(C)

Sir Ralph Hopton, = Eliz.
K.B. of
Witham, Som.
B. Hopton of
Stratton (1643)
M.P. Wells
(1596–1652)
(D)

Sir Art. Capel
B. Capel (1641)
M.P. Herts.
(d. 1649)
(E)

A. King's Lord General in the West, 1642–3.
B. Joined King at York, 1642.
C. Helped raise force to defend Sherborne Castle, Dorset, for King, Sept. 1642.
D. Hertford's lieutenant in the West, and, with Rupert, Charles's most able general.
E. King's lieutenant general in Salop, Chester, and North Wales, 1643.

APPENDIX IV

THE DISTRIBUTION OF THE
HOPTON LANDS

Just before his death in 1652 Ralph, Lord Hopton was considering compounding for his estate. The following is a list of properties noted in the *Calendar of the Committee for Compounding* (1650), 2301–5:

1. Witham Friary, Som.
2. Cogan Fleming Manor, Mon. Demised by Sir Ralph Hopton, K.B., in 1640 to Sir John Wyndham, husband of his sister Katherine, for £1,000.
3. Ewyas-Lacy, Hereford. Sir Ralph held a lease thereof for three lives under one Arnold; the lease determined on the decease of Sir Robert Hopton, Esq., Sir Ralph's father, so that it reverted to Arnold.
4. Tilshead Rectory, Wilts.
5. Llanthony Manor, Mon., and other lands and tithes, leased for ninety-nine years or three lives by John Arnold to Owen Hopton for £40 a year. Owen Hopton assigned this estate to his brother Robert, and Robert to his son Sir Ralph.
6. Ditcheat mansion house, Som.
7. Alhampton Manor, Som.
8. Lands in Witham Friary, Nunney parish, Som.
9. Bisset-le-Rose Manor, Suffolk.
10. Lands in Cardiff, Glamorgan, and St. Mellons, Mon.
11. Ewyas-Lacy, Waterston, and Trewaylan manors, Hereford.
12. Langley Fitzurse Manor, Wilts.

BIBLIOGRAPHY

I. *Calendars, State Papers, and Dockets*

Public Record Office: State Papers

Acts of the Privy Council of England, 1550–52, 1552–54, 1554–56, 1577–78, 1578–80. London, 1891 ff.

Transactions and offices of the early Hoptons.

Letters and Papers, Foreign and Domestic, of the Reign of Henry VIII. James Gairdner and R. H. Brodie, eds. London, 1894.

Calendar of Patent Rolls, Edward VI & Philip and Mary. London, 1926, 1937.

Calendar of State Papers, Domestic, 1619–23, 1625–26, 1625–49 (*Supp.*), *1641–43, 1644, 1644–45, 1645–47.*

Calendar of State Papers, Foreign.

Except for incidental mention in the 1620's, the record here on Hopton is almost a complete blank.

Calendar of State Papers, Venetian, 1642–43, 1643–47, 1650. London, 1925 ff. Allen B. Hinds, ed.

Correspondence of the Venetian Secretary, Gerolamo Agostini, to the Doge and Senate. As it is full of rumours, often received at third or fourth hand, it is generally untrustworthy unless used in connexion with more reliable sources.

Calendar of the Proceedings of the Committee for Advance Money 1642–1656. Mary Anne Everett Green, ed. London, 1888.

Of immense value for details on the sequestration of Hopton's estate and for notice of 'delinquents' who were associated with or who served under him.

Calendar of the Proceedings of the Committee for Compounding. (Mrs.) Mary Anne Everett Green, ed. London, 1891.

Useful information on Hopton's estate.

Docquets of Letters Patent and Other Instruments Passed under the Great Seal of King Charles I at Oxford in The Years 1642, 1643, 1644, 1645, and 1646. William Henry Black, ed. London, 1837.

Breviate of Hopton's patent of nobility.

Journals of the House of Commons. London, 1742 ff.

Journals of the House of Lords. London, 1742 ff.

Calendar of the Clarendon State Papers, 4 vols. Ogle, Bliss, Macray, and Routledge, eds. Oxford: Clarendon Press, 1869 ff.

Clarendon MSS. (Bodleian), XXIII, 1738: (1), (2), (3), (4), (6), (7).
Papers of military commanders:
1. Hopton's narrative: July 1642–June 1643.
2. Col. Walter Slingsby: the battles of Lansdown and Roundway
3. Slingsby: the battle of Bristol
4. Hopton: June–July 1643.
6. Hopton: the battle of Alresford
7. Slingsby: the battle of Alresford
Numbers (1), (4), and (6) comprise Hopton's narrative *Bellum Civile*. The hand is that of an official scribe.

Clarendon State Papers: State Papers collected by Edward Earl of Clarendon commencing from the year 1621, 3 vols. R. Scrope and T. Monkhouse, eds. Oxford, 1767–86.

Nicholas State Papers, 3 vols. George F. Warner, editor. Camden Society, 1886, 1892, 1897.

Thurloe State Papers, 7 vols. London, 1742.

(H.M.C.), *Calendar of the MSS. of the Dean and Chapter of Wells*.

II. *Manuscript Sources*

British Museum

Additional MSS. 18,980, 18,981, 18,982, 20,778, 28,273.
Letters of Hopton to Prince Rupert. Some of these are printed, in compressed form, in Eliot Warburton's *Prince Rupert and the Cavaliers*, q.v.
E.g. 2533, 2534. Letters of Hopton to Sir Edward Nicholas.
Harleian MSS. 986, ff. 83–90. This portion of the diary of Richard Symonds (q.v.) gives the breakdown of brigades and regiments at Aldbourne Chase, 10 April 1644.
—— 4712, ff. 33, 204. Preliminaries to the battle of Cheriton Wood: local delinquents and the state of Hopton's intelligence.
—— 6802, 6804, 6851–2. Papers of Sir Edward Walker, Royalist Secretary at War. These folios are concerned mainly with the Oxford army. But Harl. 6802, relating chiefly to transactions of the year 1644, contains numerous references to the western armies and incidentally to Hopton in a series of commissions, warrants for raising forces and fortifying garrisons, orders for receiving money, Acts of Council, etc.

Victoria and Albert Museum, South Kensington

Grenvile Letters. Nine manuscript letters, written 1626–43, by Sir Bevill Grenvile, eight to his wife Grace and one to his son Richard. Includes a vivid description of the battle of Braddock Down.

Bodleian Library

Portland Papers: Nalson Collection. Largely Parliamentarian correspondence, with many references to Royalists.

Rawlinson MSS. 395. Reports on how Hopton was supplied with munitions from Weymouth.

Tanner MSS. LIII, LIX, LX, LXI, LXII, LXIII, LXIV.

Local Archives

Bristol: Common Council Proceedings, 1642–9.

Devizes Museum: Miscellaneous Collection, No. 19. Manuscript copy of C. R. B. Barrett's *Battles and Battlefields in England* (1896), 'Chap. XXVII *Roundway Down, July 13, 1643*'.

Exeter City Library: Ancient Letters of the Corporation of Exeter. Information on city defences in Civil War.

Stafford: William Salt Library, Salt MS. 2007.

(Lord Chan) Clarendon, Book of Memoranda. Otherwise referred to as the Minute Book of the Prince of Wales's council. Describes meetings of the Prince's council held at Bristol between 22 March and 21 April 1645; and three more meetings at Bridgwater at the end of April. Some include the whole council, with dignitaries such as Prince Rupert or George, Lord Goring sitting in. Others include only two or three councillors. Hopton appears to have attended all of them. Useful information on recruiting, finance, and supply. The only detailed primary source for 1645.

Taunton, Somerset Record Office: Manuscripts of Frederick Brown, rector of Nailsea.

Hopton genealogies—92 ff.

Baptism, Lincoln College, death, letter of administration for chattels—138.

Nettlecombe Court MSS. 9 (1): Royal warrant (19 Chas. I, 22 Mar.), given to George Trevillian, Esq. to raise a regiment of foot.
—— 9 (2) 1-b. Copy of letter from Sir Thomas Fairfax, written from Bodmin 5 Mar. 1645/6; and Hopton's reply of 8 Mar., as to terms of surrender. See Carte, below.

—— 9 (2) 1–c. Articles of agreement at Truro, 14 Mar. 1645/6. See Carte, below.

Undated manuscript, probably end of June 1643, in which Hopton recounts events at Taunton, Somerton, Glastonbury, Wells, and Chewton Mendip. The manuscript is perforated and mildewed though partly decipherable with ultra-violet lamp. Fortunately, before rot set in, it was printed by the Camden Society in the *Trevelyan Papers*, Pt. iii, 235–8 (1872), q.v.

Great Torrington, Devon: The parish register, Church of St. Michael and All Angels, courtesy of the Rev. P. G. Harrison, vicar. The burial of sixty-three soldiers 16–21 Feb. 1645/6.

Truro, Cornish Record Office: Bassett MSS.

Hopton's financial transactions with Francis Basset.

—— Tremayne MSS.

Little Hoptoniana of value except for Proposition of the commissioners of Devon, the Cornish reply and counterpropositions, and extended negotiations of these parties running through the early spring of 1643.

Wells, Acts of the Corporation, 1635–44 (resuming 1662).

Useful statistics: price of ammunition, rates for quartering troops. Particularly interesting is correspondence concerning the selection of a municipal recorder, in which Hopton's influence outweighs Prince Rupert's.

Winchester, City Archives: Manuscript of a Royalist, John Trussell, 'Benefactors to Winchester'. Trussell was City Clerk of Winchester at the time of the Royalist occupation 1643–4. His account is a poem in heroic couplets, mostly a lament, but with a few broad references to conditions. A photostat of portions relevant to the Civil War is in the possession of Mr. Richard Sawyer, surveyor, of Winchester. The manuscript is on loan to the City of Winchester from James Osborne of Yale University.

III. *Tracts, Pamphlets, and Newsletters*

Catalogue of the Thomason Tracts 1640–60, 2 vols. London, 1908.

Chief News Books: Royalist: *Mercurius Aulicus*
Parliamentary: *The Perfect Diurnall*
Mercurius Britannicus
Mercurius Politicus
Kingdom's Weekly Intelligencer

Fern, H., D.D. *The Resolving of Conscience, upon this Question. Whether upon such a Supposition or Case, as is now usually made (The King will not discharge his truth but is bent or seduced to subvert Religion, Laws, and Liberties) Subjects may take arms and resist? and whether that case be now?* Cambridge and London, 1642.

Three Speeches Made by the Kings most Excellent Majesty The first to divers Lords and Colonels in His Majesties Tent, the second to His souldiers in the field; the third to His whole Army, immediately before the late Battell at Keinton near Banbury. Wherein His Majesties resolutions are declared, being sent to Master Wallis in London, in a Letter from an eminent Gentleman, Colonell Welton, one of His Majesties Commanders. London, 1642?

The Humble Petition of the Knights, Esquires, Gentry Freeholders, and inhabitants of the County of Somerset. London, 15 June 1642.

Parker, Henry. *The Danger to England Observed, Upon its deserting the High Court of Parliament.* London, 28 July 1642.

A Declaration Made by the Lord Marquese of Hertford and Other Lords and Gentlemen of the County of Somerset, 1642.
Arrest of Parliamentary deputies in Somerset.

True Newes From Somerset-shire. London, 6 August 1642.

A True and Exact Relation of all the Proceedings of Marquesse Hartford ... Sir Ralph Hopton, etc. in the publishing of the Commission of Array in ... Somerset (King's Pamphlet, E. 112, No. 33), 19 August 1642.
Descibes the ambuscade at Marshall's Elm.

A Most Exact and true Relation of the Proceedings of His Maiesties Armie at Shelborne (Sherborne Castle), *written by a Lover of Truth.* London, 1642 (B.M., E. 117.4 & 12).

Anti-Cavalierisme, or, Truth Pleading as well the Necessity, as the Lawfulness of this present War, for the suppression of that Butcherly brood of Cavaliering Incendiaries, who are now hammering England, to make an Ireland of it. London, 1642.

The Lord Marquesse of Hertford, His Letter, Sent to the Queen in Holland. Also a Letter from the Committee in Sommersetshire, to the Houses of Parliament, with copy of their Message to Marquesse Hertford ... whereunto is added certain Votes ... for the apprehending ... Sir Ralph Hopton. ... London, 8 August 1642 (B.M. 1103 e. 72).

The Copy of a Letter sent from Shirbourne relating the skirmish betweene the Earle of Bedford and the cavalliers there. London, (September) 1642.

The Declaration and Remonstrance of the Lords, Knights, and Gentry of the Countie of Cornwall. Agreed on by the whole County in generall, Oct. 10 1642. Wherein is declared the Resolution of the said Lords, Knights, and Gentry, concerning the King and Parliament. Together with their proceedings against Sir Ralph Hopton ... etc. London, 13 October 1642.

Certaine and true news From Somerset-shire; with the besieging of Sir Ralph Hoptons House, together with the valiant and manfully performed courage of Mr. Arnold Hyward Gentleman, Souldier, and Lieutenant to the Troope of young Captaine Pym, son to that worthy and well deserving Member of the House of Commons John Pym Esq. . . . etc. London, 15 October 1642.

To the Right Honourable The House of Commons The Humble Petition of Sir Hugh Pollard which was lately taken prisoner in Somerset-shire, and brought up to London, and committed to the Counter for leavying Warre against the Parliament. London, 28 October 1642.

A Remonstrance or Declaration of the names of the Knights and Gentlemen that take part with Sir Ralph Hopton, and other Delinquents, in Devonshire, and Cornewall with the number of their Forces. Also the names of the Knights and Gentlemen that stand well affected to the Parliament . . . etc. London, 29 October 1642.

New Plots Discovered, Against the Parliament and the Peace of the Kingdome. In two letters, the one sent from the Marquis of Hartford, to Sir Ralph Hopton, the other sent from Sir Ralph Hopton to the said Marquis . . . etc. London, 3 November 1642.

True Intelligence from Cornwall: Being a true Relation of the Rising of 600 Fishermen and their Wives, and falling upon Sir Ralph Hopton and the Cavaliers, wounding Sir Ralph himselfe. . . . Also how the day following Sir Ralph Hopton with 500 men took some few Fishermen, and tied them to trees, whipping them naked . . . etc. From 'J. T.' London, 10 November 1642.

True and Joyfull Newes From Exeter. Showing how Sir Ralph Hopton, Sir Bevill Greenvill, with divers of the Cornish Malignants, made their approaches thither . . . etc. London, 25 November 1642.

The Covenant entered into by the Mayor of Exeter, Deputy-Lieutenants

of that County, and Common-Councell of that City To defend the
City and County against Sir Ralph Hopton and his adherents in
this their Rebellious Insurrections . . . etc. London, 1642.

A Letter from Bristoll the tenth of December 1642. London, 1642.

Remarable (sic) Passages Newly received of the great overthrow of Sir
Ralph Hopton and his Forces; At Madburie, 12. miles from
Plimouth . . . etc. London, 14 December 1642.

The True Copie of A Letter sent from Sir Ralph Hopton, Col.
Ashburnham, and Sir John Berkeley, to Mr. Christopher Clarke,
Mayor of the City of Excester . . . etc. *With the Answer which the*
Mayor returned to them. London, 1642.

A Famous Victory Obtained before the City of Exeter, on Sunday
January 1 by Captaine Pym, Against Sir Ralph Hopton, and the
Cornish Cavaliers . . ., etc. *Being the Copie of a Letter, sent from*
Lieutenant Abell Hyword. . . . *Bearing date January 2, 1642/43.*
6 January 1643.

Speciall Passages And certaine Informations from severall places
Collected for the use of all that desire to be truely Informed. From
Tuesday the 3 of January, to Wednesday the 11 of January 1642
(1643) (Number 22).

A True Relation of a late Victorie obtained by Sir Ralph Hopton Against
My Lord of Stamfords Forces in Cornwall. Which (through the
mercifulnesse of the Generall Sir Ralph Hopton) was gotten with
little bloodshed . . . etc. Oxford, 28 January 1643.

A Continuation of certaine Speciall and Remarkable Passages from both
Houses of Parliament, and other Parts of the Kingdom. From
Thursday the 26, of January to the 2 of February, 1642 (1643).
(Number 29.) Item 12: *Of the Earl of Stamfords proceedings*
against Sir Ralph Hopton . . . etc.

Good Newes from Plymouth: Being a true Relation of the death of Sir
Ralph Hopton, and many of his Commanders, who by treachery
sought to surprise the good Towne of Plymouth. London, 20
February 1643.

A most true Relation of divers notable Passages of Divine Providence in
the great deliverance and wonderfull victory obtained by the
Parliaments Forces under the command of the Earle of Stamford,
in the County of Devon, against the Army of Cavaliers, raised by
Sir Ralph Hopton. . . . London, 1 May 1643.

Speciall Passages And certain Informations from severall places,
collected for the use of all that desire to be truely Informed. From

Tuesday the 25 of April, to Tuesday the 2 of May 1643. (Number
38.) Pp. 310–13 (B.M., E. 100.17). Chudleigh's account of
Sourton Down, dated at Okehampton, 26 April 1643.

Exploits Discovered, In A Declaration of some proceedings of Serjeant
Major Chudley, Generall of the Forces under the Earle of
Stamford: Against Sir Ralph Hopton. Fully relating the great
overthrow given to him. As it was sent in a Letter from Exon.
(Aprill 29) to a Man of Note in London, 2 May 1643.

A Full Relation of the great defeat given to the Cornish Cavalliers, By
Sergeant Major Generall Chudley, Confirmed by divers Letters
from those parts to severall Merchants in London. London, 3 May
1643. Chudleigh's own account, a separate pamphlet.

A True Relation of the Proceedings of the Cornish Forces . . . from
'J. T.', dated at Plymouth 15 May 1643. London, 1643.
Dispositions and command structure of the Cornish army just
before Stratton.

The Round-Heads Remembrancer: or, A true and particular Relation
of the great defeat given to the Rebels by His Majesties good
Subjects of the County of Cornwall, under the command of Sir
Ralph Hopton, on Tuesday May 16, 1643. Oxford, 1643.

The Copie of a Letter Sent from the Maior of Bristoll unto a Gentleman
. . . *in London, relating The great defeat given to the Cavaliers in*
those parts by Sir William Waller, and Sir Arthur Haslerig. . . .
Dated 8 July 1643.
Remote Parliamentary view of Lansdown fight.

Sir John Byron's Relation to the Secretary of the Last Western
Action. . . . York, 1643.
Eyewitness account of the battle of Roundway.

A True Relation of the late Fight between Sir Will. Waller's Forces,
and those from Oxford, with the manner of Sir Will. Waller's
Retreat to Bristoll. . . . London, 1643 B.M., E. 61 (6).

A copie of the Articles agreed upon at the surrender of the City of Bristol
. . . etc. London, 1643.

The true Copie of a Letter sent from an Inhabitant of Bridgewater in
the County of Somerset . . . *unto a Quartermaster of a Troope of*
Horse belonging to the Westerne Brigade. From Henry Davey,
dated at Bridgwater 27 October 1643.

A Narration of The Great Victory . . . *Obtained by the Parliament's*
Forces . . . *at Alton in Surrey* . . . etc. London, 1643.

A Great Over-throw: Given to Sir Ralph Hopton's whole Army by

Sir William Waller neere Farnham, with onely sixe Troope of Horse, and some Foote . . . etc. London, 1643.

An Exact and True Relation of the taking of Arundel Castle The sixt of this present January, between nine and ten of the clock in the forenoone. . . . London, 1644 (B.M., E. 81.12).

Certain Propositions made by Sir William Waller at the Surrender of Arundell-Castle Together with a List of the Names of the Commanders taken in the said Castle. . . . London, 11 January 1644 (B.M., E. 81.21).

Thirty-three Religions, Sects, Societies, and Factions, of the Cavaliers now in Armes against the Parliament. London?, 1644.

Winchester Taken together with a fuller relation of the Great Victory at Alsford, by 'E. A.', eye-witness report. London, 1644 (B.M., E. 40.1 & 40.9).

B.M., T.T., E. 40.12: letter from Captain John Jones, dated at Alresford 29 March 1644.

'Memorial of Denzil Lord Holles written . . . in Normandy 1648', *Select tracts relating to the Civil Wars in England in the Reign of King Charles I,* Baron Maseres, editor (R. Withes, London: 1815), i. 206.

B.M., T.T., E. 40.13: Sir William Balfour's letter of 30 March. London, 1644.

B.M., T.T., E. 53.10: Edward Walsingham, *Britannicus Virtutis Imago.* London, June 1644.

A True Relation of the Storming of Bristoll, And the taking the Town, Castle, Forts, etc. Letter from 'J. R.' to Speaker William Lenthall. London, 13 September 1645.

A Declaration of His Highnesse Prince Rupert with a narrative of the State and Condition of the City and Garrison of Bristoll, when his Highnesse Prince Rupert came thither . . . etc. (September) 1645.

The Rev. John Heydon, *The Discovery of the wonderfull preservation of his Excellencie Sir Thomas Fairfax, the Army, the Records of the Town, the Library, and blessed Bible under the hands of the Major, Aldermen, Captain, and Schoolmaster of Torrington in Devon.* 1647.

A True Relation concerning the late Fight at Torrington Between the Forces under the command of Sir Thomas Fairfax, and the Forces under the command of the Lord Hopton and others. 20 February 1645/6. (Original among manuscripts of the House of Lords.)

A Fuller Relation of Sir Thomas Fairfax's Routing all the King's

Armies in the West under Prince Charles, the Lord Hopton, the Lord Goring, and all the rest at Torrington: with the manner of the Fight and the number kill'd and taken on both sides. Letter from one of the clerks of the Parliamentary army to an M.P., dated 16 February 1646, midnight. Printed in London.

A List of the particulars of what was taken, and how many killed at this Victory against the Enemy at Torrington. London, 21 February 1645/6.

A Summons From His Excellency Sir Thomas Fairfax to Sir Ralph Hopton And his Forces Now in Cornwall. London, 11 March 1645/6.

A more Full and Exact Relation (Being the Third Letter to the Honorable William Lenthal Esquire, Speaker of the Honorable House of Commons) of the several Treaties between Sir Tho. Fairfax and Sir Ralph Hopton, and of his coming into the Parliament.... From 'J. R.', dated at Truro, 13 March 1645/6. London, 18 March 1645/6.

His Majesties Whole Army in the West Conquered, And all Sir Ralph Hoptons Horse and Armes delivered to Sir Thomas Fairfax: With the copies of the severall Letters that passed between them . . . etc. London, 16 March 1645/6.

A late Letter From Sir Thomas Fairfaxs Army now in Truro. Relating the severall Passages in the Treaty, And what is concluded. Communicated to both Houses of Parliament upon Munday 16. March 1645 (1646). London, 17 March 1645/6.

Sir Thomas Fairfaxs His last Letter of the Treaty with Sir Ralph Hopton, And a Declaration of the proceedings of his Majesties Agents with the Irish Rebels . . . and other Notable Observances, by way of answer to Sir Ralph Hopton. A Copy of Sir Ralph Hoptons Demands . . . etc. London, 18 March 1645/6.

Peters, Hugh. *Master Peters Message from Sir Thomas Fairfax with the Whole State of the West and all the Particulars about the Disbanding of the Prince and Sir Ralph Hopton's Army.* London, 1646.

Severall Propositions Presented To the Members of the Honourable House of Commons, by Mr. Peters, Minister of the Gospell . . . with A Discovery of two great plots against the Parliament. . . . The First, By the Queen. . . . The Second by the Lord Hopton.... London, 1 December 1646.

A Declaration Sent from the Right Honorable Ralph Lord Hopton To

The Gentlemen and Inhabitants of Cornwall, and the Counties Adjacent, concerning his Ingagement for and in behalf of Prince Charles, who now is King Charles the Second, King of Great Brittayne, &c. And Desiring their joynt Assistance to settle Him in His Crowne and Dignitie as He is their Lawfull Soveraigne. 19 February 1648/9 (B.M., E. 544.131).

A Great Fight near Pendennis Castle in Cornwall Between The Lord Hopton, and the Parliaments Forces, upon the landing of his men for the fetching in of provision; with the number killed and wounded on both sides . . . etc. 2 April 1649 (B.M., E. 549.9).

The Declaration of the Right Honorable Ralph Lord Hopton, Lieutenant Generall of all His Majesties Forces designed for the West of England to All His Maiesties loving Subjects Inhabiting in the severall Counties of Cornwall, Devonshire, Sommerset, Wilts, Bristol, Bath and Wells and the Counties adjacent. From Plymouth, 20 May 1650.

A Message sent From The Lord Hopton, and Sir Richard Greenvill to the Prince, and a fight in the Isle of Guernsey . . . etc. Noted in letter of 'T. S.', dated at Exeter, 1 June 1650. London, 7 June 1650.

A List of Officers Claiming to the Sixty Thousand Pounds, &c. Granted by His Sacred Majesty for the Relief of His Truly-Loyal and Indigent Party. . . . London, 1663 (SP 29/68/19).

IV. *Seventeenth-Century Military Books*

Cockle, Maurice J. D., ed. *A Bibliography of English Military Books to 1642.* London, 1900.

Dallington, Robert. *Aphorisms Civil and Military.* London, 1613.

Edmunds, Clement. *Observations Upon the Five First Bookes of Caesar's Commentaries.* Printed by Peter Short, 1600.

Eldred, William. *The Gunner's Glasse.* 1646.

Fourquevaux, Raimond de Baccarie de Pavie. *Instructions for the Warres.* 1589.
   One of the most famous and widely read books of its kind.

de Gheyn, Jacob. *The Exercise of Armes for Calivres, Muskettes, and Pikes.* The Hague, 1607.

Hexham, Henry. *The Three parts of the Principles of the Art Military, Practiced in the Warres of the United-Provinces . . .* etc. London, The Hague, etc., 1637–41.

Hexham was quartermaster to Col. George Goring's regiment of foot in the Low Countries.

Instructions for Musters and Arms, and the Use Thereof. London, 1623.
Twelve pages of instructions for the militia, recurrently ordered to be implemented in the years following publication. An official manual.

Markham, Francis. *Five Decades of Epistles of Warre.* London, 1622.

Markham, Gervase. *The Souldiers Accidence or an Introduction Into Military Discipline.* London, 1635.
This book furnished militia officers with much practical information. It particularly evinces familiarity with Continental military practice.

——— *The Souldiers Grammar.* 2 parts. London, 1626 and 1639.

Militarie Instructions for the Cavallrie. Cambridge, 1632.
A minute treatment of Continental cavalry organization.

Monck, George. *Observations upon Military and Political Affairs.* 1671.
Written while he was a prisoner in the Tower. Excerpts in the *J.S. Army H.R.* iii. 50–51.

Norton, Robert. *The Gunner.* London, 1628.

Rich, Barnabe. *Farewell to Military Profession.* 1581.

Ward, Robert. *Animadversions of Warre.* 1639.

V. *Periodicals*

English Historical Review.
Journal of the Society for Army Historical Research.
Devon, Notes and Queries. From 1910, *Devon and Cornwall, Notes and Queries.*
Reports and Transactions of the Devonshire Association.
Notes and Queries for Hampshire.
Notes and Queries for Somerset and Dorset.
Transactions of the Shropshire Archaeological Society.
Somerset Archaeological and Natural History Society Proceedings.
The Wiltshire Archaeological and Natural History Magazine.

VI. *Monographs and General Works*

Alexander, J. J. and Hooper, W. R. *The History of Great Torrington in the County of Devon.* Sutton, Surrey, 1948.

Alumni Cantabrigienses. John Venn and J. A. Venn, eds. 4 vols.
Cambridge University Press, 1922, 1924, 1927.
Alumni Oxonienses. Joseph Foster, ed. Oxford and London, 1891,
1892.
Atkyns, Richard. *The Vindication of Richard Atkyns Esquire, as also
A Relation of Several Passages in the Western War.* London, 1669.
A humorous, highly idiosyncratic personal account, with some
pungent descriptions. The military parts of this work have been
edited by Lieutenant-Colonel Peter Young in 'The Praying
Captain—a Cavalier's Memoirs', *J.S. Army H.R.* xxv (1957), q.v.
Aubrey, John. *Brief Lives.* Oliver Lawson Dick, ed. London, 1949.
Social anecdotage.
Bailey, John E. *Life of Thomas Fuller.* London, 1874.
Fuller was Hopton's chaplain.
Bampfield, Joseph. *Colonel Joseph Bamfeild's Apologie.* The Hague?,
1685.
Barnes, Thomas Garden. *Somerset, 1625–40: A County's Government
During the Personal Rule.* Harvard University Press, 1961.
Excellent for Hopton as deputy lieutenant.
Barrett, C. R. B. *Battles and Battlefields in England.* London, 1896.
No documentation, but useful for pictorial sketches of battle-sites:
Stratton, Lansdown, Roundway.
Bartholomew's Survey Gazetteer of the British Isles. Seventh edition.
Edinburgh, 1927.
Bates-Harbin, Sophia W. (Mrs. Cosmo W. H. Rawlins). *Members of
Parliament from the County of Somerset.* Taunton, 1939.
Background on the first Sir Ralph Hopton, Knight Marshal, and
his brother Sir Owen, Lieutenant of the Tower, with Hopton
coat-of-arms.
Bayley, A. R. *The Civil War in Dorset, 1642–1660.* Taunton, 1910.
Berlin, Isaiah. *The Hedgehog and the Fox.* New York, 1957.
Bibliotheca Somersetensis. Emanuel Green, ed. 3 vols. Taunton, 1902.
Blore, Thomas. *The History and Antiquities of Rutland.* London,
1684–7.
The Rev. E. J. Bodington, 'The Battle of Roundway Down', *Wilts.
Arch. & Nat. Hist.* xxxvii (1912), 593–602.
Bracken, C. W. *A History of Plymouth and Her Neighbours.* Plymouth,
1931, 1934.
Brunton, Douglas and Pennington, D. H. *Members of the Long
Parliament.* London, 1954.

Burne, Lieutenant-Colonel A. H. *The Battlefields of England.* London, 1950.

—— *More Battlefields of England.* London, 1952.

Burne, Lieutenant-Colonel Alfred H. and Young, Lieutenant-Colonel Peter. *The Great Civil War.* London, 1954.

Campbell, Mildred. *The English Yeoman.* New York, 1942, 1960.

Carte, Thomas. *Original Letters.* London, 1739.
  Hopton's account to the Prince of Wales for 15 January–13 April 1646 (see pp. 109–26).

Certificate of Musters in the County of Somerset. Emanuel Green, ed. Printed for the Somerset Record Society (vol. xx). London, 1904.

Chevalier, Jean. 'Journal et Recueil des choses les plus remarquables en l'isle de Jersey, arrivées pendant les Guerres Civiles sous les regnes des Rois Charles Premier et Charles Second', Historical Manuscripts Commission, Appendix to Second Report. London, 1870.

Churchill, Winston S. *The World Crisis, 1911–1914.* London, 1923.

Clarendon, Edward Hyde, Earl of. *History of the Rebellion and the Civil Wars in England.* W. Dunn Macray, ed. 6 vols. Oxford, 1888.
  Sections on the war in the west are taken straight from Hopton himself, who served as a critic and adviser for this work.

von Clausewitz, Karl. *Principles of War.* Hans W. Gatzke, ed. Harrisburg, Pa., 1942.

Coate, Mary. *Cornwall in the Great Civil War.* Truro, 1933, 1963.

Cobbett's Parliamentary History, i and ii. London, 1806, 1807.
  To be used with caution for the Civil War period.

Collinson, John. *The History and Antiquities of the County of Somerset.* 3 vols. Bath, 1791. Index and supplement: Taunton, 1898.

The Complete Peerage (of George E. Cokayne). Vicary Gibbs, *et al.,* eds. 12 vols. London, 1910–59.
  The most complete capsule account of Hopton.

Complete Parochial History of the County of Cornwall. Truro, 1872 (J. Lake, printer).
  Note supplementary papers.

Curtis, Mark H. *Oxford and Cambridge in Transition.* Oxford, 1959.

Curtis, William. *History of Alton.* London, 1896.

Davies, Godfrey. *The Early Stuarts.* Oxford, 1937.

Diary of Sir Henry Slingsby. Daniel Parsons, ed. London, 1836.

Useful, but sketchy. Sir Henry's cousin Walter Slingsby was one of Hopton's regimental officers.

Dictionary of National Biography. Oxford, 1908.

See vol. ix, pp. 1241–4 for sketch of Hopton by Sir Charles H. Firth. A good summary, though dated.

Dugdale, Sir William. *Baronage of England.* London, 1675–6.

—— *The Life, Diary, and Correspondence of Sir William Dugdale* . . . W. Hamper, ed. London, 1827.

Summary notation of important events and movements in sketchy calendrical form.

Emmison, F. G. *Tudor Secretary: Sir William Petre at Court and Home.* Harvard University Press: Cambridge, Mass., 1961.

Firth, Sir Charles H. *Cromwell's Army.* London and New York, 1902.

Indispensable for military background: organisation, weapons, etc.

—— 'The Capture of Bristol by Lord Fairfax in 1645, and the vindication of Nathaniel Fiennes by Cromwell and the officers of the New Model', *Notes and Queries,* seventh series, ix. 181–2 (1890).

Fisk, William L. 'The Straffordians—a Cross Section of Conservative Political Thought', *The Historian,* xxvi. 341–55. August, 1959.

Forster, John. *Arrest of the Five Members by Charles I.* London, 1860.

A Whig historian uses Hopton to refute Clarendon's statement that the Commons was entirely in the hands of the 'popular' party after the arrest of the Five Members.

—— *The Grand Remonstrance.* London, 1860.

Describes the encounter in the Commons between Hopton and Sir Simonds D'Ewes, reflecting the attitude towards the 'Ancient Parliament Man' (Hopton) of one who really knew Parliamentary procedure.

Fortescue, J. W. *A History of the British Army.* 13 vols. London and New York, 1899 ff.

Freeman, Douglas Southall. *Lee's Lieutenants.* New York, 1949.

Fuller, Thomas. *History of the Worthies of England.* 3 vols. London, 1840.

Fuller served as Hopton's regimental chaplain for a few months in 1643–4.

Gardiner, Samuel Rawson. *History of England to 1642.* 10 vols. London, 1887 ff. Edition of 1901–3 is best.

—— *History of the Great Civil War.* 4 vols. London, 1893 ff.

—— *Letters and Papers Illustrating the Relations Between Charles the Second and Scotland in 1650.* [date ?]

Gerard, Thomas. *The Particular Description of the County of Somerset, 1633.* E. H. Bates-Harbin, ed. Somerset Record Society (vol. xv). Frome, 1900.

Gibb, M. A. *The Lord General: A Life of Thomas Fairfax.* London, 1938.

A eulogy of Fairfax, though it does not denigrate Hopton. Might be useful for comparison of the stereotypes 'noble Puritan' and 'noble Cavalier'.

Godolphin, Sidney. *Poems.* W. Dighton, ed. Oxford, 1931.

Godwin, G. N. *The Civil War in Hampshire.* Southampton and London, 1904.

Not formally documented and savouring somewhat of the gentle country antiquary. Good for local background. Portrait of Hopton in his peer's robes.

De Gomme, Sir Bernard. 'Bristol taken by Prince Rupert: Julye 26, 1643.' Transcribed in *J.S. Army H.R.* iv. 180–203 (1925), with an introduction by Prof. Sir Charles H. Firth and notes by Lieutenant-Colonel J. H. Leslie (Maps and Plans).

De Gomme was one of the foremost military engineers of his day. His account, which is detailed, is a thoroughly businesslike and professional piece of work.

Granville, George, Lord Lansdowne. *A Letter to the Author of Reflexions Historical and Political. . . .* London, 1782.

Charles I's letter of thanks to the Cornish.

Granville, Roger. *The History of the Granville Family.* Exeter, 1895.

Useful background on Sir Bevill Grenvile.

—— *The King's General in the West.* London and New York, 1908.

The 'King's General' here is Sir Richard Grenvile, who might be compared with Hopton as the 'King's Man'. The work is admittedly an apology.

Green, Emanuel. *On the Civil War in Somerset.* Somerset Archaeological and Natural History Society, 1869.

Green, Mary Anne Everett. *Elizabeth, Electress Palatine and Queen of Bohemia.* London, 1855, 1909.

Incidental mention of the 'postilion' episode, in which the 'Queen of Hearts' rides behind Hopton, then a young cadet, in the flight from Prague, 1620. It adds nothing, however, to David Lloyd's meagre account.

Guizot, François Pierre Guillaume. *L'Histoire de la Revolution D'Angleterre*. Paris, 1826 ff. Translation by William Hazlitt, 1846.

Hall, A. R. *Ballistics in the Seventeenth Century: A Study in the Relations of Science and War*. Cambridge University Press, 1952.

Harrison, the Rev. P. G., *Vicar of Great Torrington*. Torrington Parish Church, undated brochure.

Particulars on the partial destruction of the church in the battle of Torrington, 16 February 1646.

Hill, Christopher and Dell, Edmund. *The Good Old Cause*. London, 1949.

Hillier, G. *The Sieges of Arundel Castle, In the County of Sussex, By Sir Ralph Hopton, Commander of the Royalist Army, in December, 1643–4. And By Sir William Waller, General for the Parliament, in January, 1644*. London, 1854.

According to the author, this narrative was taken from a manuscript compiled 'several years before' for the Duchess of Norfolk. He lists other sources, all printed: *The Parliament Scout, Scottish Dove, Mercurius Civicus, Weekly Account, True Informer*, Waller's Letters to Lenthall, Waller's *Vindication* (1793), the *Sussex Archaeological Journal*, and 'the entire series of tracts of the time'. There is little mention of Hopton *per se*.

Hoare, Sir Richard Colt, Bart. *Monastic Remains of Witham, Bruton, and Stavordale, Com. Somerset*. Frome, 1824.

Fifty copies only, privately printed. Contains Hopton pedigree.

Hopton, Ralph, Lord. *Bellum Civile: Hopton's Narrative of His Campaign in the West, and other Papers*. C. E. H. Chadwyck-Healey, ed. For Somerset Record Society. Frome, London, 1902.

This is the main source for the first half of the western war, covering the period from 1 August 1642 at Shepton Mallet to 29 March 1644 at Alresford, drawn from the Clarendon MSS., XXIII: 1738 (1), (4), and (6). Miss D. M. Barrett of the Bodleian Library confirms that the manuscript is neither Hopton's own hand nor that of William Edgeman, Sir Edward Hyde's secretary. It appears simply to be a 'fair copy' by an anonymous scribe.

Hugo, Victor. *Les Misérables*. 2 vols. H. M. Caldwell Co., New York and Boston, n.d.

Hunt, W. *The Somerset Diocese, Bath and Wells*. London, 1885.

Hurstfield, Joel. *Elizabeth I and the Unity of England*. New York, 1960.

Inderwick, Frederick A. *The Interregnum (1648–1660): Studies of the Commonwealth, Legislative, Social, and Legal.* London, 1891.

Journal of Sir Simonds D'Ewes. From the Beginning of the Long Parliament to Strafford's Trial. Wallace Notestein, ed. Yale University Press, *et al.*, 1923.

—— *From the First Recess of the Long Parliament to the King's Withdrawal from London.* Willson Havelock Coates, ed. Yale University Press, *et al.*, 1942.

The Journeys of Celia Fiennes. Christopher Morris, ed. London, 1947. Useful for vignettes of a western journey made in 1698 by a daughter of Colonel Nathaniel Fiennes, Parliamentary Governor of Bristol in 1643.

Kaufman, Helen Andrews. *Conscientious Cavalier.* London, 1962. Based on the diaries and letters of Colonel Bullen Reymes, M.P., F.R.S. (1613–72), who served under Hopton in the west. Useful for the last phase of the campaign, though Hopton does not often appear.

Keeler, Mary Frear. *The Long Parliament, 1640–41: A Biographical Study of Its Members.* Philadelphia, 1954. First secondary source to record the real year of Hopton's birth (1596).

Kershaw, R. N. 'The Elections for the Long Parliament, 1640', *E.H.R.* xxxviii (October 1923), 496–508.

Lloyd, David. *Memoirs of Excellent Personages.* London, 1668. Receive with caution. Lloyd erroneously states that Hopton was born in Monmouthshire in 1601. Presumably, however, he had some personal knowledge of him. In addition to short accounts of the battles of Braddock and Stratton, there is a marginal note on the episode with the Queen of Bohemia.

Locke, Audrey. *The Seymour Family: History and Romance.* London, 1911. Incidental mention of Sir Owen Hopton, Lieutenant of the Tower, Sir Ralph Hopton's great-grandfather.

Lodge, Edmund. *Portraits of Illustrious Personages of Great Britain. . . .* London, 1821–34. See vol. iii for portrait of Hopton in his peer's robe.

Ludlow, Edmund. *Memoirs.* Vivoy, 1698–9; London, 1720–1; Edinburgh, 1751; Oxford, 1894 (2 vols.): C. H. Firth, ed. Details on the Civil War in Wiltshire, 1643–5. Ludlow, a Parliamentarian, concedes that Hopton on several occasions acted with magnanimity against the licence of his own troops.

Luke, Sir Samuel. *Journal of Sir Samuel Luke*. Transcribed and edited with an introduction by I. G. Philip, Secretary of the Bodleian. Issued by the Oxfordshire Record Society for the years 1947, 1950, 1952, and 1953. They cover the years 1642/3 to 1644 (to 29 March). 3 vols. Pagination continuous:
Vol. i (pp. 1–86): 9 February 1642/3–3 May 1643
Vol. ii (pp. 87–184): 1 June 1643–31 October 1643
Vol. iii (pp. 185–288): 1 November 1643–29 March 1644
Luke was scoutmaster-general of the main Parliamentary army under the Earl of Essex. Concerning Hopton, these reports are generally accurate with respect to his immediate past movements, but confusing and unreliable with respect to his designs.

Luke, Sir Samuel. *Letter-Books of 1644–45*. Edited, with an introduction, by H. G. Tibbutt. Bedfordshire Historical Record Society Publications, vol. xlii, Bedford, and H.M. Stationery Office, York House, Kingsway, London.
Brigadier Peter Young, of the Royal Military College, Sandhurst, says: 'The most important single source-book for the Civil War . . . since the end of the second world war.'

Markham, Clements R. *A Life of the Great Lord Fairfax*. [date ?]

Metcalfe, Walter C. *Book of Knights Banneret, Knights of the Bath*. London, 1855.

Military Memoir of Colonel John Birch. Written by Mr. Roe, his secretary. The Rev. John Webb and the Rev. T. W. Webb, eds. Printed for the Camden Society, 1873.

Nichols, John Gough, ed. *Literary Remains of King Edward the Sixth*. Edited from his autograph manuscripts. London, 1857.

Notestein, Wallace. *The English People on the Eve of Colonization*. New York, 1954.

Oman, Sir Charles. *Art of War in the Middle Ages*. New York, 1937. Includes a short section on the seventeenth century.

—— *A History of the Art of War in the Sixteenth Century*. New York, 1937.
A useful chapter on Tudor armaments, organization, ranks, etc.

Parkes, Miss Joan. *Travel in England in the Seventeenth Century*. Oxford University Press, 1925. Reviewed in *J.S. Army H.R.* iv. 178.
Sorry state of roads and problems of army transport.

Peacock, Edward, F.S.A. *The Army Lists of the Roundheads and Cavaliers*. London, 1863, 1874.

Phillips, William, ed. *The Ottley Papers Relating to the Civil War*. Transactions of the Salop. Archaeological Society, 2d series, vol. vii, Pt. ii, 1875.
Letter from Hopton to Sir Francis Ottley concerning recovery of butts of wine.

Prest, J. M. 'The Campaign of Roundway Down', *Wilts. Arch. & Nat. Hist.* liii. 277–93 (June 1950).
Almost entirely derivative, citing Boddington and Burne, as well as Clarendon and Hopton. But useful photoplates of Roundway Down (one showing new wooded growth) and sketch maps based on Ordnance Survey.

Quarter Session Records for the County of Somerset, Charles I. E. H. Bates-Harbin, ed. Somerset Record Society (vol. xxiv). London, 1908.
Useful for Hopton's record as J.P.

Rait, Robert S. *Five Stuart Princesses*. New York, 1902.

'Recollections by Sir William Waller', printed as an appendix to *The Poetry of Anna Matilda*. Published by J. Bell, 1788.
A highly romanticized account, of little historical value.

Roberts, Michael. *Gustavus Adolphus*. London and New York, 1958.

Rogers, Inherman, 'Barnstaple, Bideford, and Torrington During the Civil War', *Devon, Repts. & Trans.* lix. 323 ff.

Rowe, Violet. 'Influence of the Earls of Pembroke . . .'. *E.H.R.* l. 240–56.
The scope of power of Hopton's Parliamentary patrons.

Roy, Ian. 'The Royalist Army in the First Civil War'. Unpublished D.Phil. thesis. Oxford, 1963.

—— 'The Royalist Council of War, 1642–6', *Bulletin of the Institute of Historical Research*, No. 35 (November 1962), 150–68.

The Rump: An Exact Collection of the Choicest Poems and Songs relating to the Late Times. 1662.

Rushworth, John. *Historical Collections*. . . . 8 vols. London, 1680–1722.

Saintsbury, George. *Minor Poets of the Caroline Period*. Oxford, 1906.

Sanford, John Lanyton. *Studies and Illustrations of the Great Rebellion*. London, 1858.
Royalist letters of 1645: Culpeper, Capel, Digby. Most unsympathetic to reforming Royalists in the Long Parliament.

Sealy, Lucy. *The Champions of the Crown*. London, 1911.
The only attempt at a comprehensive sketch of Hopton, apart from

Firth's *D.N.B.* article, that our own times can show. Based mainly on David Lloyd's *Memoirs*, it is undocumented.

Seral, Thomas. 'On the Strodes of Somersetshire', *Som. Arch. & Nat. Hist.* xiii (1865–6), Pt. ii, 14–15.

Seyer, Samuel, the younger. *Memoirs historical and topographical of Bristol and its neighbourhood from the earliest period down to the present time.* 2 vols.
Vol. ii, pp. 295–467, covers the Civil War.

Short Title Catalogue. Donald Wing, ed. Columbia University Press, 1945 ff.

Somerset Assize Orders, 1629–40. Thomas G. Barnes, ed. Printed by Butler & Tanner, Frome, for the Somerset Record Society (vol. lxv), 1959.

Sprigge, Joshua. *Anglia Rediviva.* (Original: London, 1647.) Harry T. Moore, ed. Gainesville, Fla., 1854.
A puritan gives the Parliamentary view of the war down to 'England's Recovery'. Contains the articles of the treaty between Hopton and Fairfax at Truro in March 1646. Also duplicate of Hopton's letter in Carte (q.v.).

Stewart, Colonel David, 'Military Surgeons in the Sixteenth and Seventeenth Centuries', *J.S. Army H.R.* xxvi. 151–7.
Little information on Royalist medical service in Civil War, other than that most of the surgeons were in London, and so unavailable to the King.

Sturgess, Herbert Arthur Charlie. *Middle Temple Record.* London, 1949.
Register of admissions to the Honourable Society of the Middle Temple from the fifteenth century to the year 1944.

Symonds, Richard. *Diary of the Marches of the Royal Army During the Great Civil War.* Charles E. Long, ed. Printed for the Camden Society (No. 74), 1859.
Published from B.M., Add. MSS. 17,062, this record covers the period 10 April 1644–17 December 1644 and 24 April 1645–11 February 1646. It is accurate, but a meagre account on the whole. Contains useful descriptions of towns and distances between them.

Thomas, Hugh. *The Spanish Civil War.* New York, 1961.

Tibbutt, H. G. *The Life and Letters of Sir Lewis Dyve, 1599–1669.* Bedford Historical Society (vol. xxvii), 1948.

Tolstoy, Leo. *War and Peace.* New York, 1942.

Toynbee, Margaret, ed. *The Papers of Captain Henry Stevens,*

Waggon-Master-General to King Charles I. The Oxfordshire Record Society. Printed for the Society in 1961 and issued in 1962.

Tregellas, Walter H. *Cornish Worthies.* 2 vols. London, 1884.
Sketches of the Arundells, Bassets, Godolphins, and Grenviles. Incidental mention of Sir Nicholas Slanning and the Trevanions. Faulty dating and sketchy documentation make this a source to be handled with care.

Trevelyan Papers. Sir Walter Trevelyan, Bart., and Sir Charles Trevelyan, K.C.B. 3 vols. Camden Society, 1872.
Two Hopton letters of 20 June and 30 June 1643 to his friend George Trevelyan, or Trevillian, of Nettlecombe, Somerset, recommending officers. Also contains an account of events from Taunton to Chewton, which may be compared with Atkyns's account (q.v.).

Underdown, David. *Royalist Conspiracy in England, 1649–1660.* Yale University Press, 1960.

Victoria History of the Counties of England. H. Arthur Doubleday, William Page, L. F. Salzman, eds. London, 1900 ff.

The Visitations of Cornwall. Comprising the heralds' visitations of 1530, 1573, and 1620. Additions by Lieutenant-Colonel J. L. Vivian. Exeter, 1887.

Visitation of the County of Devon in the year 1620. London, 1872 (Harleian Society, vol. vi).

The Visitations of the County of Devon. J. L. Vivian, compiler. Exeter, 1895.
Genealogical background of Sir Nicholas Slanning.

Visitations of Somerset in the Years 1531 and 1573. F. W. Weaver, ed. Exeter, 1885.

Visitation of the County of Somerset in the Year 1623. F. T. Colby, ed. London, 1876 (Harleian Society, vol. xi).
See endpapers for Hopton family tree. Needs to be supplemented and corrected from Blore, Hoare, and Keeler (q.v.).

Walker, Sir Edward. *Historical Discourses upon several occasions.* . . . London, 1705.
Walker was Charles I's Secretary at War. This compendium of several works, edited by H. Clopton, is a stodgy, but accurate, account of the years 1644–5. The material for 1644 was 'corrected' by the King himself and used by Clarendon. It begins where Hopton's *Bellum Civile* leaves off—at the battle of Alresford.

Walton, Isaac. *Lives*. London, 1825.

The *War in Wiltshire*. Wiltshire Archaeological Society, Records Branch, 1940.

Warburton, Eliot. *Memoirs of Prince Rupert and the Cavaliers, Including Their Private Correspondence*. London, 1849.
Ably edited on the whole, though much of the correspondence has been compressed and shortened.

Wedgwood, C. V. *The King's Peace*. London, 1955.

—— *The King's War*. London, 1958.

Whitelock, Bulstrode. *Memorials*. Oxford, 1853.

Windeatt, Edward. 'Totnes and the Civil War', *Devon, Repts. & Trans*. xlv (1913), 220 ff.

Wood, Anthony. *Athenae Oxoniensis*. London, 1721.
His material must be considered in terms of contemporary reports: tradition close to sources; his personal animosities, misanthropy, and High-Church Tory bias can be discounted.

Wordsworth, the Rev. C., 'List of Clergy in Wiltshire Outed, Sequestered, or Silenced 1643–60', *Wilts. Arch. & Nat. Hist*. xxxiv. 166–7.

Wormald, B. H. G. *Clarendon: Politics, Historiography and Religion 1640–1660*. Cambridge University Press, 1951, 1964.

Wyndham, H. A. *A Family History*. 2 vols. Oxford, 1939.

Young, E. H. 'Okehampton During the Civil War', *Reports and Transactions of the Devonshire Society*, lx. 277.

Young, Brigadier Peter and Adair, John. *Hastings to Culloden: Battlefields in Britain*. London, 1964.

Young, Peter. 'King Charles I's Army of 1642', *J.S. Army H.R.* xvii (1938), 102–9.

—— 'King Charles I's Army of 1643–1645', *J.S. Army H.R.* xviii (1939), 27–37.
Three important lists:
1. Regiments at Aldbourne Chase, Berks., 10 April 1644.
2. King's army in Cornwall, late summer, 1644.
3. Prince Maurice's foot, 1644, including several Cornish regiments.

—— ed. 'The Praying Captain—a Cavalier's Memoirs', *J.S. Army H.R.* xxxv (1957): 3–15, 53–70.
The 'Praying Captain' is Richard Atkyns, Esq., author of the *Vindication* (q.v.).

Young, Brigadier Peter. 'The Prince of Wales's Regiment of Horse, 1642–46', *J.S. Army H.R.* xxiii (1945), 107–13.

R

—— 'The Royalist Army at the Battle of Roundway Down, 13th July, 1643', *J.S. Army H.R.* xxxi (1953), 127–31.
Contains as an appendix Sir John Byron's 'Relation', which Young calls 'by far the best of the contemporary narratives'.
Zagorin, 'The Court and the Country: A Note on Political Terminology in the earlier Seventeenth Century', *E.H.R.* lxxvii, No. 303 (April 1962), 306–11.

INDEX